Winter Trails™: New York

Help Us Keep This Guide Up to Date

Every effort has been made by the authors and editors to make this guide as accurate and useful as possible. However, many things can change after a guide is published—new products and information become available, regulations change, techniques evolve, trails are changed, etc.

We would love to hear from you concerning your experiences with this guide and how you feel it could be improved and be kept up to date. While we may not be able to respond to all comments and suggestions, we'll take them to heart and we'll make certain to share them with the author. Please send your comments and suggestions to the following address:

The Globe Pequot Press
Reader Response/Editorial Department
P.O. Box 480
Guilford, CT 06437

Or you may e-mail us at:
editorial@globe-pequot.com

Thanks for your input, and happy trails!

winter trails™

New York

The Best Cross-Country Ski
& Snowshoe Trails

by
JOHANNA and **RON FARRA**

The
Globe
Pequot
Press

GUILFORD, CONNECTICUT

Copyright © 2001 by The Globe Pequot Press

Cover photographs: top, courtesy Tubbs Snowshoe Co., Stowe, Vermont
Cover and interior design: Nancy Freeborn
Trail Maps created by Equator Graphics; © The Globe Pequot Press
State map: Lisa Reneson
Photo credits: P. x, photo by Mike Groll/*Buffalo News,* courtesy New York State Parks, Recreation and Historic Preservation; p. 155, courtesy New York State Parks, Recreation and Historic Preservation; p. xiv, courtesy Lapland Lake Cross-Country Ski and Vacation Center; p. xv, photo by Darcy Kiefel, courtesy National Sports Center for the Disabled; p. xxi, photo by Guy Thibaudeau, courtesy Saratoga Mountain Ski Touring Center; p. 179, photo by Jack Lynch, courtesy Saratoga Mountain Ski Touring Center; pp. xxvii, 132, photos by Roger D. Weston; p. 1, photo of frozen falls, courtesy Minnewaska State Park Preserve; p. 8, courtesy Bark Eater Lodge; p. 13, courtesy Glens Falls Recreation Department; p. 17, photo by Larry Wicke, courtesy Garnet Hill Cross-Country Ski Center; pp. 21, 122, photos by Irene Szabo, Finger Lakes Trail; p. 35, courtesy Adirondack Park Agency and Visitor Interpretive Center, Newcomb; p. 50, photo by D. J. Zlomek, N.Y.S.D.E.C.; p. 65, courtesy Great Glen Trails Outdoor Center; p. 70, photo by Matthew Seaman, courtesy Mohonk Mountain House; p. 78, courtesy Williams Lake Resort; pp. 82-83, courtesy Chenango Valley State Park; p. 89, photo by Robert J. McMahon; p. 97, courtesy Rogers Environmental Education Center; pp. 102, 112, 140, 171, courtesy Tubbs Snowshoe Co., Stowe, Vermont; p. 106, photo by Dave Riordan; p. 136, photo by Scott S. Graber, courtesy Fahnestock Winter Park; p. 145, photo by Gary Lawton, courtesy Connetquot River State Park Preserve; p. 165, courtesy Long Path North Hiking Club; pp. 190-91, courtesy Saratoga National Historical Park, National Park Service; p. 201, courtesy Salmon Hills Resort; p. 223, photo of deer by Jeff Nadler, Burnt Hills, New York. The remaining photos are courtesy of Johanna and Ron Farra.

Library of Congress Cataloging-in-Publication Data

Farra, Johanna.
    Winter trails New York : the best cross-country ski & snowshoe trails /
  by Johanna and Ron Farra.
      p. cm. — (Winter trails series)
    Includes bibliographical references (p.).
    ISBN 0-7627-0557-4
      1. Cross-country skiing—New York (State)—Guidebooks. 2. Snowshoes and snowshoeing—New York (State)—Guidebooks. 3. Trails—New York (State)—Guidebooks. 4. New York (State)—Guidebooks. I. Farra, Ron. II. Title. III. Series.

GV854.5.N45 F37 2001
917.4704'44—dc21
                                       00-056148

Manufactured in the United States of America
First Edition/First Printing

It is with great pride and pleasure

that we dedicate this book to five champion skiers:

Kathleen, Eileen, Michael,

Christine, and John.

New York

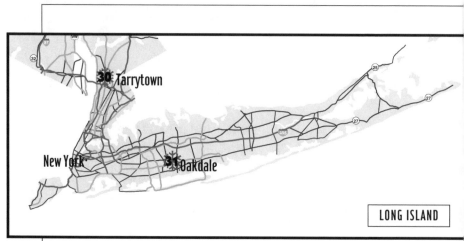

Tarrytown

New York

Oakdale

LONG ISLAND

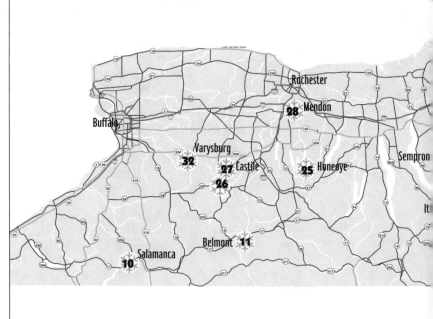

Rochester

Mendon

Buffalo

Warysburg

Castile

Honeoye

Sempron

Belmont

Salamanca

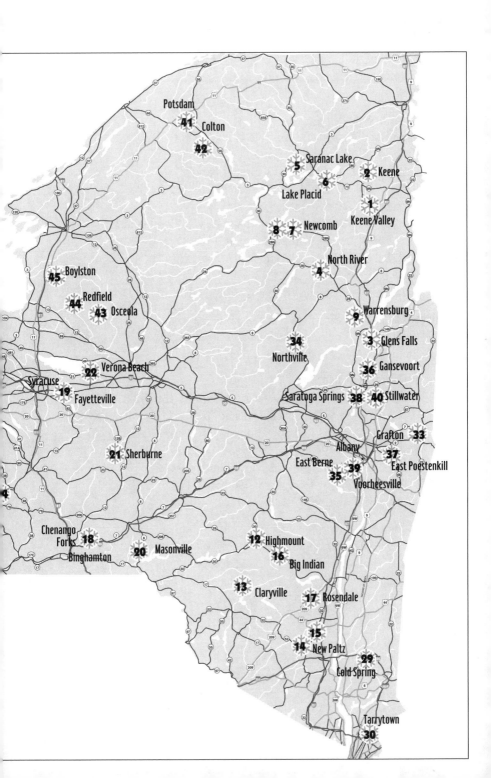

Contents

Foreword, x
Acknowledgements, xi
Introduction, xiii

Foreword

Bernadette Castro.

On behalf of Governor George E. Pataki, the State of New York, and the Office of Parks, Recreation and Historic Preservation, I would like to enthusiastically congratulate Johanna and Ron Farra for their outstanding efforts in writing a book describing winter trails in New York State. We are excited that the authors visited many state parks that offer visitors wonderful skiing and snowshoeing opportunities. We are pleased they selected more than a dozen popular state park trails to include in their book, *Winter Trails: New York*. From the extensive Art Roscoe cross-country ski trails in Allegany State Park to the Yellow/Red Trail Loop at the Connetquot River State Park Preserve on Long Island, the authors provide an excellent snapshot of what New York's state parks have to offer winter trail users.

Governor George Pataki has long been not only a supporter of state parks but also one of the greatest users of our wonderful trail system. Whether he is using the trails to snowshoe, hike, or bird-watch, the Governor clearly understands the importance of public trails. Through his leadership, New York State has dramatically increased the amount of open space, parkland, and trail opportunities for all to experience.

I encourage the readers to visit not only the parks highlighted in this book but as many of our 158 state parks and 35 historic preservation sites as possible throughout the year. Although some of our state parks and preserves are closed in winter, many others offer skiing and snowshoeing trails when conditions permit. We have 774 cabins, some of which are available for rent in the winter. At some parks the access roads leading to our 8,362 campsites are also open for skiing and snowshoeing since they are not plowed in winter. These campsite roadways join more than 1,350 miles of state park trails for you to traverse.

If you return for a visit during the summer, we offer seventy-six developed beaches and fifty-one swimming pools throughout the state for your pleasure. Moreover, please do not forget our twenty-seven golf courses, sixteen nature centers, and seventeen heritage areas.

To learn more about our magnificent state park system, visit our Web site at www.nysparks.com or one of our regional park offices. If you plan on staying overnight at one of our parks, please make a reservation by calling (800) 456–CAMP.

Bernadette Castro, Commissioner
New York State Office of Parks, Recreation and Historic Preservation

Acknowledgments

Writing a book is never a one-person affair. The authors had a great deal of help from friends and associates in the world of skiing and snowshoeing. We applaud the efforts of all the volunteers and professionals who have labored so well in creating the many winter trails throughout New York State. It has been a privilege and inspiration to work with so many dedicated individuals as they shared the trails with us and helped gather the materials for these pages. We would like to acknowledge the following people for their unselfish assistance during the research phase of writing *Winter Trails: New York*.

Adirondack Region: Tony Goodwin (Ausable Club and Jackrabbit Trail), Joe Pete Wilson (Bark Eater Lodge), Chris Merrill (Crandall Park), Dick Carlson (Garnett Hill Resort), Bob Rafferty (Mt. Van Hoevenberg), Andy Blanchette (Santanoni Preserve), Rynda McCray, Ruth Olbert (Visitor Interpretive Center-Newcomb), Patrick Beland (Warren County Trails).

Allegany Region: Greggory Spako, Dan Davis, Mike Miecznikowski (Art Roscoe Trails), Dave Zlomek (Phillips Creek).

Catskill/Palisades Region: Lynn Brittian, Rosie Haverson (Belleayre Nordic Trails), Leigh Draper, John Thomas, Kristi Foster (Frost Valley YMCA), Tom Cobb (Minnewaska State Park and Preserve), Eric Lowheide, Heidi Jewett, Kim Ladanyi (Mohonk Mt. House), Bill Rudge (Rochester Hollow Preserve), Anita Peck (Williams Lake Resort).

Central Region: John Michalski (Chenango Valley State Park), Tom Maxian, John Livingston (Green Lakes), Rick Dunbar (Oquaga Creek), Marsha Guzewich (Rogers Environmental Education Center), John Lowe, Al Gorton (Verona Beach State Park).

Finger Lakes Region: Stephen Davison (Bear Swamp Forest), Dan Karig (Hammond Hills), Wally Dyer (Harriet Hollister Spencer Recreation Area).

Genesee Region: Eileen Kennedy, Roger Weston (Mendon Ponds Park), Irene Szabo (Finger Lakes Trail), Doug Bassett (Letchworth State Park).

Hudson Valley/Taconic Region: Paul Kuznia (Fahnestock Winter Park), John Middlebrooks (Rockefeller Preserve).

Long Island Region: Bill Bergin, Inge Becker (Connetquot River Preserve).

Niagara Region: Scott Miedenbauer (Byrncliff Resort).

Saratoga/Capital District: Tom Conklin (Grafton Lakes State Park), Ann Hirvonen (Lapland Lake Resort), Mike Willsey (Long Path), Connie Hyat, Gary Hill (Moreau Lake State Park), Walter Kirsh (Pineridge

Nordic Center), Mike Venuti, Jeff McCrevey, Mike LeBaron, Barbara Frasier (Saratoga Spa State Park), Nancy Engel (Thacher Park), Joe Craig, Gina Johnson (Saratoga National Historical Park).

Thousand Islands Region: Dick Mooers, Chris Ritter, Jenny Lane (Clarkson University Trails), John Wood, Ed Fuhr, Judy Fuhr (Higley Flow State Park), Hugh Quinn (Osceola Tug Hill), Hans Giuliani, Liz Giuliani, Mike Kearney (Salmon Hills Resort), Jay Chapman (Tug Hill Tourathon Trails).

On the editorial side of this project is the fine staff at The Globe Pequot Press. We would like to extend special words of praise and appreciation to Laura Strom, Lafe Low, and Shelley Wolf.

Introduction

For some people winter is a time of dread and fear. Many older citizens and less athletic people fear that they will be cold or sick, that they may fall on the ice or get their automobiles stuck in snow. But for many others, it can be a time of excitement, a time of change from the heat of the preceding seasons to the cool and clear air of winter. Winter for them is a beautiful time when Mother Nature covers the earth with a pure white blanket, which our northern ancestors found to have qualities well suited to sliding activities. It is the sliding quality of snow that excites skiers. Just as people enjoy the thrill of roller coasters and other fast rides at amusement parks, there is an exhilarating feeling associated with sliding across snow. It's especially satisfying when the movement is produced by your own energy.

Rather than fear the snow and the cold, people first used it for transportation and later for recreation. Skiers learned to glide over the snow by driving their legs forward on skis and pushing back with poles. For many generations Nordic skiing was the only form of skiing.

New Yorkers with Scandinavian backgrounds were eager to locate places to ski and began cutting trails wherever they could get permission. At first ski and snowshoe trails began to appear throughout the metropolitan region, including New York City's Central Park. Farmland and country roads, which were abandoned in winter, soon became known to the Europeans as places for skiing and snowshoeing. To find more consistent snow, many winter enthusiasts traveled further north. The famous ski trains from New York City and Schenectady brought the masses to North Creek, where they could ride in trucks and cars to the top of the mountain for the thrill of skiing down the trails. There were no Alpine skiing areas then, only ski trails on private property, closed roadways, public parks, and woodlands. As more ski trails were cut, more New Yorkers learned about winter trail sports. Today there are more miles of winter trails for cross-country skiing and snowshoeing in New York State than in any other Mid-Atlantic state.

One of the nicest features of cross-country skiing is the freedom to do it wherever there is enough snow. Many of us love to ski through unbroken snow, setting our own tracks and breaking trail with our skis. Snowshoeing is a bit less difficult than cross-country skiing. In fact, one of the most popular features of snowshoeing is the opportunity for children and

Spring skiing on the cross-country trails is great fun.

adults—even grandparents—to walk along a snow-covered trail at the same pace without feeling the frustration of being "held back" by slower participants. In skiing, on the other hand, more experienced skiers definitely feel limited by slower companions, often creating an unpleasant journey for one or more of the adventurers.

It was difficult indeed for us to single out forty-five trails for inclusion in *Winter Trails: New York.* This is one of the largest northern states, boasting hundreds of winter trails suitable for cross-country skiing and snowshoeing. Some winter trails are located in villages, cities, or state parks, many can be found on golf courses, and others are in forests and wilderness areas. Winter trails cross open fields and pastures, travel through wooded and forested areas, and follow abandoned roads, rail beds, shorelines, streams, and riverbanks. Trails can be as simple as a ski loop in your backyard, a school playground, or a professionally designed Olympic trail. Almost anywhere there is snow you'll find a place for cross-country skiing or snowshoeing. Except for those on private property or at commercial ski centers, winter trails are usually open to the public free of charge.

This guidebook aims to bring public attention to hundreds of trails in New York. It features some of the best winter trails selected from among the fifty-six counties throughout the state, offering a diversity of environments to attract novices and beginners to the sport as well as informing experienced skiers and snowshoers about the trails. We have included winter trails in some regions of the state that receive very little snowfall, but whose managers encourage the use of these trails when snow does arrive. We also discuss a couple of nationally significant inter-state trails that cross New York, including the 2,100-mile Appalachian Trail and the 3,200-mile North Country Trail. There are chapters on ski-able sections of some of the longest trails within the state, including the Finger Lakes Trail System, the Northville/Lake Placid Trail, the New York State Canalway Trail, and the New York/New Jersey Long Path.

There are winter trails described here for every age group and talent. Most are suitable for the in-track classic (kick-and-glide) ski technique, while others are used for skate skiing. This newer nordic ski method employs the faster-paced, side-to-side skating movement. Skate skiing can not be used on all ski trails since it requires packed snow and a wider area. Commercial ski centers provide trails for both skiing techniques. Snowmobile trails and those packed by snowshoers are often ideal for skate skiing. It is important for "skaters" to avoid damaging the classic cross-country ski tracks. Some of the trails featured in the guide are short jaunts in local parks; others may be quite long, often traversing county or state forests that cover thousands of acres. Many of New York State's winter trails are public-access trails on city, county, or village lands; some are located on state and federal lands and land designed for recreation and open space preservation. Almost all of the winter trails are multiuse trails where skiers and snowshoers share the non-motorized winter routes with bikers, equestrians, hikers, hunters, and walkers. A few of the selected winter trails are partially shared with snowmobil-ers. Although most cross-country

A disabled skier enjoys a day in the snow with her coach.

skiers and snowshoers would rather avoid the offensive noise and odor of snowmobiles on the trail, skate-skiers find the firm, packed snowmo-bile trails a joy to ski. We also include several popular commercial cross-country ski areas, also known as Nordic centers, where ski-shaped grooves are cut into the snow with heavy-duty grooming machines. Nordic centers use a variety of grooming attachments to rework the snow and ice to offer the best ski surfaces for their customers.

Although hundreds of the state's winter trails are available for snow-shoeing, many are not. This is true especially at areas where groomed ski tracks have been made by track-setting machines. With the rapid growth in snowshoeing many Nordic centers now designate certain winter trails for the sport.

Some trails have sponsors who can often provide more information and some, such as the Finger Lakes Trail Council and the New York-New Jersey Trails Conference have detailed guidebooks available (see appendix). Unfortunately, one guidebook can not include all the great winter trails in the state. There are many more excellent trails in New York State, including some we have experienced and many we have only read or heard about (see appendix).

Using *Winter Trails: New York* as a guide to the ski and snowshoe trails throughout New York State could open the road to a very unique experience for you. Traveling to more than forty winter trails throughout New York might be an impossible goal considering the size of the state, but, to ski or snowshoe at all the trails in one or more of the eleven regions (those nearest your home) may be doable. In this guidebook, for example, we describe eight trails in the Adirondack Region. If you set out to visit all of these in one season not only would you have a great fitness experience, but you would have the opportunity to learn much about the cities, towns, and villages surrounding the trails you visit. You might catch the spirit of the great Hudson River if your goal is to cross-country ski or snowshoe at all the trails described and listed in the Catskill/Palisades or Hudson Valley Region. If you were to include overnight stays in some of the villages in the region, you would have time to investigate the attractions of the area.

Rating the Winter Trails

Because the surface of the earth varies so widely, it is natural to find wide variations of landforms and terrain along the trails selected for inclusion in this guidebook. There can not be any absolutes in assigning a difficulty level to the trails. Those described in *Winter Trails: New York* are rated in general according to a three-category system: easiest, more difficult, and most difficult.

Here are the telltale tracks of a skier and snowshoer.

Trails rated *easiest* are selected with beginners in mind. They are usually quite flat, with some gentle inclines and declines along the way. Changes in the terrain are generally gradual and subtle. These trails are shorter in mileage and duration; most can be completed in a half day or less, some of the easiest in an hour or two.

Trails rated *more difficult* have one or more steep pitches, causing increased downhill speed and requiring additional slowing and stopping skills. The uphill climbs are more taxing on the arms and legs, requiring more physical exertion. These trails are generally longer in mileage and duration and require participants to have good map-reading skills.

A few of the state's *most difficult* winter trails are included in *Winter Trails: New York* for experts and advanced skiers and snowshoers. They are usually found in the backcountry and mountainous areas at higher altitudes. Users of these trails will encounter very difficult climbs as well as steep and fast downhill runs with sharp turns along the way. Users must have accurate map and compass skills as well as a good knowledge of other survival techniques. Participants need to be in the best physical shape for climbing the often long and steep section on the most difficult trails.

Equipment

Equipment for cross-country skiing and snowshoeing has changed drastically in recent years due to lighter and stronger materials now available to the manufacturers. The purchase of good equipment is important for enjoyable and safe use of the winter trails.

The equipment needed for cross-country skiing or snowshoeing on the winter trails described in this guide will vary greatly depending on such factors as the age and skill level of the user. Equipment for beginning skiers or snowshoers is different from those who use the trails for exercise or ski racing practice. Beginners are encouraged to ask a salesperson at a reputable ski or sports shop for help in selecting the proper equipment.

Modern *snowshoes* come in a variety of styles with easy-in, easy-out bindings, making it possible for all members of the family to go snowshoeing. Made of lightweight aluminum or plastic, modern snowshoes come in three general types. Recreational shoes are for short hikes on terrain that is not too steep or rugged. Mountaineering shoes are more technical in design, with high-quality gripping devices. They offer more aggressive traction for the steeper, icier conditions found on longer hikes and in the mountains and backcountry. Snowshoes for conditioning are made of very light and durable materials. They are aerobically designed for fitness training and competition on packed trails. Although wooden snowshoes perform well and still offer one of the finest experiences on snow, they require a fair amount of maintenance and are more susceptible to breakage.

Proper *snowshoe bindings* are as important as good snowshoes. The bindings are the only controlling device between you and the snowshoes. If the binding doesn't function well, the snowshoe won't either, no matter how good it is. Choose a binding that holds your foot securely with little or no sideways movement. Be sure your foot can't slip forward or backward. Bindings must be "mitten friendly," making it as easy as possible to get in and get out, especially in cold weather. The traditional decking material of laced rawhide has evolved into solid sheets of synthetic materials such as polypropylene or plastic. These decks are stronger, lighter, and better at shedding snow, offer greater flotation and require virtually no maintenance.

This baby hitches a ride with dad.

Ask the salesperson at your local sport shop to explain the various models and costs. Many shops have snowshoe "demo days" for trying different snowshoes and some shops and cross-country ski centers have snowshoe rental programs so you can try before you buy.

"If you can walk, you can snowshoe," a slogan used by snowshoe manufacturers to promote the sale of their products, is basically true. You can enjoy snowshoeing in all kinds of winter conditions, however, you should learn how to use the shoes. No matter how good your equipment or how capable you are, proper snowshoeing technique will help you climb more quickly and much more efficiently. Proper snowshoe technique can be learned on your own with practice and the help of a good book, or with a bona fide instructor. Many hiking clubs and ski clubs own several pairs of snowshoes and offer tours and instruction (see appendix).

Today's smaller, lighter snowshoes can also be helpful to cross-country skiers for climbing over rough terrain or going off-piste (off the trail). If the trail turns to mush, or to mud in springtime, having a pair of snowshoes to trade for skis can be a great way to travel. A small pair of snowshoes open up new trails to cross-country skiers by allowing them to do what has been called *ski-shoeing*. One simply skis from the parking lot to the base of a steep mountain trail, then exchanges skis for snowshoes for a more efficient means of climbing. Modern ski manufacturing has produced equipment that is far superior to the wooden skis of the past.

Although most older skis are still usable, fiberglass and other modern materials make the skis much lighter and stronger. Buying the least expensive equipment is probably a waste of money; it most likely will not fit well and will be more susceptible to breaking. We recommend that you buy the best equipment you can afford, not necessarily "the top of the line."

Turning your skis on the winter trails is quite important. When buying Nordic ski equipment, keep in mind that shorter skis turn more easily than longer skis. Wider skis are better suited to all-around trail use; the skinny racing skis are considerably lighter and very fast. For the more difficult climbs on skis, especially in the backcountry, you will want wider, heavier skis with steel edges. You should also consider carrying a set of *skins* to attach to your skis for very steep and slippery trail conditions. They are lightweight and could make the difference between a pleasant ski trip and a miserable one.

If you are a first-time skier planning a winter trails outing, it is probably a wise idea to rent the equipment rather than buying it before ever experiencing the activity. As with other outdoor sports, skiing is a personal activity that may or may not fit you and your lifestyle. There is a wide variety of ski equipment to fit the many styles and personal needs of users. If you rent first, you will give yourself a chance to experience the various makes, models, and types for yourself. Although there are aspects you may like, not everyone will immediately take to skiing. Once you decide what best fits your personality and style, you can purchase the equipment that will serve you for many years.

Choosing the right skis is a bit more complex. There are several types of *cross-country skis* available, depending on the intended use. You should take your time choosing the right Nordic ski equipment; the decision will be based upon how you will use it, as well as how often and where you will ski. Most commercial ski centers will deduct the cost of rentals for those who "try and buy" equipment. Many hiking clubs and ski clubs also have winter equipment available for loan or rent.

Recreational skis, racing skis, and backcountry skis come in waxable and waxless varieties. There are models of recreational and racing skis for the classic kick-and-glide style of skiing and the newer skating technique. Backcountry skis are wider, stiffer, and usually equipped with metal edges. Beginners need a bit more grip and less emphasis on the glide; the opposite is true for advanced skiers and cross-country ski racers. If you ski in parts of the state where ice and crusty snow are common, metal-edged skis will add a lot of security on downhills as well as when traversing. They're especially important for backcountry skiing. Wider skis are a must when carrying a heavy load.

Although skis seem to get all the attention, the *ski boots* you choose can make the biggest difference. Warm, comfortable boots are the most important component in the equipment package. Look for a boot with insulation between the inner lining and outer shell. Touring boots, which offer lots of support, may be best for beginners and intermediate skiers. If you acquire the skill to ski very fast, then you can select racing boots. The warmest boots, however, may be of no use if they don't fit well. When fitting boots, bring the appropriate layer of socks for your personal needs. If you wear orthotics for running, jogging, or walking, bring them to the fitting. Try each boot to be sure your toes are not cramped and that your heel is held down firmly. Because new boots will stretch a bit, make sure the lacing eyelets don't meet when the boots are tightened. Many manufacturers are now making cross-country ski boots to accommodate women's feet.

A pair of good quality *ski poles* is also a must on the winter trails. They are essential for good ski technique and as safety devices in certain weather conditions. Modern cross-country ski poles are sculpted of lightweight alloys featuring comfortable and efficient ergonomically designed handgrips. Snowshoers should also carry ski poles. They not only encourage upper body movement, but are great for helping to maintain your balance, or (failing that) returning to your feet after a fall. These can be ski poles, trekking poles, or poles designed specifically for snowshoeing. Telescoping poles are best, as the length can be changed to fit the snow condition or terrain (i.e., side hill traversing) and they pack up easily when not in use.

Most people like to go cross-country skiing and snowshoeing on warm and sunny days in winter, but they must also be prepared to stay warm and dry in wind, snow, sleet, and rain. Because weather conditions can change rapidly on the trail, a properly supplied *backpack* becomes your "winter survival kit." The size of the backpack or fanny pack will depend on the length of the tour and how long you might be out in inclement weather conditions. Obviously, a short trip around the trail at a city park will require you to carry less in your pack than an all-day tour in a forest or on a wilderness trail. The following supplies are suggested for winter trails:

- Food: A high-energy snack can boost energy when hungry, tired, cold, or lost.
- Clothing: For extended trips, a full change of clothing is recommended. Bring extra socks, hat, gloves, and underwear, as well as a waterproof windbreaker and wind pants.
- Compass: Understand its use. It may save your life.
- First-aid kit: Include Band-Aids, sponges, aspirin, cough drops, and sunscreen.

- Flashlight or headlamp: Be sure to have extra batteries and bulbs.
- Pocketknife or multi-use tool: These are useful in a variety of situations.
- Space blanket: They're inexpensive and lightweight, and may save your life.
- Trail map: Take time to read it.
- Water: A quart per day is recommended.
- Watch: Know what time the sun sets and plan accordingly
- Waxing supplies: Carry silicon for waxless skis.
- Whistle: It's easier to blow than to yell.

Dressing for the Winter Trails

Cross-country skiing and snowshoeing generally differ in their requirements for dressing properly. For instance, the amount of energy used to propel skis forward on a snow-packed trail will differ greatly from the energy needed to walk down the same trail on snowshoes. On the other hand, if the snowshoer is running on the trail, as in a race or a fitness program, then the clothing requirement will be about the same. In both cases, the age-old theory of layering applies. Layers of clothing that can be removed or added are far superior to one or two heavy garments for keeping you warm and dry while skiing or snowshoeing. On the trails, the right clothing can be as

Jo and Ron dress in layers to stay warm and dry.

important as the right skis. Although it is possible to go for a short ski or snowshoe trip on a clear and warm winter day wearing regular street clothes (slacks, sweater, parka), it is wise to consider the clothes designed especially for winter athletes and winter trail users.

The type of clothing you wear during winter depends to a great extent on the activity in which you will be engaged. During activity the body produces heat, which keeps you warm while active but is uncomfortable and can even be dangerous when you slow down or discontinue the activity. The difference between body temperature and the outdoor temperature in winter can be 100 degrees or more. Clothing is used to regulate the heat and cold as the activity changes. Winter clothing doesn't have to be fancy, but it must be able to keep out external moisture like rain and snow as well as keep away internal moisture caused by the body's reaction to the physical activities. This is a seemingly difficult task for Nordic skiers and snowshoers because of the great amount of heat produced by the strenuous activity of climbing hills, followed by rapid cooling while going downhill or slowing the pace.

Layering is the key to comfort and safety during winter activities, helping you to be prepared for changes in both the body's temperature and the outdoor temperature. Preventing cold-weather discomfort or injuries depends on your ability to control heat loss and to regulate the body's core temperature. You can do this with clothing that insulates your body, but you must also regulate moisture and keep the insulating material dry. To dress for ski or snowshoe tours you should start with lightweight underwear made of one of the polypropylene-based "miracle fibers," which are said to shun moisture. These materials "breathe" and do not absorb body moisture like other fabrics. The moisture escapes through the fibers into the air or is absorbed by a second layer of clothing. Good-quality underwear wicks (carries) the moisture away and traps the dry, warm air next to your skin.

You should add an absorbent layer on top of the underwear, such as a fleece or wool shirt or sweater. Some winter trail users prefer a zippered turtleneck shirt as the second layer, which can be opened to cool the neck and chest area. Avoid cotton and choose an absorbent material. Wool and fleece maintain their insulating quality even when they get wet.

Finally, you will cover the second layer with the outside layer, which should be wind- and water-resistant to be most effective. A lightweight, easily removed shell serves well as the outside layer. A lightweight parka or heavy insulating layer that can be rolled up and stuffed in a backpack is also very popular for extended trail activities or for covering up during stops or emergencies.

Keeping your head, hands, and feet protected is especially important, as they can be the primary areas through which body heat is lost. The layering process works for the hands and legs as well, although for some people, the legs don't require as much insulation as the upper body. Ideally, pants covering long underwear should be of absorbent materials and have zippers for easy on and off. A shell layer for legs should be easily removed. Covering the hands in layers is also the best practice in winter, starting with thin glove liners of polypropylene. Wool or fleece mittens covered with a protective shell will keep hands warm. Mittens are better than gloves for very cold temperatures.

Keeping feet warm can also be a challenge. Sweaty feet affect people differently, but changing socks during the day can help. Keeping boots dry is also important. After a day of skiing, boots are often damp inside and may need help to dry in time for the next day's activities. You may

Classic-style skiing and skate skiing require different surfaces.

want to purchase a boot dryer. There are also boot covers to slip over your cross-country ski boots for extra warmth on subzero days. And be sure to carry several extra pairs of dry socks on your adventures.

Navigating the Winter Trails Safely

Owners and managers of commercial Nordic centers make sure it is easy for their customers to follow the trails without getting lost. Directional trail signs designed by Cross Country Ski Areas Association (CCSAA) are hung with care to guide skiers and snowshoers along the trails to their chosen destinations. Skiers carry detailed trail maps, making it easy to check and recheck their locations as they enjoy the trail. In addition to the directional signs, color-coded signs of durable material are attached to trees and posts indicating the degree of difficulty: green (easiest), blue (more difficult), black (most difficult). The three colors also suggest beginner, intermediate, and advanced skill levels.

Unfortunately, the same degree of navigational safety is not available at all the ski and snowshoe trails in the state. In fact, there are some trails where it would be a travesty to destroy the natural environment with such colorful signs! Wilderness trails in general are not marked trails, but, almost all other trails officially designated for public use are marked with "blazes" of some kind. Paint is the most common blaze material. Some old-time trails are blazed with slashes made in trees by an ax, machete, or other tool. These are often painted with brush strokes or spray painted. More than one brush mark indicates a turn in the trail. Some trails in city and state parks, forest preserves, and other noncommercial areas have directional signs of wood, tin, plastic, or other durable material.

It is generally not easy to get lost on the trails, but it does occur all too frequently. Winter trail users need to stay on the designated trails, following the blazes or directional signs at the various intervals. With trail maps and trail directions given in *Winter Trails: New York*, you should happily reach your destination without incident. However, as previously discussed, winter weather can be very unpredictable. A winter storm can play havoc with your outing, at times making it very difficult to see the trail signs or blazes. In a whiteout you'll be happy to see the trail at all. The wisest choice in such situations is to turn around, retracing your own tracks back to safety. We must also caution you that signs are sometimes vandalized or stolen. Although we may have noted that a given trail was "well marked" at the time of publication, you may not find that to be the case. Missing signs can cause some winter trails users to become disoriented or lost. It is best to check your direction frequently with the trail map and be prepared to backtrack to get accurate bearings from a previous checkpoint. Turning around is always encouraged, rather than getting cold or exhausting oneself when the trail is long and when there are no shortcuts or cutoffs. If an accident occurs, report it to the appropriate personnel. For after-hour assistance dial 911 for local, state, or park police.

The key to safe navigation on the winter trails is preparation. Call ahead to ask about snow conditions and whether the trails are open for skiing or snowshoeing. Always let someone know your travel plans—where you are going and when you plan to return. Dress appropriately and carry necessary trail supplies (see equipment section for backpacking tips). Select trails to match your ability and the amount of daylight remaining. Be sure to sign in and out at all trail registers and stay on the selected trails.

Learning how to read trail maps and use a compass is probably the best security against getting lost. Check your trail map frequently to help avoid directional problems and always be prepared to return home. Many of today's winter trail users also carry a cell phone. This modern option has caused some to be lulled into a false sense of security on the trail. Some savvy hikers and trail enthusiasts are also experimenting with the new GPS technology for safer trail travel. We strongly recommend that you first become skilled at map and compass reading before relying on electronic devices.

Some of the private and public lands described in *Winter Trails: New York* pass through areas legally open for hunting during the proper seasons. Usually the big-game hunting seasons are closed before the ski trails are covered with snow. Although it would be rare to find hunters on the trails, a variety of small game may be hunted throughout the winter. Trail users should check in advance with the managing authorities regarding use of the specific trails. You may want to consider wearing blaze orange while using trail sections that pass through hunting lands.

Dogs on the Trail

It is said that the simple act of petting a dog can lower blood pressure and that daily exercise strengthens the cardiovascular system. It therefore seems reasonable to conclude that cross-country skiing or snowshoeing with your dog might add years to your life, and life to your years! In *Cross-Country Ski Vacations*, author Jonathan Wiesel says, "Dogs love to ski and I listen when my two Newfoundlands wish to take me outdoors." He goes on to list places where dogs are welcome on the winter trails with their masters. In our research we have noted that dogs are permitted on many public and private winter trails in New York State, although many others regulate against bringing such pets onto the trails. The main concern is for the welfare and safety of all trail users. Several cross-country ski centers and Nordic resorts now encourage dog owners to bring their dogs so they can enjoy the trails and the facilities together.

With dogsledding and skijoring becoming increasingly more popular throughout the snow belts of the country, dog owners are seeking more places for these activities. Although backpacking and wilderness hiking with dogs is fairly common, not much has been written to prepare skiers and snowshoers for taking dogs on the winter trails. Rules forbidding pets on the trails stem from the ski center's experience with animals tripping skiers, defecating on the trails, chasing wildlife, and leaving paw prints in the carefully groomed snow.

"Proper trail manners and ethics apply to our canine companions as well as ourselves," says author Gary Hoffman in *Happy Trails* (see appendix). All places offering the opportunity for dog owners to bring their pets expect the masters to be responsible pet owners. Several areas provide "Mutt Mitts" and other collection containers for dog owners to use on the trails. New York state parks require pets to be on a leash (not exceeding 6 feet in length) and under control at all times. Proof of rabies inoculation may be requested.

More about Snowshoeing

Throughout *Winter Trails: New York* we refer to "ski and snowshoe trails" as a convenience, not to suggest that skiing and snowshoeing are the same skills. They are not. Skiing requires a much more complicated set of skills. Although both activities are frequently done on the same trails, snowshoers are urged to stay away from the machine-made and man-made tracks used for classic cross-country skiing. On the other hand, the pawlike prints left by snowshoers are often quite helpful for those who need packed trails for the Nordic skate skiing technique.

Today there is a major resurgence of interest in snowshoeing trig-

The trail guide leads a weekend snowshoe tour at Moreau Lake State Park.

gered by the introduction of small, lightweight aluminum snowshoes and easy-to-use supportive binding systems. The new materials, improved bindings, crampon systems, and ergonomically shaped frames make the shoes much easier to control and maneuver. The maintenance-free frames with wear-resistant decking add to their popularity, making them remarkably easy to use and master. Snowshoeing has been called "the great equalizer" because all members of the family can participate equally without a great deal of instruction. There are no books to study, no classes to take, or exams for which to bone up, and there are no difficult skills to learn. Grandma and Grandpa snowshoe at the same pace as the other family members. Everyone can socialize as they "walk" along a winter trail.

As in any sport, however, you will want to tackle steeper terrain and more challenging trails. That's when having a little more technique will help you avoid falls and perhaps injury. "Snowshoeing technique" may sound like an oxymoron, but surely there are techniques for climbing steep hills and narrow paths, as well as skills for traversing snow-laden backcountry passes or descending precipitous mountain trails. Because the activity does not place undue stress on muscles, bones, and ligaments, many summer athletes (swimmers, cyclists, runners, triathletes, and other fitness enthusiasts) are now turning to snowshoeing in winter to maintain the conditioning and diversity of their indoor workouts. Snowshoes offer a low-impact workout that builds strength, endurance, and aerobic capacity. Winter hikers, campers, and mountaineering folks make up another group of snowshoe enthusiasts.

Ski and snowshoe clubs such as the Adirondack Mountain Club offer snowshoe workshops and clinics throughout the season. Also mark your calendar for the third weekend in February for the annual National Snowshoe Weekend when the American Hiking Society and several snowshoe companies present "Winter Trails Weekend." You will be able to try a pair of snowshoes for free and take guided trail hikes at local golf courses, nature centers, or city and state parks. Call (301) 565–6704 for more information. There is a nationwide on-line resource for finding snowshoe trails (www.tubbssnowshoes.com). We also recommend that you check area cross-country ski centers to inquire about any upcoming snowshoe events and activities. See the appendix for several good books about snowshoeing.

Winter Sports on Cross-Country Skis

Cross-country skiing is only one of the activities you can do on skinny skis, one of the so-called Nordic winter sports. Since it is such a fun activity, it's easy to imagine that the other Nordic activities involving cross-country skis are also fun. Imagine, for instance cross-country skiing with an archery bow and a quiver full of arrows over your shoulder, or a .22-caliber rifle on your back, or a map holder with a topographic map in front of your chest. Also try to imagine what it would be like to fly off a ski jump with Nordic skis and land in a perfect telemark position. Or to make beautiful telemark turns in the pristine snow of the backcountry.

Cross-country ski racing is very popular at many New York State ski trails.

How about being pulled by your dog across a snow-covered lake on cross-country skis? These winter activities contribute to many exciting adventures to be experienced on cross-country skis. Each of these Nordic activities has a group of enthusiastic supporters who are always ready to encourage and assist those interested in trying a new winter sport.

If you enjoy hunting or target shooting, you might try *biathlon*, the sport of cross-country skiing and rifle marksmanship. Biathlon instructors will assist you in learning to shoot and in finding places to practice and compete. Biathlon has become a year-round activity, enjoyed by runners in the warmer months.

Archery, another very popular shooting activity, has been combined with cross-country skiing to create the new sport of *ski archery*. As in biathlon, ski archery participants ski 1 or 2 miles before shooting at targets. With the pulse racing, skiers steady their bodies, take aim, and shoot their arrows before continuing to the finish line or to the next shooting station. The New England Ski Archery Championships are held each year at Bretton Woods, New Hampshire. The National Ski Archery Championships and World Trials are held in Stowe, Vermont.

Good map-reading skills and quick decision making are essential qualities of those who enjoy the sport of *ski orienteering*, another Nordic sport. Cleverness is usually more important than cross-country skiing ability in this sport, as participants study their maps to decide on the best route to the control points and to the finish line. Most foot orienteering clubs now have "ski-o" programs, while local, state, national, and international ski-o competition is also becoming quite popular in the world of Nordic skiing.

Put your dog on a leash and he will instinctively begin to pull. Dogs that love to pull are easily harnessed for towing their masters on cross-country skis. Called *skijoring*, this winter activity can be a simple recreational adventure with your canine pet, or an exciting skijoring race at a regional or national sled dog competition. Professional Ski Instructors of America (PSIA) offers a program of instruction for those who seek to learn this new method of cross-country skiing.

You can also take lessons in *ski jumping* at specialized facilities throughout the snowbelt, including weekend ski jump camps offered every winter at Kodak Park in Lake Placid. More girls are taking up this Nordic sport since the U.S. Ski Association approved a competitive classification for women. At the first ever ski jump competition exclusively for women at Rumford, Maine, an 18-year-old girl broke the old hill record held, of course, by a male. Both men and women also compete in an Olympic sport combining ski jumping and cross-country skiing called *Nordic combined*.

To learn more about these Nordic skiing disciplines contact the following organizations:

New England School of Archery, 109 School Street, Concord, NH 03301; (803) 224–5768.
U.S. Biathlon Association, Camp Johnson, Colchester, VT 05446; (802) 864–1316.
Orienteering North America, 23 Fayette Street, Cambridge, MA 02139; (617) 868–7416.
Ski Jump Camps, c/o Kodak Park, Lake Placid, NY 12946; (800) 463–6235.
U.S. Telemark Ski Association, 2552 East 1700 South, Salt Lake City, UT 84108; (801) 582–8621.
Skijoring, c/o Roy Smith, 2626 Route 29, Johnstown, NY 12095; (518) 581–8103.
Nordic Division, Professional Ski Instructors of America, 1-A Lincoln Avenue, Albany, NY 12205; (518) 452–6095.

About the maps

U.S. Geological Survey maps—topographic maps—form the underlying basis of the trail maps in this book. The U.S. Geological Survey is in the process of converting its topographic maps from feet to meters. Because this is an ongoing project, not every U.S. Geological Survey map has been converted. Therefore, you will find that on some maps in this book, elevations appear in feet while on others they appear in meters. A box on the map tells you if the elevations are in meters.

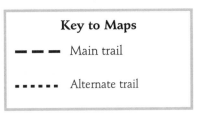

new york

Lake Road Trail

The Ausable Club, Keene Valley, New York

Type of trail:	▬▬▬ ⬤
Also used by:	Hikers, backcountry skiers
Distance:	8.2 miles, plus 0.5-mile side-trip option
Terrain:	Mostly flat and rolling
Trail difficulty:	Easiest
Surface quality:	Ungroomed, user tracked
Facilities and food:	There are no winter facilities at the Ausable Club. You may stock up at nearby grocery stores in Keene and Keene Valley: Valley Grocery (518–576–4477), Stewart's Shop (518–576–2056). The popular Noonmark Diner (3 miles) serves home-cooked meals (518–576–4499). Try the Trails End (518–576–9860) or Bark Eater Inn (518–576–2221) for lodging. Fast-food venues, restaurants, and tourist attractions may be found in Lake Placid (10 miles).
Phone numbers:	Adirondack Ski Touring Council, (518) 253–1365.
Fees:	There are no fees to use the trails.
Caution:	This is a long tour; be prepared to turn around. There are no patrols on these trails. Stay on the trail and off the ice at the lake. There is a strictly enforced ban on dogs and other pets on the property.

In 1886 the residents of Keene Valley and a growing colony of summer visitors became alarmed over the threatened purchase of the Upper and Lower Ausable Lakes and the surrounding mountains. The purchase by large lumbering interests was to include the adjacent forest and the road leading to the Beede House, the site of the present Ausable Clubhouse. By October 1887, twenty-nine stockholders had formed the Adirondack Mountain Reserve, Inc. (AMR), which purchased outright 25,000 acres of unspoiled forest, mountain, streams, and lakes.

Almost a hundred years later a sale of land to New York State left the AMR with approximately 7,000 acres, consisting principally of the area surrounding the Clubhouse, the river above the club, the Upper and Lower Lakes, and a portion of their headwaters. The sale was combined with the grant of a conservation easement to the State, whereby the AMR agreed not to develop the land retained in the Reserve. This is one of the six principal trailheads in the six-million-acre Adirondack Park.

In 1906 the AMR bought the inn, establishing it as the Ausable Club. Although the Reserve owned the "Club" and the two operations were

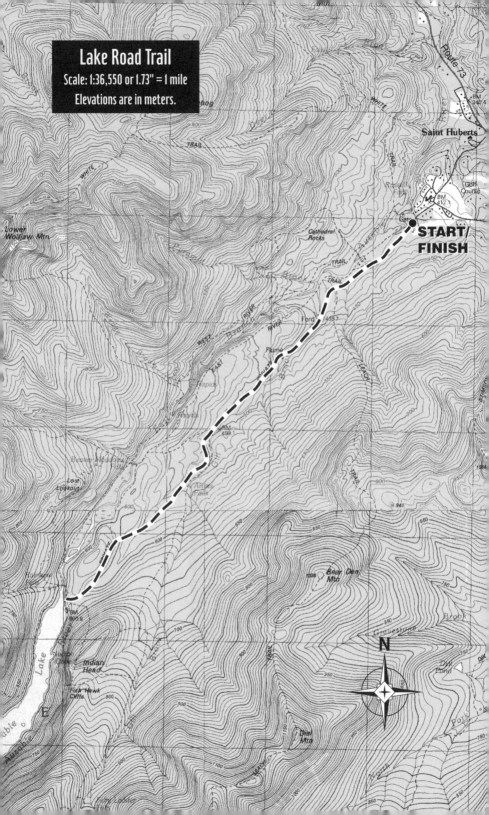

The lodge at the Ausable Club stands silent in winter.

mutually supportive, it was not until some years later that the two were completely integrated. But perhaps most important of all in retrospect, the Adirondack Trail Improvement Society (ATIS) was founded independently in 1897. This marked the beginning of a 90-mile trail system, opening up a wild and wonderful wilderness to hikers and nature lovers alike for years to come.

This ski tour is entirely on private land. You may encounter snowmobiles, which are used to supply several private camps at the interior of this 7,000-acre property. Heavy-duty vehicles such as bulldozers sometimes use the road, leaving a less than perfect surface for skiing. Such traffic is infrequent, however. The AMR has managed the property for more than a century as a preserve for the land and for wildlife. You are likely to observe a variety of animals along these trails because a ban on dogs

Directions at a glance

0.0	Park at the public parking lot on Route 73.
0.6	Sign in at the registration box.
0.7	Pass the entrance gate.
1.9	Cross Gill Brook.
2.5	Pass the reservoir (left).
4.0	Marked junction for optional journey to Rainbow Falls.
4.1	Reach Lower Ausable Lake. Return via the same route.
8.2	Finish at parking lot.

is strictly enforced and hunting is prohibited. This trail is especially popular early in the season and in low snow years.

To access the Lake Road Trail to Lower Ausable Lake, park in the public parking lot on Route 73, about a half mile from the Ausable Club. If snow conditions permit, you can ski from the parking lot, otherwise you need to walk to the clubhouse and the entrance to the trail.

Just before reaching the main building at the Ausable Clubhouse, turn left and pass between two tennis courts, continuing about 300 yards to the registration station. Everyone using the trails is required to sign the register before entering the AMR property. You will soon see the unique entrance sign and gate constructed of cedar trees with rustic letters identifying the Ausable Club and Lake Road. The Lake Road Trail, a gravel-based access road, is relatively flat and suitable for beginners. It ascends gradually from the beginning all the way to the lake. Its scenery is always lovely, with a number of junctions intersecting the roadway leading to some of the popular High Peak trails. These side trails are more difficult and should not be attempted by beginners and novices. There is, however, a difficult hiking trail to Rainbow Falls, an experience that should not be missed. It may be well worth the annoyance of removing your skis or snowshoes in order to take the optional 0.5-mile side-trip, which leaves the trail shortly before the 4.1-mile turnaround point.

Along the Lake Road Trail you will cross Gill Brook, followed by an intermediate climb for approximately 2 miles. You'll see a small reservoir on your left before a short descent to the lower lake. There are no ski patrols or other officials in winter to advise you of the lake's condition. According to local sources, the lake is frequently *unsuitable for skiing;* strong winds and ice conditions often render the surface too rough or icy. The boathouse area is off-limits to the general public, but there is a nice viewpoint looking 100 yards up the trail to Indian Head, which diverges left at the top of the hill just before the side trip to Rainbow Falls. Here you might enjoy the viewshed and some refreshments before returning to the clubhouse and your car. The return trip will be even more delightful, as it is a gentle descent all the way. You might make it back to the trailhead and clubhouse in less than half the time!

How to get there
From the Adirondack Northway (I–87) take Route 73 west to St. Huberts. Travel 5.9 miles past the junction of Route 9 and Route 73. Park in the designated parking lot at the bottom of the hill on Route 73.

Ridge Trail Loop

Bark Eater Lodge, Keene, New York

Type of trail:	▬ ◄
Also used by:	Hikers, walkers, and equestrians
Distance:	6.4 miles
Terrain:	Hilly, mountainous
Trail difficulty:	More difficult
Surface quality:	Groomed and packed for classic and skating techniques
Food and Facilities:	The Bark Eater Lodge serves home-cooked meals. The public is welcome and may order meals or enjoy a brown bag lunch at the Nordic center. Food and supplies are available at nearby grocery stores in Keene and Keene Valley: Stewart's (518–576–2056), Valley View Groceries (518–575–4477). The popular Noonmark Diner is just a few miles away (518–576–4499). Fast-food vendors, restaurants, and lodging may be found 10 miles away in Lake Placid.
Phone numbers:	The Bark Eater Lodge, (518) 576–2221. Visitors Bureau, (800) 447–5224.
Fees:	There is a fee for use of the trails.
Caution:	Novices and beginners should be prepared to remove skis or turn around if the skiing becomes too difficult.

Once a farmhouse that served as a stagecoach stopover for meals, the Bark Eater Lodge is almost two centuries old. "Bark Eater" comes from a Native American term for the Iroquois' longtime foes, the Algonquin. Visitors enjoy great views of the Sentinel Mountain Range and the Adirondacks' 4,000-foot peaks, especially from the polo field that doubles in the winter as an instructional area for skiers. The Sentinel Mountain Range stands guard over a small glacial valley that forms one of the passes through the mountains between the Ausable Valley and the plains of North Elba.

Joe Pete Wilson is host of the inn and the Wilson Stables. Wilson's grandparents worked for a lumber company and ran the largest business operation on the Placid side of the range, he as a farmer and driver and she as a camp cook. At the same time his great-grandparents worked at one of Lake Placid's most famous hotels.

Wilson, a former Olympic and world competitor in Nordic skiing, biathlon, and bobsledding, carries on the tradition of the country inn his parents established in the 1940s. The resort features an old farmhouse with two fireplaces, three spacious common rooms, antiques every-

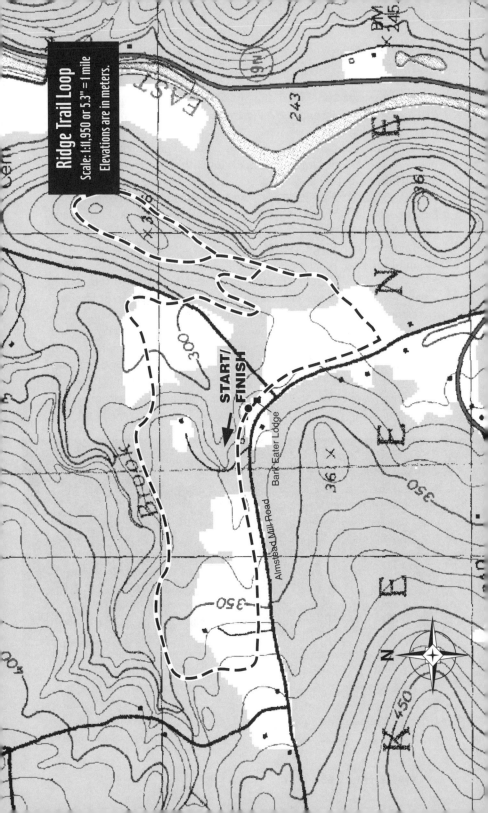

Ridge Trail Loop
Scale: 1:11,950 or 5.3" = 1 mile
Elevations are in meters.

START/
FINISH

Bark Eater Lodge

Almstead Mill Road

Brook

EAST

9N

BM
245

243

300

350

350

400

450

36

where, seven bedrooms with shared baths, a renovated carriage house with four bedrooms and private baths, and a log cabin deep in the nearby woods.

Having grown up in a farming family, Wilson works the same fields that today include ski and snowshoe trails, a professional polo field, and horseback riding trails.

The cross-country ski trail system is groomed and tracked, with sections for skate skiing. Ungroomed trails for both skiing and snowshoeing loop off the main trail at many points. Snowshoers are requested not to walk in the set tracks. The Ridge Trail Loop, a combination of trails, is a favorite of cross-country skiers who frequent the Bark Eater trails because of its easy access to some of the most spectacular views in the Adirondacks. The Ridge Trail Loop provides a quick visual geography lesson of the High Peaks region.

To access the Ridge Trail, start at the ski shop next to the Lodge, where you will find the entrance to the Clifford Brook Trail. Heading west, this trail passes the Wilson Riding Stables (open year-round) then crosses a small private road that leads to the Log Cabin. You can use the Clifford Brook Trail for a "warm-up" as it climbs over a plateau and descends through mixed hardwoods and softwoods with views of a fast-moving stream below. After about 0.5 mile, you'll find the junction (left) for the Deer Run Loop. At about 1.25 miles is the junction (left) for a very steep drop-off trail to the Clifford Brook, old logging trails, and the for-

Horse-drawn sleigh rides and ski trails are popular at the Bark Eater Lodge and Wilson Stables.

Directions at a glance

0.0   Begin at the ski shop.

0.1   Reach trailhead for the Clifford Brook Trail.

0.2   Cross private roadway.

0.35   Bear right at junction for Deer Run.

0.8   Pass junction for Sugar Works Trail System.

1.1   Turn left onto Brandywine Trail.

1.7   Turn left at T intersection.

1.8   Cross Lime Kiln Road.

2.1   Switchback (180 degrees left) at Ridge Trail.

2.5   Turn left at plateau on Ridge Trail.

2.7   Bear left at Y intersection and continue to Outlook I, II, and III.

3.5   Return to beginning of Y intersection.

4.2   Pass junction for Meadows Trail.

4.45   Turn right at Alstead Road.

5.0   Follow Meadows Trail and return to ski shop.

mer Sugar Works Trail System. This short, steep option, known by locals as "Killer Hill," is truly a trail for experienced skiers, telemarkers and backcountry enthusiasts. Continue instead to the run-out at the Meadows ahead of you. It is challenging enough, and taking off the skis is permitted at any time.

At the next junction, follow the Brandywine Trail (left), which rolls along about a half mile on a lower plateau, crossing a stream and joining the Meadows Trail. Turn left when you reach the T at the Meadows Trail and cross Lime Kiln Road, a quiet country lane named for an old lime quarry established here many years ago. As you approach a large meadow—a professional polo field in season—take the switchback (left) to the Ridge Trail, a fairly steep climb made easy by long sweeps and careful grading. It can be fun to come back downhill here if you're looking for a little extra practice with your telemark turns. The gentle hills next to the meadow are another good spot for practicing telemark turns.

At the next junction, turn left and ski along the ridge for some very spectacular views of the Adirondack High Peaks Region. Bearing left at the Y in the trail will bring you to an immense boulder and a nearby vista overlooking the Ausable River and Route 9N, which leads to Elizabethtown, the county seat.

At the top of the ridge there is an outcropping of bedrock on the upper side and a precipitous, seemingly endless pitch on the other. The loop heading north along the top of this incredible geographic spine is an easy, up-and-down run through mostly mixed hardwoods. At Outlook I the Inn and the Clifford Brook Trail can be seen far below, along with glimpses of Oak Mountain and other low mountains lining the river. Outlook II offers a great view of the meadows below and the Ausable River. At Outlook III you are presented with a spectacular view of the Sentinal Range to the west and Canada to the north.

Continuing along the ridge, the trail descends gradually to Alstead Mill Road, where you will turn right and follow the Meadows Trail along the roadway and polo field, returning to the Inn and Nordic center.

The Bark Eater Lodge and Cross-Country Ski Touring Center have separate trails designated specifically for snowshoeing. Some are parallel to the Ridge Trail, others are south of the lodge. It is suggested that you call the Bark Eater Lodge to verify snow conditions.

How to get there

From the south take the Adirondack Northway (I–87) to exit 30. Take Route 73 to Keene (17 miles). Turn right onto Alstead Mill Road and follow it a half mile to the inn.

From the north take the Adirondack Northway (I–87) to exit 34. Take Route 9N south to Keene. Turn right on Route 73 and go west 1 mile to Alstead Mill Road. Follow it a half mile to the inn.

From the west take Route 86 to Lake Placid. Take Route 73 south toward Keene 12.5 miles to Alstead Mill Road. Turn left and go a half mile to the inn.

Competition Trail Loop

Crandall Park, Glens Falls, New York

Type of trail:	
Also used by:	Bikers, hikers, walkers, runners
Distance:	3.1 miles with optional cutoffs
Terrain:	Flat to hilly
Trail difficulty:	Easiest to most difficult
Surface quality:	Machine groomed and tracked
Food and facilities:	There are no facilities at the park. The YMCA is adjacent to the trail and has rest rooms and warming areas. The Inside Edge Ski Shop, also adjacent to the trail, offers equipment rentals, accessories, and lessons. Fast-food vendors, restaurants, grocery stores, and lodging may be found in the city of Glens Falls and nearby Lake George and Saratoga Springs: Nice N' Easy Shop (518–743–0081) and Stewart's Shops (518–792–3357) for groceries, Queensbury Hotel (518–792–1121) for lodging.
Phone numbers:	Glens Falls Recreation Department, (518) 761–3813. Chamber of Commerce, (518) 798–1761. (In 2000 look for Crandall Park Trails on the web under "National Recreation Trails.")
Fees:	There is no charge for using the ski trails.

The city-owned cross-country ski trails at Crandall Park in Glens Falls were professionally designed and are well maintained throughout the skiing season by a group of local volunteers called Friends of Cole's Woods. The snow is machine groomed for both classic skiing and the newer skating style of cross-country skiing. The International Cross-Country Ski Trails at Crandall Park are open to the public free of charge every day and are lighted nightly. The trails are monitored and patrolled by the National Park Service, by local volunteers, and by City Recreation Department employees.

The trails at Crandall Park had the honor of being the first lighted cross-country ski trails in North America, according to Tom Jacobs, owner of the ski shop bordering the trails. Set in the lovely Cole's Woods area of the city, the trail system was dubbed "The Glens Falls International Ski Trails" in 1971 when Jacobs and John Caldwell, members of the 1952 U.S. Olympic Ski Team, arranged for members of the U.S. Nordic Ski Team to compete against several European and Canadian racers at the first international nighttime ski race. A unique trophy engraved by Tiffanys of New York was presented to the city at the dedication ceremonies. Winners' names are engraved on the trophy every year at the

START/FINISH

Inside Edge

Route 9

BM 339

338

CRANDALL PARK N

DIXON RD

350

Competition Trail Loop
Scale: 1:7,877 or 8.04" = 1 mile

conclusion of the annual International Ski Races. The names on the trophy read like a Who's Who of the U.S cross-country skiing champions.

After six years of public skiing on the 2-kilometer trail, the city purchased an adjacent thirty-five-acre parcel and completely updated the trail system with the aid of volunteers and city employees. Many competitive skiing programs are promoted at the park for youngsters, high school and college ski teams, adults, and master racers. The Glens Falls Recreation Department also offers cross-country ski lessons for residents of Glens Falls and the region.

All trails are wide enough to accommodate a groomed track and a skating lane. There is sufficient space for faster skiers to pass slower trail users. Races are often held here while recreational skiers are also using the trails. The trail map, available at the YMCA and Inside Edge Ski Shop, shows the location of the more difficult and most difficult sections on the trail.

Night skiing is very popular on the International Cross-Country Ski Trails at Crandall Park.

Access to the Competition Trail Loop can be gained from four parking lots; the main trailhead is located at the Little League Baseball Center on Glen Street. It is recommended that you begin your 5-kilometer (3.1 miles) tour on the Competition Loop here. Follow the signed trail to the Four Corners Junction. This is fairly flat skiing. Turn right and begin a moderate descent crossing the Halfway Brook via the first of four bridges.

Shortly after crossing the bridge there is a slight climb to a left cutoff junction. Beginners and the less skilled intermediate skiers are encouraged to take this alternate 1.3-mile trail back to the Glen Street trailhead and parking lot. Others will continue past the bridge on the Competition Loop, skiing along a mostly flat and undulating section to the Bonnie and Clyde Hill, a moderate climb. Less skilled skiers may need to use the herringbone technique here. The trail begins to twist and turn gently until you reach a short downhill section. Intermediate and advanced skiers will be able to negotiate this more difficult section but, as on any downhill, everyone will want to exercise caution. There is a short cut-off trail here for the fainthearted.

The Competition Loop continues to meander gently through the "Gap" and behind the Aviation Mall to a very twisting section, appropriately called the "Snake," until it reaches the famous "Wall." Here even the expert skiers have to herringbone on a long and very challenging uphill.

Several cutoff trails have been constructed here and at the next steep hill, Camel Back, for noncompetitors and less skilled skiers.

Those who continue on the Competition Loop through the Wall and Camel Back sections of the trail will enjoy the very pretty Cole's Woods. The trail makes a long continuous turn right to a junction near the second bridge, then turns sharply left and over Halfway Brook to the Grand Junction and the property line.

Turning left the trail takes skiers to another bridge and through the forest of tall pines. It flattens out before reaching a nice wide and gentle run down Dead Fox Hill to another bridge crossing. The trail continues through a mostly flat section called Main Street. Arriving back at the Four Corners Junction the trail turns right and you'll "head for home" skiing past the YMCA. Circle the Little League Baseball Center and return to the start/finish line for the end of your tour on the popular Glens Falls International Ski Trail.

Directions at a glance

0.0   Begin trailhead at Glen Street.

0.2   Turn right at Four Corners Junction.

0.3   Cross bridge.

0.4   Reach cut-off for shortened loop.

1.0   Reach cut-off at Bonnie and Clyde Hill.

1.5   Turn left at end of the Gap.

1.8   Reach the Snake area.

2.0   Reach the Wall.

2.4   Cross second bridge.

2.6   Cross third bridge.

2.7   Cross fourth bridge.

2.9   Return to Four Corners.

3.1   Return to trailhead.

How to get there

From Exit 19 of the Adirondack Northway (I–87) head east (past Aviation Mall) to Route 9. Turn right (south) on Route 9 for approximately 1 mile. Turn right on Fire Road. There are several locations here for skier parking: the YMCA, the Glens Falls Recreation Center, and at the end of Fire Road. Parking is also available behind the Inside Edge Ski Shop on Glen Street or at the Aviation Mall.

Balm of Gilead Trail Loop

Garnet Hill Lodge Cross-Country Ski Center, North River, New York

Type of trail:	▬▬▬▬ ⬮
Also used by:	Hikers, backcountry skiers
Distance:	2.0 miles
Terrain:	Hilly, mountainous
Trail difficulty:	More difficult to most difficult
Surface quality:	Ungroomed and backcountry skiing
Food and facilities:	The resort offers a full-service Nordic ski center for day and night skiing and snowshoeing. The fully staffed ski shop provides sales and rentals of ski and snowshoe equipment and accessories. Lessons are available for beginners to experts. The cafeteria at the Nordic center offers light fare and provides tables for those who bring a bag lunch. Fine food and first-class accommodations are offered at The Garnet Hill Lodge. Fast-food vendors, groceries, restaurants, and lodging may be found in the nearby village of North Creek. For groceries try Grand Union (518–251–4669) or North Creek Deli (518–251–2977).
Phone numbers:	Garnet Hill Lodge and Ski Center (518) 251–2444. Chamber of Commerce, (800) 888–GORE.
Fees:	There is a fee to use the trails.
Caution:	Garnet Hill borders Siamese Wilderness Area. The trails in this area are not patrolled and should not be attempted by beginners or novices.

Located about forty-five minutes north of the small city of Glens Falls is the tiny hamlet of North River. The region is known for its garnet mines, established in 1907. This beautiful red mineral is still mined today in Warren County's "garnet hills." Visitors to the Garnet Hill Lodge will marvel at the display of beautiful handcrafted jewelry made with the deep red transparent variety of garnet. When not covered by snow, trail users can see examples of the colorful garnet ore embedded in outcroppings and ledges along the trail as well as in rocks found in the streambeds.

The Garnet Hill Lodge is a complete winter resort with 55 kilometers of trails for skiers of all abilities. Some trails are designated for snowshoers only, others are open to skiers with dogs. Garnet Hill offers a wide variety of side trips and alternate loops for snowshoers and the more adventurous skiers. Multicolored topographic maps of the trails are available at the Garnet Hill Lodge or the Nordic center. The center also offers

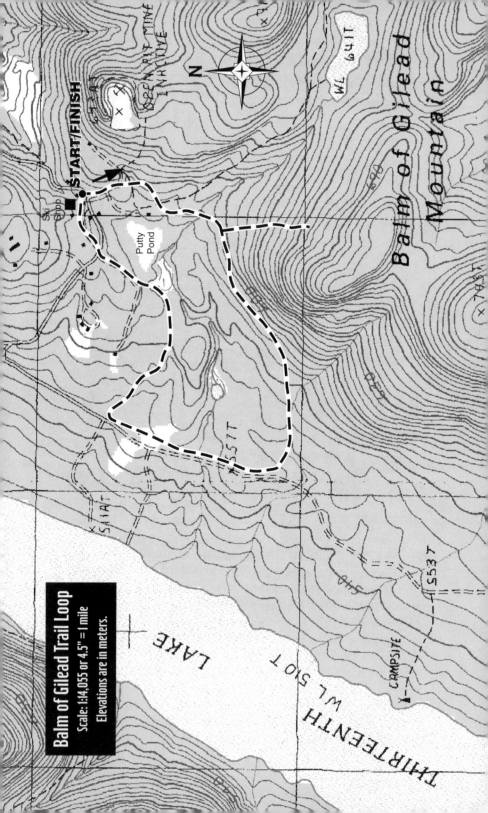

Balm of Gilead Trail Loop

Scale: 1:14,055 or 4.5" = 1 mile
Elevations are in meters.

Skijoring has become increasingly popular with both skiers and canines.

refreshments and light meals; guests of the Lodge enjoy home-cooked gourmet meals. A variety of housing arrangements is available at the Lodge and several cottages. Some accommodations are available for skiers with dogs.

The Nordic center offers a full-service shop, ski and snowshoe rentals, and lessons with ski instructors certified by Professional Ski Instructors of America (PSIA). Guided tours of the backcountry are also available for small groups, including lift-serviced Nordic skiing at nearby Gore Mountain. Garnet Hill Lodge provides a unique shuttle service for guests who choose to ski at the privately owned Barton Garnet Mines and Highwinds Inn.

We have selected an ungroomed trail to the summit of Balm of Gilead Mountain. A wilderness adventure for snowshoers as well as skiers (intermediate/advanced only) it includes "the best scenic view in the Adirondacks for the least amount of work expended," according to local sources. Balm of Gilead is a name given to a variety of poplar trees with large, fragrant buds that yield a sticky, fragrant resin. This probably accounts for the name of the mountain and trail.

The Balm of Gilead Trail Loop comprises three trails: Balm of Gilead, Overlook, and Hagen Trails. Begin your tour at the Nordic center, crossing the parking lot and walking up a plowed driveway past the tennis courts. Here you'll find directional signs to the former Hooper Garnet Mine and the trailhead to the Nature Trail. You may take a copy of the *Wilderness Nature Trail Guidebook* from the covered box found at the trail junction and plan for a future self-guided tour of this interpretive trail.

When you have adjusted your equipment (skis or snowshoes), follow the trail as it passes a private home and crosses onto state land. A few yards further you'll find a former miner's shack. You might stop to observe the tiny pieces of garnet embedded in the old stone fireplace still standing. You will then pass the junction to the Nature Trail and William

Directions at a glance

0.0   Begin at the Nordic center.

0.2   Turn off plowed road toward Hooper Mine to the Nature Trail.

0.5   Pass junction for Nature Trail and William Blake Pond Trail.

1.6   Go left on Balm of Gilead Trail.

2.0   Reach summit of Balm of Gilead and overlook.

2.4   Turn left on Overlook Trail.

2.8   Turn right on Wilderness Trail.

3.0   Turn right on Hagen Trail and pass Putty Pond Trail junction.

5.0   Finish at Nordic center.

Blake Pond Trail on your left. Continuing straight ahead for several yards you will cross a stream and find a sign for the Balm of Gilead Trail and trees blazed with red. It is about a half mile of gradual uphill climbing to the summit and overlook from here.

After taking in the spectacular view of Thirteenth Lake and the mountains of the Siamese Pond Wilderness from the open face of Balm of Gilead Mountain, return downhill on the same trail to the first junction. Turn left here onto Overlook Trail and follow it to Wilderness Trail, a wide woods road. Turn right and continue skiing until you reach the Hagen Trail. At this point we remind you not to panic, the distance may not seem right, but if you know you are headed in the right direction (check your compass) keep going until you reach the destination indicated on your trail map.

The Hagen trailhead is located at the edge of a town road and is blazed with blue. Turn right and enjoy this gentle climb with several nice twists and turns. Hagen Trail loops back to the Wilderness Trail at the junction of Putty Pond Trail. Continue on the Wilderness Trail to the Nordic center.

How to get there

From the south take the Adirondack Northway (I–87) to Exit 23. Take Route 9 north to Route 28. Bear left on Route 28 and travel through North Creek to North River. Turn left onto 13th Lake Road and follow the signs to Garnet Hill Lodge.

From the north take I–87 to exit 26 at Pottersville. Travel south on Route 9 and west on Route 8 to Weavertown. Turn right on Route 28 and travel to North River. Turn left onto 13th Lake Road and follow the signs to Garnet Hill Lodge.

Jackrabbit Trail
Saranac Lake, New York

Type of trail:	▬▬▬ 🚙
Also used by:	Hikers, snowmobilers
Distance:	4.0 miles round-trip
Terrain:	Hilly
Trail difficulty:	Easiest
Surface quality:	Ungroomed, skier tracked
Food and facilities:	There are no facilities associated with the trail, but a wide variety of eateries and sleeping accommodations is available at many locations close to the trail. Fast-food venues, restaurants, and grocery stores may be found in the nearby village of Saranac Lake. For groceries: Grand Union Company (518–891–4345), Lakeview Deli and Market (518–891–2101), Stewart's Shop (518–891–6687). Lodging is available at Hotel Saranac (518–891–2200).
Phone numbers:	Adirondack Ski Touring Council, (518) 523–1365.
Fees:	There is no charge to use the Jackrabbit Trail unless you choose to ski at one of the commercial ski areas along the trail (see text).
Caution:	The Jackrabbit Trail crosses roadways in several places. Use extreme caution if you cross the road.

The Jackrabbit Trail (JRT), one of the most popular ski/snowshoe trails in the north country, is 25 miles long, linking the Village of Keene at its western end with the northern village of Saranac Lake in the High Peaks region of the Adirondack Mountains. The JRT was conceived and constructed by members of the nonprofit Adirondack Ski Touring Council (ASTC) beginning in 1986. This unique trail includes a section that takes skiers through the main street of Lake Placid, the famed Olympic Village. You may see winter athletes who train and compete here in Olympic sports.

The Jackrabbit Trail is named in honor of Herman "Jackrabbit" Johannsen, a pioneer of cross-country skiing in Lake Placid (1916–1928), who laid out many of the routes used on today's Jackrabbit Trail. Johannsen died in 1987 in his native Norway at the age of 111 years, reportedly attributing his long life to cross-country skiing. According to sources, Jackrabbit continued to cross-country ski well beyond his hundreth birthday. This trail features a wide variety of terrain with sections for Nordic skiers and snowshoers of every ability. The European-style

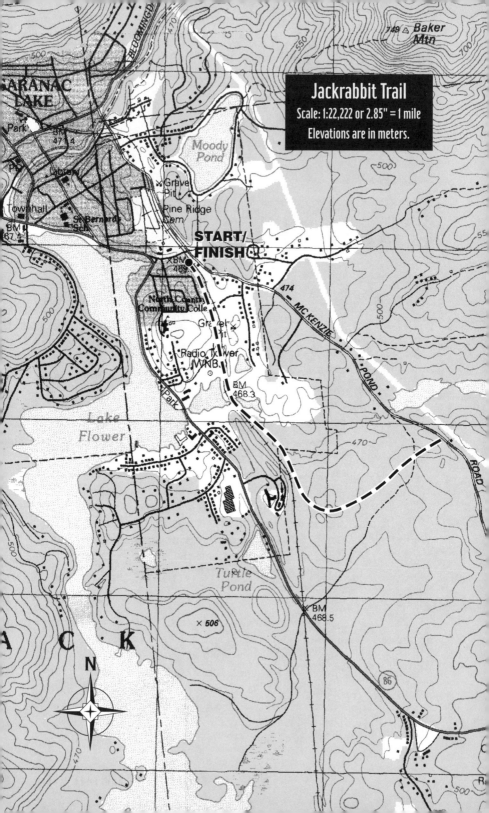

Pets sometimes lead the way on winter trails.

trail transverses wilderness areas, open meadows, golf courses, and the expertly groomed trails of three commercial cross-country ski centers as well as several small towns and villages. Skiers and snowshoers may be accompanied by their dogs on the JRT.

As with other trail systems, users have a variety of options. You may choose to travel on the Jackrabbit Trail for an hour, a day, or several days. Perhaps you will stay overnight at the Rock & River Inn or Bark Eater Inn near the trailhead at Keene. The next day you might head west to the historic village of Lake Placid, where there are always dozens of activities in which to participate. You might then spend the night at a motel, tourist home, or B&B, skiing the next day to a lean-to on the trail for lunch or wilderness camping. After that, you could continue straight on to the western trailhead at the village of Saranac Lake or take a side trip deep into the wilderness of the Adirondack Mountain's High Peaks region.

The ultimate goal of the Jackrabbit Trail organizers is to continue the ski trail from Keene to the village of Tupper Lake, with such side trails as the Adirondack Park Visitor's Center (VIC) at Paul Smiths, New York. When completed, this trail is expected to extend to several other north country communities, encompassing nearly 60 miles of unbroken trail and offering a round-trip tour of almost 120 miles. Many users leave one car at their desired destination along the trail, returning to the start to retrieve their other vehicle at the end of the tour; others ski to a set destination on the trail and return over the same route.

There are numerous access points along the 25-mile trail, some with paved and lighted parking lots and others on the side of dirt roads in the backcountry. There is no charge for skiing on most sections of the Jackrabbit Trail, but you are requested to make a donation to the Adirondack Ski Touring Council to help maintain the unique ski trail. Coming from the Keene end of the trail you may proceed as far as the lodge at Cascade Cross-Country Ski Center without paying a fee. To continue on the groomed section of the trail between here and Lake Placid, however, a daily trail fee applies. Called the Lake Placid Interconnect Ticket, it is honored at all ski centers on the Jackrabbit Trail plus the Olympic Trails at Mt. Van Hoevenberg.

For this guidebook we have selected the western trailhead in Saranac Lake, one of the most popular access points on the Jackrabbit Trail. The 4-mile section described here, beginning at the gymnasium at North Country Community College, is fine for beginners and novices, but you are welcome to adjust the length of the trip to suit your needs. The trip from the college to the Nordic ski center at the Whiteface Club Resort is about 7.5 miles one-way. More advanced winter trail users may consider going beyond the resort to Lake Placid or Keene.

You may choose a side-trip to the village of Saranac Lake before heading out on your ski tour. Turning left at the old railroad light and crossing sign, you can reach Riverside Park and Main Street. Here you'll find shopping and several types of eateries, including the popular restaurant at Hotel Saranac where students of Paul Smiths College are in training.

Back at the college gym, start your trip by following the abandoned railroad bed to the right. The trail is identified with large red rectangular trail signs with the logo of the Adirondack Ski Touring Council. You'll soon cross a bridge over a small stream where you can catch a glimpse of Lake Flower (right) beyond a small pond. Continuing along the railroad bed through a wetland area you will note a McDonald's Restaurant located just a few hundred yards off the trail to the right. Some skiers access the Jackrabbit Trail from here, a good meeting place. About 0.75 mile past McDonald's, the railroad bed begins a sweeping turn to the right. It is here that you leave the railroad bed, making a sharp left turn to begin a gentle climb into a pine grove on state forest land. After a brief climb the Jackrabbit Trail descends gradually to join a Department of Environmental Conservation (DEC) snowmobile trail. Bear left here and follow the trail about 0.8 mile before it turns right and finishes at McKenzie Pond Road (about 2 miles). To complete this tour you must retrace your tracks back to the college parking lot.

Another popular access point to the Jackrabbit Trail is just across McKenzie Pond Road (about 100 feet to the right) with parking permitted along the roadside. A Jackrabbit Trail sign posted at this trailhead marks the beginning of a 5.5-mile wilderness section leading to the Nordic Center at the Whiteface Club Resort in Lake Placid. Here you can also choose to take a lovely and very picturesque side trip to McKenzie Pond (approximately 2 miles). Trail maps and additional information about the Jackrabbit Trail are available from the Adirondack Ski Touring Council, Box 843, Lake Placid, NY 12946.

How to get there

From Exit 30 of the Adirondack Northway (I–87), take Route 73 to Lake Placid (approximately 30 miles). In Lake Placid take Route 86 west to Saranac Lake. Follow signs to North Country Community College. Park in the parking lot at the gymnasium.

Flatlander Extension Trail Loop
Mt. Van Hoevenberg, Lake Placid, New York

Type of trail:	═══ ◄
Also used by:	Hikers, mountain bikers
Distance:	1.5 miles
Terrain:	Mostly flat
Trail difficulty:	Easiest
Surface quality:	Machine groomed and tracked
Food and facilities:	Mt. Van Hoevenberg Lodge is a comfortable warming lodge with rest rooms, snack bar, gift and rental shop, waxing room, and showers. Fast food, restaurants, grocery stores, and lodging may be found in nearby Lake Placid. For groceries: Whispering Pines Country Store (adjacent to trails, 518–523–9322), Grand Union (518–523–9627), and Stewarts Shop (518–523–7825). Mt.Van Hoevenberg B&B (518–523–9572) is adjacent to the trails.
Phone numbers:	Mt. Van Hoevenberg, (518) 523–2811. Olympic Regional Development Authority (ORDA), (800) 462–6236.
Fees:	There are fees for use of the trails.

The Olympic ski trails at Mt. Van Hoevenberg in Lake Placid were designed in 1976 for athletic competition at the 1980 Olympic Winter Games. The length, contour, and steepness of the trails is prescribed by Olympic rules and regulations. Since then additional ski trails have been created for recreational skiers of varying skills and capabilities. The Mt. Van Hoevenberg trails are machine groomed and tracked for both classic and skating techniques. The trails are not open for snowshoeing.

You may purchase your trail pass at the ticket booth in the large parking lot before proceeding to the ski lodge and stadium. You can dress for skiing, wax your skis, or sign up for a ski lesson in the comfort of the lodge while watching other skiers in the stadium through the picture windows. You may wish to study the very large trail map on display in the Olympic stadium before beginning your tour of the trails. Be sure to pick up an official trail map to take with you on the trails.

To access the novice trails, begin at the ski lodge and stadium. Ski to the far end of the stadium where the connecting trails are marked with colors and arrows. Turn left and follow the trail for Flatlander Extension, identified with green and black markers. The trail here is wide with a gradual decline as it meanders through a softwood forest. At the first junction, Flatlander Trail (green markers) continues to the right. Stay on

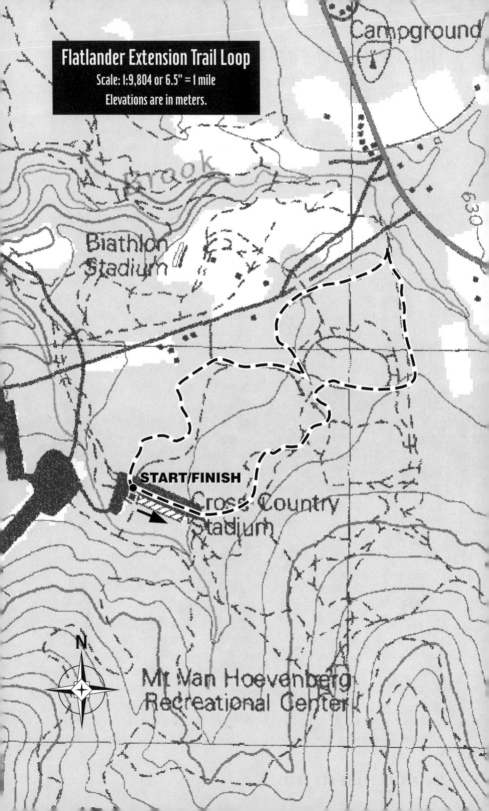

Flatlander Extension Trail Loop
Scale: 1:9,804 or 6.5" = 1 mile
Elevations are in meters.

Campground

Brook

Biathlon
Stadium

START/FINISH

Cross Country
Stadium

N

Mt Van Hoevenberg
Recreational Center

630

the Flatlander Extension, which goes left and climbs gradually to an overpass.

You will turn right at the end of the land bridge onto a wide woods road with a slight rise and a wide, sweeping turn. At the junction for the Campground Trail, turn right then left, following the signs for the Flatlander Extension. The trail narrows here, following the private property line of the South Meadow Farm. You'll catch a nice view (on the right) of the valley between Cascade Mountain and Pitchoff. Skiing further, you will turn left again and reach an open meadow and a great stopping place with a few picnic tables along the trail (near junction 17). Turning left again the trail dips gradually then approaches a short, steep climb where sidestepping or herringbone technique may be needed. At the top of this short climb is a four-way intersection with the footbridge over Bob Run Road to your right. Do not turn here, but follow Flatlander Extension along a unique trail-dividing fence, skiing to your right. This is a nice long run-out to a very long flat section.

Turn right at junction number 18 and follow the signs directing you back to the lodge and stadium. Continue on Flatlander Extension, passing the maintenance building (right) while enjoying the ease of skiing an almost perfectly flat trail through an old spruce and fir grove to the sta-

An athlete works on his skating technique on the world class Olympic Ski Trails at Mt. Van Hoevenberg.

Directions at a glance

0.0 Begin at Gloria Chadwick Ski Lodge.

0.1 Turn left at end of stadium.

0.4 Follow Flatlander Extension Trail. Ski over the overpass.

0.5 Turn right at end of ramp.

0.7 Turn left at campground junction.

1.0 Continue straight at four-way intersection and footbridge over Bob Run Road.

1.2 Follow Flatlander Extension to stadium.

1.5 Return to stadium and ski lodge.

dium. At the last turn you will reach the spectator bridge where, during an Olympic event, hundreds of people gather to cheer the athletes. At the end of your tour you may wish to enjoy the camaraderie and comfort of the ski lodge across the stadium before returning to the parking lot. At the lodge, you'll see a plaque dedicating the structure to Gloria Chadwick, as well as a photo of the authors' son, Olympian John Farra.

How to get there

From the south take Exit 30 of the Adirondack Northway (I–87). Turn left on Route 73 and travel through Keene and Keene Valley to the Olympic Sports Complex. Turn left on Bob Run Road and follow the signs to the Cross-Country Ski Center.

From the north take Exit 34 of the Adirondack Northway (I–87). Take Route 9N south through Ausable Forks to Keene. Turn right on Route 73 and travel through Lake Placid to the Olympic Sports Complex. Turn left on Bob Run Road and follow the signs to the Cross-Country Ski Center.

Lake Road Trail

Camp Santanoni Forest Preserve, Newcomb, New York

Type of trail:	▬▬ ⬭⬭⬭
Also used by:	Hikers, bikers, equestrians, hunters
Distance:	9.4 miles round-trip
Terrain	Flat
Trail difficulty:	Easiest
Food and facilities:	Although there are some covered facilities for taking cover from the weather and a few rustic outhouses, this trail and Great Camp have no modern facilities for winter trail users. Fast-food vendors, restaurants, groceries, and lodging may be found in the hamlet of Long Lake (12 miles). Try Stewart's Shop (518–624–4796) or Kickerville Mini-Mart & Deli (518–624–2178) for groceries. Mike's Newcomb House, adjacent to the trail, serves pizza, burgers, and sandwiches (518–582–4401).
Fees:	There are no fees to use the trails.
Caution:	This is a long tour. Be prepared to turn around. Sign the register at the beginning of the trail. Do not go off the trail or onto the ice. There are no patrols.

The Santanoni Preserve is situated at the edge of Vanderwhacker Mountain Wild Forest in the tiny hamlet of Newcomb. Arriving at the preserve, you cross a wooden bridge over a narrow section of Harris Lake to see the magnificent Gate House Complex. The Gate Lodge, closed in winter, includes a massive stone and wood archway, caretaker's home, boathouse, and assorted sheds and barns. This is only part of the Great Camp Santanoni, regarded at the turn of the nineteenth century as "the grandest of the Adirondack Great Camps."

The Santanoni Preserve was originally part of the 12,900-acre multi-building estate of a wealthy Albany banker, Robert C. Pruyn (1847–1934). The massive lakeside camp was constructed in 1892–93. A farm complex was completed in 1902, followed by the Gate Lodge Complex in 1905. The main camp was situated on Newcomb Lake, nearly 5 miles away from the Gate House and the town. Camp Santanoni has been characterized as one of the most sophisticated and distinguished of all the surviving Great Camps.

In 1953 Pruyn's heirs sold Camp Santanoni to the Melvin family, who continued to maintain and enjoy the camp for almost twenty years, although on a simpler scale. In 1971 the Melvins' eight-year-old grand-

Lake Road Trail

Scale: 1:30,864 or 2.05" = 1 mile
Elevations are in meters.

Newcomb Lake

Santanoni
Great Camp
Complex

Upper
Duck Hole

N

Farm
Complex

CAMPGROUND

CAMP
GROUND

BOAT RAMP

BEACH

HARRIS LAKE

WL 473.8

Gate
House
**START/
FINISH**

RESTRICTED

PICNIC
GROUND

BEACH

PICNIC
GROUND

BOAT
RAMP

LANDING
STRIP

BM 478.9

Newcomb

Winter trail users pass this unique and historic barn on their way to one of the Adirondack Great Camps—Santanoni.

child was lost in the forest and never seen again. The family had no wish to return to the scene of this tragedy and quickly sold the camp and its forty-five buildings to the Nature Conservancy. Santanoni was resold to the State of New York and was incorporated into the State Forest Preserve, subject to the state's "forever wild" mandate.

The Lake Road Trail, a multiuse trail, is an old carriage road leading from the Gate Lodge at the property's entrance to Pruyn's Great Camp on Newcomb Lake. Built by the Pruyns for horse-drawn carriages, the trail is wide enough for two carriages to pass side by side. A registration box is situated at the beginning of the 4.7-mile trail. It is important for winter trail users to sign in and sign out in the registration log book. There are always risks in the wilderness and there are no patrols on this unusually long winter trail.

After the Department of Environmental Conservation (DEC) registration kiosk there is a long flat section and a gentle downhill before you begin a long, gradual climb to the Santanoni Farm Complex, which once comprised more than two dozen buildings on 200 acres of cleared land. The layout and working systems of the Farm Complex were designed by Edward Burnett, who was considered an expert on "scientific farming."

Burnett had designed barns for the Vanderbilts, Whitneys, and other wealthy landowners. The farm provided dairy products, meat, vegetables, and fruit for the Pruyn family, farm workers, and guests at both Camp Santanoni and the Pruyn home in Albany.

On the right side of the trail you will come to a unique dairy barn with a round silo extending through the roof rather than being attached to the side of the barn. Through the lower-level windows you can still see the stanchions that held cows at the turn of the nineteenth century. Across the Newcomb Lake Road is a stone building, a former creamery. On the porch is a picnic table for enjoying a snack or bag lunch.

Four other structures, ruins of other agricultural buildings and archaeological remains, are located along the road approximately 1 mile from the Gate House Complex. The still-standing structures include three farmhouses: the Gardener's Cottage, the Herdsman's Cottage, the Farm Manager's Cottage, and a smokehouse. The residential buildings exhibit the typical rustic features of many Adirondack Great Camps, including porches with whole peeled logs and under-eave braces. The smokehouse (next to the road), used for preserving meat produced at the farm, is the last structure you'll see on the road as you continue your trip toward Newcomb Lake and the Santanoni Great Camp.

The road is quite wide here. It descends only to rise and then gradually descend again. There are no extreme climbs or descents to be found along the 5-mile roadway; rather many long downhill runs with several wide turns at the bottom, followed by long and gradual uphills. These are great places to "let your skis run" without fear of getting out of control. Winter trail users may also enjoy the sounds of several small streams crossing in culverts under the road.

After coming around a bend you will cross a stone bridge over a fairly large stream with a number of small waterfalls visible from the trail. The stream is likely to be covered with nature's ice creations during winter. You may also notice DEC markers identifying this trail as a horse trail. At 2.2 miles you will arrive at the intersection for Moose Pond and the High Peaks Wilderness Area. Bikes and motor vehicles are prohibited beyond this point. Although most visitors come to see the Great Camp, skiers and snowshoers may find this junction to be an ideal location to return to the beginning, making it a 4.4-mile round-trip tour.

Those who choose to continue will bear to the right toward Newcomb Lake, about 2 miles according to the posted trail map. The sign also indicates that it's an additional 2.7 miles from here to the Great Camp. As the trail continues to meander through a hardwood forest toward the camp and lake, you'll pass a giant glacial boulder and get your first glimpse of Newcomb Lake through the trees. It is always a welcome sight. You will cross a second stone bridge, followed shortly by another. A narrow hiking trail also crosses here. At this point the trail descends gradually toward the lake then becomes steeper but quickly levels off again. Upon careful observation you'll note an old wooden outhouse on your left as you continue toward your destination, followed by an open meadow overlooking the lake. A picnic table and several hitching rails for horses are located here. The road crosses over a long wooden bridge between the lake and the Upper Duck Hole, then turns and follows the shoreline about a quarter of a mile before you finally arrive at the Great Camp and its complex of buildings. This was the main camp complex for the heart of the Pruyn family's wilderness retreat.

Directions at a glance

0.0   Begin at the registration kiosk and gate.

1.0   Arrive at Camp Santanoni Farm.

2.2   Reach the intersection for Moose Pond and High Peaks Wilderness.

4.0   Arrive at Newcomb Lake.

4.7   Arrive at Santanoni Camp Complex. Return via the same route.

You may want to rest here for a while, perhaps to have a snack or bag lunch. You will surely want to take a tour of the Great Camp and the Lodge, which is composed of five cottages under one massive roof, before retracing your tracks and returning on the trail to your car. Several of the historic buildings are being restored with funding from the Town of Newcomb, the Adirondack Architectural Heritage, and the Department of Environmental Conservation.

How to get there

From the south, take exit 26 of the Adirondack Northway (I–87). Travel through Minerva on Route 28N to Newcomb. Follow signs to Camp Santanoni.

From the north, take exit 29 of the Adirondack Northway (I–87). Follow Route 2 to Route 28N to Newcomb. Follow signs to Camp Santanoni.

From the west take Routes 28 and 30 to Long Lake. Take Route 28N to Newcomb. Follow signs to Camp Santanoni.

Rich Lake and Peninsula Trails

Adirondack Park Visitor Interpretive Center, Newcomb, New York

Type of trail:	⬭
Distance:	1.9 miles
Terrain:	Mostly flat; some hills
Trail difficulty:	Easiest to more difficult
Surface quality:	The snowshoe trail is packed by staff and other users.
Food and facilites:	The Visitor Interpretive Center is a modern facility with a large lobby area, an exhibit room, a multipurpose room, and rest rooms. Visitors are allowed to have bag lunches in the lobby area. Fast-food vendors, restaurants, groceries, and lodging may be found in nearby Long Lake (12 miles). For groceries try Stewart's Shop (518–624–4796), Kickerville Mini-Mart & Deli (518–624–2178). Mike's Newcomb House, adjacent to the trail, serves pizza, burgers, and sandwiches (518–582–4401). Northwoods Diner and General Store offers soups and sandwiches (518–582–3731).
Phone numbers:	The VIC, (518) 582–2000. For emergencies dial 911.
Fees:	There is no fee for trail use.
Caution:	Snowshoeing is prohibited on the lake. Dogs are not allowed on the trails. Do not start on the Peninsula Trail after 3:30 P.M. The trails and the center close at 5 P.M.

The Visitor Interpretive Center (VIC) at Newcomb is one of two interpretive centers operated by the New York State Adirondack Park Agency, which was created by legislative action to provide educational programs for the public in a wilderness setting. The 365-acre site on Rich Lake has been leased from Syracuse University and the SUNY College of Environmental Science and Forestry (ESF). This site includes a mile-long forested peninsula, distinctive wetlands, old-growth forests, lake vistas, scenic outlooks, and a 3.5-mile trail system. Trail users will note that this property is used for a variety of environmental research and educational projects. Students and faculty may be seen here collecting data for scientific research. The VIC offers the public a variety of winter programs, including snowshoeing.

The interpretive trails at the VIC are open in the winter for snowshoeing only. Snowshoers are required to sign in and out at the center. The VIC has a snowshoe-lending program, with a variety of sizes for children and adults. Sign out equipment at the desk, leaving a driver's license as security.

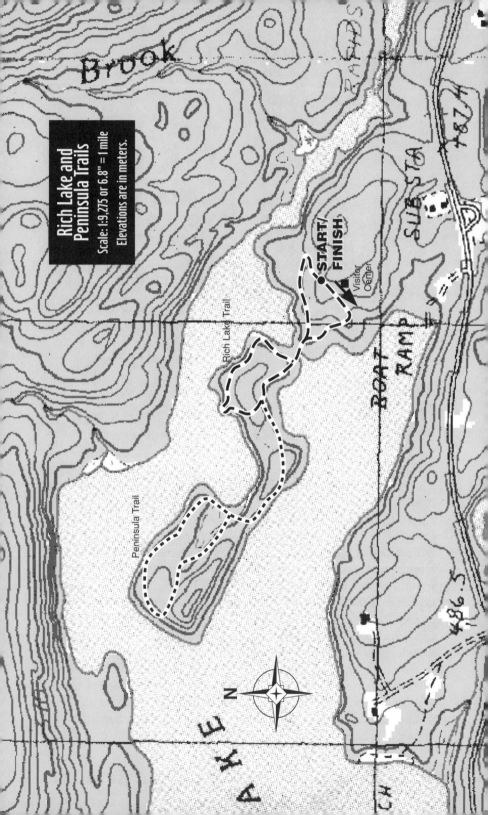

Although the VIC offers three trails, we recommend taking the Rich Lake Trail first, adding the Peninsula Trail if you wish to go further. Follow the red markers from the trailhead located at the back of the Interpretive Center. The trail begins to descend toward Rich Lake from the VIC, with several switchbacks to make the going easier. The trail is gentle, well marked, and well maintained by the staff of the VIC. During other seasons this trail is wheelchair accessible.

Using the trail map and the trail marker system, continue to follow the red trail in the direction indicated. Soon you will arrive at a long wooden boardwalk (with railings) crossing the Cedar Wetlands and leading you to a deck overlook at Rich Lake. As you stand at this magnificent overlook, you may see Goodnow Mountain to the southwest, with its hiking trail and fire tower. To the west is another scenic overlook, located on the Peninsula Trail.

Several of the VIC's interpretive stations can be found along the route. The Graveyard Bay Overlook is clearly in view to your right. After crossing the boardwalk and bridge, the trail descends gradually to a Y on the Rich Lake Loop. Follow the arrows and the red markers to the right as the trail winds through the woods on gently rolling terrain. There are a number of benches along the route for those wishing to stop and enjoy the peace of these surroundings.

The winter trails at the Visitor Interpretive Center at Newcomb are reserved for snowshoers only.

It is important that you stay on the trail for the protection of the plants and habitats of the animals.

At trail marker 6 on Rich Lake Trail you will find a second overlook. To the west you will see the lake, a marsh area, and the floating boardwalk on the Peninsula Trail. To the north and around the lake is the outlet to Rich Lake. The trail continues to meander and turn through a conifer forest and along the shoreline to the Peninsula Trail junction. At this point you may wish to return to the VIC, retracing your steps on the Rich Lake Trail for a total distance of approximately 0.6 mile. Turn right onto the Peninsula Trail if you wish to continue snowshoeing for an additional mile.

The Peninsula Trailhead is located across from an enormous boulder (glacial rock). It is much more difficult than the Rich Lake Trail. You will find several very steep sections on this trail. Snowshoers need to exercise extreme caution, especially going downhill. Be careful not to lean backward on the snowshoes.

At the beginning of this trail, you'll travel up a small knoll and descend along the lakeshore. As you begin to ascend a steep hill you will come to a Y in the trail. Stay to the left and you will arrive at the deck of the third outlook, called the Graveyard Bay Outlook. Looking to the southeast you should see Graveyard Bay, not visible from the first overlook on the Rich Lake Trail. The bay is named after the small cemetery located across the highway. You will be unable to see the cemetery. This magical spot is quiet and often protected from the wind. Winter visitors may be fortunate enough to observe the unique ice formations created by the wind and wave action. If you listen carefully, you may be able to hear the tinkling and chiming of the moving ice, but more often you may hear groaning of ice forming or, in springtime, of ice going out.

From the Graveyard Bay Outlook retrace your steps back to the Y and continue on the right fork. The trail will take you over several hills before you descend steeply into a grove of gigantic Eastern hemlocks whose canopy gives a cathedral feeling. Extra caution is required here. Following the green markers, the trail turns sharply right before reaching a long floating boardwalk crossing a marsh. The trail continues to a conifer forest. Winter trail users are cautioned to avoid going out on frozen bodies of water. Ponds, lakes, and especially rivers can be extremely dangerous as the current creates uneven thickness and unstable ice. Furthermore, it is important to remember that these trails are located on private property, and snowshoeing is prohibited. Trail users are required to stay on the trail.

Near the furthest end of the Peninsula Trail you will find a scary-looking downhill, but don't be intimidated as the trail turns, descends gently, and quickly levels off. The trail brings you close to the shore of Rich Lake as it turns left toward a high rock wall. Here you will find a "stilt"—a tree that has grown on top of a large boulder while its roots have grown down around the rock. After leaving this interpretive station, you will see a staircase leading to the top of the rock wall. In winter the stairs are off-limits and roped off. Turn left and travel through a wilderness section (off the regular trail) which is only used in winter. It will bring you alongside the marsh and back onto the boardwalk. It is important that you take the left turn. *Do not go onto the ice.* Rich Lake is extremely dangerous. This portion of the lake holds the beginning current, which flows to the lake's outlet. Although it may look solid, it has uneven thickness and is quite unstable.

Turning right, retrace your tracks through the steep section of the Peninsula Trail. As before, you will find the trail well marked with green markers and arrows. Returning to the boulder at Rich Lake Trail junction, turn right and follow the signs back to the Visitor Interpretive Center.

How to get there

From the south, take exit 26 of the Adirondack Northway (I–87) at Pottersville. Take Route 9 north for 0.4 mile, then turn left onto Olmstedville Road. Travel 7 miles through Minerva to the intersection with Route 28N. Turn right on 28N and continue approximately 19 miles to Newcomb. Follow signs to VIC.

From the north, take exit 29 of the Adirondack Northway (I–87). Take left ramp onto Blue Ridge Road (Route 2) approximately 25 miles to Route 28N. Turn right and continue through Newcomb. Follow signs to VIC.

From the west take Routes 28 & 30 to Long Lake. Take Route 28N east approximately 14 miles to Newcomb. Follow signs to VIC.

Hudson River Trail

Warren County Nordic Ski Trail System, Warrensburg, New York

Type of trail:	▬▬▬ ⬭
Also used by:	Hikers, walkers
Distance:	2.0 miles
Trail difficulty:	Easiest
Terrain:	Mostly flat
Surface quality:	Groomed and tracked for classic skiing. Snowshoers must avoid damaging the classic ski trails.
Food and facilities:	A few picnic tables and stone fireplaces are the only facilities at this day-use park. Fast-food vendors, grocery stores, restaurants, and lodging may be found in the nearby village of Warrensburg, about 2 miles from the trails. Groceries are available at Grand Union (518–623–3114) and Stewart's Shop (518–623–9848). For lodging try the Super 8 Motel (518–623–2811) or Country Road Lodge (518–623–4363).
Phone numbers:	Warren County Parks and Recreation, (518) 623–2877. Department of Environmental Conservation (518) 623–3671 or 623–5576. For emergencies dial 911.
Fees:	There are no fees for use of the trails.
Caution:	Winter trail users are cautioned to avoid going near the Hudson River ice floes.

Warren County is the home of one of nation's most famous lakes, the 32-mile Lake George, "Queen of American Lakes." Discovered in 1646 by the French missionary, Father Isaac Jogues, the lake was first called Lac Du Saint Sacrament but was changed by a British General, Sir William Johnson, in 1755. The region was bitterly contested between the French and British (1669–1763) in wars known as the King William's War, the Queen Anne's War, the King George War, and the French and Indian War. The Lake George region played a major role, becoming the scene of momentous warfare. Today museums and replicas of forts tell the story of the development of this region of New York State.

In the early 1800s the Lake George area became a major vacation spot, with the railroad coming to the head of the lake and the tiny village. Many travelers continued north by boat and stagecoach. With the coming of the automobile and better roads, the region grew rapidly and the tiny village of Lake George was incorporated in 1903. Warrensburg, a few miles north of Lake George, was known as the "Queen Village of the Adirondacks."

Hudson River Trail
Scale: 1:10,667 or 5.93" = 1 mile

N

800

700

1000

700

640

START/FINISH

Hudson Street Ext.

700

700

RIVER

Golf
Course

ROAD

H

700

RIVER

AND

BM
656

800

800

Heath
Mtn.

From the time the first settlers are said to have arrived in the region (1773) to the turn of the nineteenth century, only a few hardy pioneer families survived the struggle in the shadow of the great Hackensack Mountain. Lumbering became the leading industry, with great spruce, hemlock, and pine forests surrounding the village. Historians believe the village was named for James Warren, who arrived in 1804 and operated a potash factory, a popular tavern, and a general store.

The sign at the entrance to the parking area for the Warren County Nordic Ski Trail System refers to the site as the "Lake George Wild Forest." Located just off Hudson Street outside the village of Warrensburg, the sign further identifies the trail system as part of the Hudson River Recreation Area. Originally part of the Bissell Farm, the property comprising cross-country ski trails, bike trails, and the county's self-guided nature trail was purchased by Niagara Mohawk Power Corporation for a planned hydroelectric project along the Hudson River. When the power company abandoned the project, the land was gifted to the Conservation Fund and subsequently to New York State to be managed as part of the Adirondack Forest Preserve. The county continues to maintain the hiking and skiing trails as a joint venture with the New York State Department of Environmental Conservation (DEC). There is also an agreement with the owners of adjacent Cronin Golf Resort for use of the golf course in winter for cross-country skiing and snowshoeing. Employees of the Warren County Department of Parks and Recreation use sled groomers as snow conditions dictate to provide a 6-mile network of winter trails.

The Warren County winter trails travel over a wide variety of terrain, ranging from the flat, open golf course trails of the south to the hilly woodland slopes of the north. This network of groomed trails offers countless loop possibilities for all levels of ability. Adjacent to the Hudson River, these unique trails provide numerous opportunities for up-close observations of the serene beauty of the Adirondacks and the very active and often noisy river. Particularly interesting is the rare ice meadow, shaped by the Hudson during thousands of years, over which huge chunks of river ice are periodically driven downstream. It is common for residents to see tremendous ice jams on the river after a midwinter thaw, sometimes congesting the river for several miles. North of Warrensburg the river is quite wide and often freezes to depths of 8 to 10 feet in winter. When the ice begins to break up, large sections float downstream in the swift river current, frequently getting caught where the river turns or narrows, blocking passage of thousands of other ice floes. Huge ice blocks and iceberg-like sheets bang into the blockage, building to a point where the river flows around the jam and over it, causing havoc for homes and roads along the banks. Years of great snow-

Winter trail users are treated to a spectacular view of the ice floes on the Hudson River at the Warren County Trail System.

fall make the situation worse, and River Road must often be closed. Winter trail users marvel at the spectacular and magnificent scenes created here by this annual show, compliments of Mother Nature.

Upon arriving at the parking area, look for the covered kiosk that includes a bulletin board and wooden plaque engraved with a trail map (in color) of the Nordic ski trail system. There is a welcome sign indicating the cooperative sponsorship of the project between the DEC and the county. The Hudson River Trail follows the county Nature Trail, beginning at the kiosk and traveling straight toward the Hudson River at the rear of the property. To the left is the intersection for the South Loop that will later be part of your tour. The main trail, originally a farm road leading to the Bissell Farm, is 10 to 12 feet wide, cutting through an old white pine forest. Although most of the trail is flat, there are some undulating sections. You will notice a few areas where the forest has been thinned as part of a reforestation plan. Bordering the trail is an old stone wall that once served as a meadow fence and property line. The area was farmed by Allie J. Bissell until the early1930s.

In winter, you can see through the pine grove on the left to the neighboring Cronin Golf Resort. A couple of connecting paths allow winter trail users to enjoy miles of easy golf course skiing. Because the Hudson River Trail is also a nature trail (in season) you will note the numbered posts at the interpretive stations along the trail. At post 3 (marked with blue) there is a left junction leading to the golf course. Soon the trail turns sharply right at post 4 and begins a long straightaway following the mighty Hudson River. At this point there is a small, steep path leading to the edge of the river, which should not be attempted on skis.

Here you can look down at the spectacular ice floes in the river as you travel along the wide, long, and flat trail. The trail follows the base of a hill to the end of the roadway/trail, reaching a large clearing that includes a rock ledge overlooking the river. You may wish to ski onto this "Foundation of the Adirondacks," as described in the nature trail booklet. If not covered by snow, you may see the rare green and blue veins in the ledge rock. The igneous rock found in this ledge was formed when underground molten magma was pushed to the surface. Once exposed, it cooled and hardened. If you could see the rock under the snow you'd find the uppermost rocks to be granite with veins of iron ore running through them. This area provides a nice setting for a snack or bag lunch while enjoying the surrounding beauty of the area.

The trail narrows as it turns to the right and continues around the base of the hill, leaving the river behind you. Shortly you'll come to a junction where the North Trail Loop bears off to the left, climbing high above the river and along the hilly northern route to a trail rated for experts only. Although black is the appropriate color for expert trails, the North Trail Loop is marked with blue blazes, perhaps because it is later joined by an intermediate trail.

The Hudson River Trail continues to be narrow as it travels along the base of two small hills. It meanders through the forest, curves to the right, and continues around the ridge between the hills. The trail passes through an old pine plantation, thought to be planted by the Civilian Conservation Corps (CCC) in the 1930s. There are several paint marks on the trees that should be ignored because they have no significance as trail markers. Soon the main trail is intersected on the right by an intermediate trail. Continuing straight on the main trail you will come to a short rise as the trail ascends gently on the side of a hill and continues through the woods. You will soon come to a stone wall separating the two parcels and hills. Shortly beyond you will notice blue blaze markers on the left, indicating the southern trailhead of the expert and intermediate trail loops. As you near the parking lot (post 9) the trail turns right and crosses the picnic area, returning you to the kiosk at the end of the Hudson River Trail. There are several picnic tables and stone fireplaces available here for year-round use.

Directions at a glance

0.0 Begin at the kiosk.

0.1 Pass intersection for South Loop.

0.4 Pass intersection for golf course.

1.0 End straightaway at rock ledge.

1.1 Reach intersection of expert trail.

1.6 Begin South Loop.

2.0 Finish at kiosk and parking lot.

We recommend that you extend your tour for an additional half-mile on the secondary loop (South Loop) with its panoramic view of the river valley and distant hills. You can access this loop at the end of the parking lot, as shown on the trail map. Travel south a few hundred yards from the parking lot, turning right and passing under the power line. You will reach a four-way intersection where the trail accesses miles of golf course trails. Continue straight ahead along the power line toward the Hudson River for a great view of the Hickory Hill Ski Center and the "Three Sisters" mountain peaks across the field and river. The ski center is located on Pine Mountain (left) with Bald Mountain on the right. The middle peak seems to be unnamed. Here the trail turns sharply right before rejoining the Hudson River Trail. Travel in the opposite direction from your earlier trip on this trail and return to the kiosk and parking lot.

How to get there

Take I–87 (north or south) to exit 23. Proceed on Route 9 north through Warrensburg to the traffic light at the five-way intersection at the center of town (bandstand on left). Bear left onto Hudson Street and continue approximately 3 miles to the parking lot for the Warren County Nordic Ski Trails (left).

Sweetwater Trail Loop

Art Roscoe Cross-Country Ski & Mountain Bike Area, Allegany State Park, Salamanca, New York

Type of trail:	▬▬▶
Also used by:	Hikers, bikers, hunters
Distance:	3.4 miles
Terrain:	Hilly
Trail difficulty:	Easiest
Surface quality:	Groomed and tracked
Food and facilities:	The Art Roscoe Cross-Country Ski Center has a comfortable lodge with tables and snack bar. Guests may purchase food here or bring a bag lunch. Fast-food vendors, restaurants, grocery stores, and lodging may be found in nearby Salamanca (4 miles): The Deli (716–945–5111), Parkview Supermarket and Deli (716–945–1226), Napoli Pizza (716–945–1002), Red Garter Playhouse Restaurant (716–945–2503).
Phone numbers:	Park Office, (716) 354–9101. Park Police, (716) 354–9111. Ski Center, (716) 945–0523. Chamber of Commerce, (716) 945–2034. For Emergency dial 911.
Fees:	There is a vehicle use fee to enter the park on weekends. This is a carry-in, carry-out facility.

Since 1921 when land was first purchased for its development, the Allegany State Park has served as a four-season recreational center for the residents of western New York State. The winter trails at the Art Roscoe Cross-Country Ski and Mountain Bike Area in the 65,000-acre park are among the very best the state has to offer.

The legendary Art Roscoe, a longtime forester at the park, loved the thrill of skiing. He was a champion downhill ski racer and actively promoted skiing in the park. Through his efforts the Civilian Conservation Corps (CCC) constructed two ski jumps on the hill behind the Red House Administration Building during the 1930s. For several decades these jumps featured state and international ski jumping events that attracted world-class competitors and large crowds from throughout the region.

Art Roscoe and the CCC also helped to establish the Bova Ski Slopes for downhill skiing in the park, one of the first public downhill ski areas in the state. Downhill skiing remained a popular winter sport in Allegany Park until the Bova Slopes were closed in the early 1980s. Roscoe's efforts in helping to create the feature winter attraction in Alleghany State Park

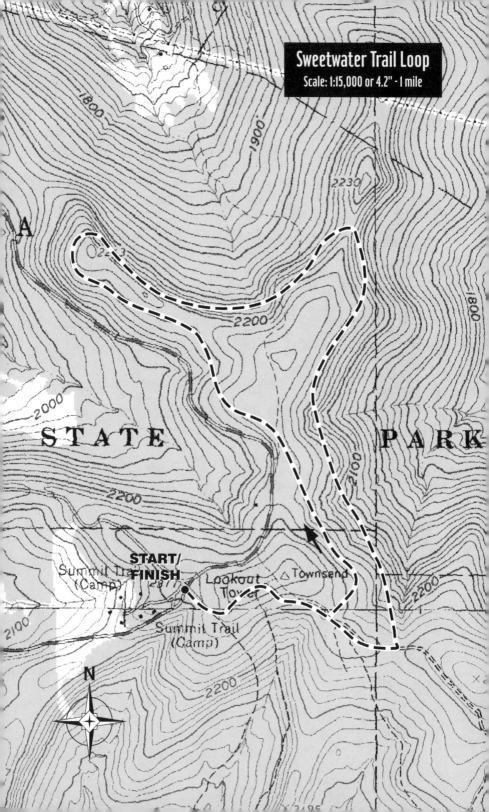

were recognized in 1979 when officials dedicated the extensive cross-country ski trail system in his honor.

Although skiing and snowshoeing are permitted on all hiking trails throughout the immense park, most of the cross-country ski trails in the Art Roscoe area have been designated for skiers only. However, snowshoeing is permitted on the 2.2-mile Stone Tower Trail. The Snowsnake Trail and the Stone Tower Trail are considered skate skiing trails and are packed for the newer cross-country skiing technique.

The Mountain Shop at the Art Roscoe Area on ASP Route 1 includes a very well-equipped rental area with modern snowshoes and ski equipment for both skating and classic cross-country ski techniques. Ski instruction and guided ski tours may be arranged through the concessionaire. The cozy knotty pine warming room equipped with picnic tables includes a snack bar where winter trail users may purchase hot soup, chili, and other refreshments or enjoy a bag lunch.

An elaborate, colorful trail map greets visitors at the popular Art Roscoe Trail in Allegany State Park.

All the designated ski trails begin at the parking lot of the Mountain Shop and are identified on the trail map. Brochures with trail maps are available at the Mountain Shop and the Red House Administration Building. A large trail map, beautifully illustrated with five colors, stands at the entrance to the trail system, giving trail users an additional orientation to the winter trails. There are also large directional signs hanging from posts at the trailheads that clearly identify the trails. These signs can be used in conjunction with the park's trail map, which gives the distance of each route in the trail system.

Access to the Sweetwater Trail is gained just past the stone pillars at the edge of the parking lot. Travel straight ahead on this two-way trail about 100 yards to where it splits. Beginners should take the right hand "flatlander" portion to the Sweetwater Trail Loop; the more experienced winter trail users may bear left and up an incline about 400 yards to an old fire tower. Plans are in the works to restore the fire tower.

From the fire tower, the trail descends on a gentle grade and reconnects shortly with the "flatlander loop." Continue skiing about a quarter mile to a sign directing you to turn left at the entrance to the Sweetwater Trail. Also hanging from the signpost is a large laminated map for trail users to review before beginning the 2.7-mile loop.

This section of the trail starts off with a very long but gradual decline.

Directions at a glance

0.0   Begin at the trailhead at the parking lot.

0.1   Bear left at the V in the trail.

0.2   Pass the old fire tower.

0.3   Turn left at first junction for the Sweetwater Trail.

1.0   Trail turns before the overlook for return.

2.7   Junction at Christian Hollow Loop.

3.1   Return to first Sweetwater Trail Loop junction. Continue 0.3 mile to the parking lot.

It is quite wide (10 to 12 feet) and is covered with grass in the summer, which helps to hold the snow in winter. You will ski through a very tall hardwood forest with many black cherry trees. After a mostly flat and straight run, the trail turns sharply left. At this point skiers may pick up a little speed, but once you're around the turn the trail flattens. This trail is well designed with wide turns, making it easy for beginners and novices to navigate.

Now comes a rolling section and a slightly steeper climb. Although there are no extremes on this trail, first-timers may have to rely on the herringbone technique at this point. Beginners should also be aware that this trail is a long loop with no cutoffs. Turning around before tiring, getting cold, or being injured is encouraged.

At about 1 mile the trail turns sharply to the right and begins to head back toward the trailhead. Here you will find an overlook (left), a good spot to stop for a rest or snack. As you continue to travel along the ridge at an elevation of 2,152 feet, you will view the valley below and the hills beyond. The trail here is quite flat and wide, apparently an old logging road.

Soon the trail turns and you begin a long gradual downhill run that levels off at the end, as do all of the downhills on the Sweetwater Trail Loop. As you near the end of the trail and begin yet another long but gradual incline, you will note the trailhead signs ahead for the Christian Hollow and Sweetwater Trails. Turn right at this junction and return 0.3 miles to where the Sweetwater Trail began. Continue straight ahead for another 0.4 miles, passing the fire tower and several old stone fireplaces before returning to the parking lot and Mountain Shop.

How to get there

From the Southern Tier Expresssway (Route 17) take exit 19 or 21 for the Red House Area. Follow signs to ASP Route 1 and the Mountain Shop.

Yellow Trail Loop

Phillips Creek Trail System, Belmont, New York

Type of trail:	══ 💠
Also used by:	Hikers, bikers, equestrians
Distance:	1.46 miles
Terrain:	Mostly flat and rolling
Trail difficulty:	Easiest
Surface quality:	Ungroomed, skier tracked
Food and facilities:	There are no facilities at the Phillips Creek Trail System. A map box with trail maps is attached to the kiosk at the parking area. Fast food, groceries, restaurants, and lodging may be found in nearby Alfred (4 miles). For convenience items and gas: College BP (607–587–9112). College Inn (607–587–8107), Manhattan West Restaurant (607–587–9363).
Phone numbers:	Department of Environmental Conservation–Belmont, (716) 268–5392. Forest Ranger, (716) 567–2187 or 437–2914. For emergencies call 911.
Fees:	None.
Caution:	There is no patrol and no telephone. Winter trails users should use the buddy system. Always be prepared for deteriorating weather conditions.

The Phillips Creek Trail System, located in the Phillips Creek State Forest, is designed for skiing, snowshoeing, and horseback riding. Snowshoers are welcome to use the trails, but are expected to stay out of the ski tracks.

Phillips Creek Trail System actually involves three state forests: Palmers Pond, Phillips Creek, and Turnpike. Together it comprises 11,098 acres of the West Almond Management Unit in Allegany County. Located just 4 miles from Alfred and 9 miles from the DEC Office of Lands and Forest at Belmont, the trails are frequently used by equestrians and hikers as well as cross-country skiers and snowshoers.

The trails at Philips Creek were laid out by Professor Raymond Yelle of SUNY Agriculture and Technical College at Alfred. Where possible, they follow old fire lanes that were put in place with the planting of millions of trees by the Civilian Conservation Corps (CCC) in the 1930s. The state later acquired abandoned farmlands in the area for reforestation, wildlife management, and other conservation needs. Subsequent land acquisitions have emphasized establishing and maintaining forests

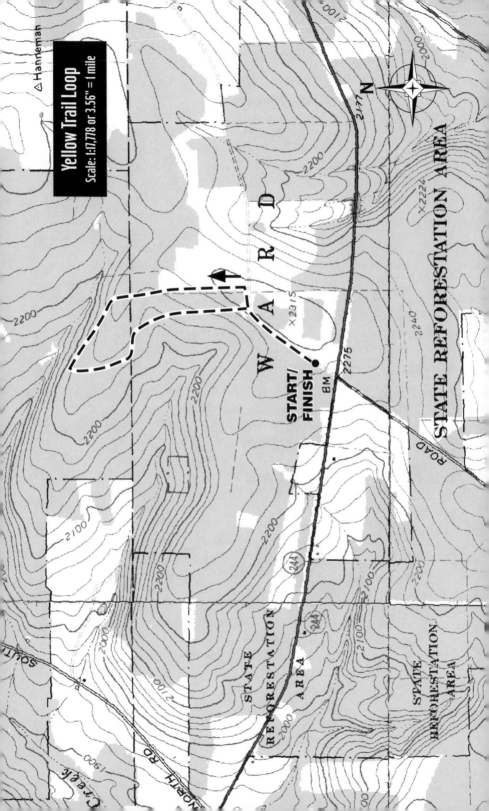

Yellow Trail Loop
Scale: 1:17,778 or 3.56" = 1 mile

△ Hahneman

N

START/
FINISH

BM

W A R D

×2315

2275

STATE REFORESTATION AREA

ROAD

244

STATE
REFORESTATION
AREA

STATE
REFORESTATION
AREA

NORTH RD

SOUTH

Creek

2100

2200

2000

2100

1900

2240

2224

×2224

2200

2100

for watershed protection, production of timber and other forest products, and recreation.

During the summer of 1976, high school students working in the Youth Conservation Corps constructed the trails under the leadership of Maurice Hannon of Allegany County BOCES at Belmont. In 1987 the trails were improved to accommodate horses (June through September). The trails pass through conifer plantations (larch, pine, spruce) and hardwood groves of various age classes, from seedling-sapling to poles and sawtimber. Results from recent harvesting may be seen by winter trail users, from clear-cuts to third row red pine removal. Selective hardwood cutting leaves trees important for wildlife, such as den trees.

Parking for the Phillips Creek Trails is at Stuck Hill Road and Route 244, where you'll find a large billboard map printed in color and a covered picnic table for the convenience of trail users. There are also several hitching rails for horses. All ski trails begin at the trail map, which identifies five trails, two for beginners, two for intermediates, and one for experts. To access the trails, travel straight ahead beyond the picnic table and hitching rails on a very wide trail (40 feet). This former town road will lead you to the trailheads of several ski and snowshoe trails.

About 200 yards beyond the parking area (on the left) is the start of

Snow piles up along the winter trails at Phillips Creek Trail System.

trail #2 (red) and trail #6 (blue). Note that the blue trail is not for skiing. To reach the Yellow Trail Loop, stay on the old roadway for another 200 yards. On the left you will find the combination trails 1 and 2 that loop back to the parking area. After another fifty yards you will turn sharply left for the beginning of the Yellow Trail Loop. The trailhead is also the return of trail #3 for intermediate-level skiers.

The Yellow Trail passes through mixed pines and then hardwoods. The timber here was planted in 1955 and every third row was harvested in 1995. After a short distance the intermediate trail #3 joins on the right. As you begin a long, gentle downhill run, you'll see a mixed pine plantation on your left. The Scotch pines are quite distinguishable with their orange bark. Black locusts, with their dark, deeply grooved bark, and black cherry trees with flaky bark line both sides of the trail. There is still debris here from an ice storm in 1991.

As the trail flattens you will see some red pines on the right that have tipped over due to shallow, poorly drained soil. You soon enter a hardwood area, leaving the protection of the pines. The trail narrows and is designated by white paint blazes. The red oak trees along this trail were left during a timber and hardwood harvest because the tops generally decay, returning nutrients to the soil.

Continuing up a slight incline, the trail takes a sharp left turn and heads west along the top of a ridge, passing some black cherry trees. The trail begins winding slightly downhill past the remnants (stumps and tops) of large "wolf" hard maples that were harvested to give younger, better trees the needed growing space. Look for a large, poor hard maple on the left, about 30 feet off the trail that was double chain-saw girdled. This was done to kill the tree, but it will remain standing and continue to be beneficial to wildlife. As it gradually decays and falls harmlessly to the ground, it will not damage the younger trees around it.

Continue to a large log landing (clearing), a place where the logs were stockpiled during the 1995 harvest. The landing was seeded to establish a cover on the bare soil and to benefit the wildlife. You now are entering the darkness of a Norway spruce and white pine plantation. It will get lighter when you encounter more hardwoods and two large red pines on the left. As you leave this area you will reach Blue Trail #6, which goes right and down a steep hill. There is a parking area sign with a left arrow as the Yellow Trail Loop takes a sharp left, following a fire lane before heading south. The trail is level and straight. It bends left and goes downhill slightly. The Yellow Trail joins the Red Trail, making a 90-degree turn to the left, and loops back through the Norway spruce and white pine. You will pass a distinctive clump of basswood trees on the left and notice the white blazes on the large red oak, hard maple, and white ash trees along the trail.

Directions at a glance

0.0 Begin at parking lot.

0.2 Pass junction for trails 2 and 6.

0.3 Pass junction for return of trails 1 and 2.

0.4 Turn left onto Yellow Trail.

0.5 Continue straight as intermediate trail 3 (red) goes right.

1.0 Make a sharp left turn at the junction of trail 6.

1.2 Turn left at junction with trail 2.

1.4 Turn right at end of Yellow Trail Loop.

1.46 Finish at parking lot.

An old ski trail crosses the Yellow Trail. You'll notice a huge red oak tree with a "W" (wildlife tree) before coming to an area with a gentle, west-facing slope. Here you'll be subjected to the wind before reaching the protection of pine trees on both sides of the trail. The area sloping to the west on a long gradual uphill is a fire lane. Near the top of the grade, several black locust trees appear on the right, followed by black maple trees. On the left is an old foundation, surrounded by buckthorn and thorn apple trees. As the Yellow Trail Loop comes to an end there is a long gentle rise and an opening in the trees where you will note a directional sign ahead. Turn right at the posted sign and return to the parking lot. If you would like to try another beginner trail before ending the day, see Red Trail #2. It's just a little over a mile long and quite enjoyable. Maps and other information can be obtained by contacting the Belmont office of the DEC (see appendix).

How to get there

From the Southern Tier Expressway (Route 17), take exit 30 to Route 19. Travel south 3 miles to Route 244. Turn left and follow the signs to the Phillips Creek parking area.

A and AA Trails

Belleayre Cross-Country Ski Trails, Highmount, New York

Type of trail:	▬▬ ⬭
Also used by:	Hikers, bikers
Distance:	1.5 miles
Terrain:	Flat to hilly
Trail difficulty:	Easiest
Surface quality:	Ungroomed, user tracked
Food and facilities:	There are no facilities at the Belleayre Cross-Country Ski Trails. However, the Discovery Lodge (Lower Lodge) can be reached from the cross-country ski trails, or via a very short drive from the Nordic parking lot. It offers all the modern amenities of the Alpine center, including a full-service cafeteria, warm rest rooms, and first-aid services. The Ski Shop offers cross-country ski equipment for rent, while the Ski School provides cross-country ski lessons. A wide variety of restaurants and lodging can be found in the nearby communities of Highmount and Pine Hill. One of our favorite eateries is the Key West Cafe in Pine Hill, featuring traditional and vegetarian cuisine (914–254–4592). For groceries try the Belleayre Plaza Grocery & Deli in Pine Hill (914–254–4753). Belleayre Mountain offers a lodging service (800–431–4555)
Phone numbers:	Belleayre Mountain, (914) 254–5600.
Fees:	There is no fee to use the Nordic trails.
Caution:	The Nordic trails are not patrolled. Trail users should not ski or snowshoe alone and should stay within their ability. The winter trails are open for skiing and snowshoeing only. Hikers and bikers are not permitted on the trails when there is snow.

The ski trails at Belleayre Mountain were used by hikers and skiers before 1885 when they were declared "forever wild" as a result of the creation of the New York State Forest Preserve. According to historians, hiker Oliver Shipps drew a map in 1931 of his ski route to the summit of Belleayre Mountain and left it with the local hotel owners so others could follow. A 1939 guidebook refers to the ski trails at "Bell Ayr" as "the best in the Catskills." Ten years later, the narrow trails from the mountain's summit were widened to accommodate hundreds of skiers at a time. The state's first chair lift was added to a series of electrical rope tows, and the operation of the state-owned ski center was turned over to the New York State Department of Environmental Conservation (DEC).

START/
FINISH

A Trail

AA Trail

Highmount

Barch

1800

1700

1700

1800

1800

28

Bellayre Mountain Access Road

A and AA Trails
Scale: 1:10,971 or 5.8" = 1 mile

Trail maps and a trail board greet skiers and snowshoers at
Belleayre Cross-Country Ski Trails.

Belleayre Mountain is one of only a few Nordic ski facilities in the state where skiers and snowshoers may enjoy the amenities of a modern Alpine ski lodge. Winter enthusiasts find Belleayre Mountain an ideal destination for enjoying both Alpine and cross-country skiing as well as other winter activities provided by the ski center. The cross-country ski trails are located in the quiet woods of the forever wild Catskill Forest Preserve near the entrance to the popular Alpine ski center. The trails are also open to snowshoers, who are reminded to avoid damaging the tracks made by skiers. The cross-country ski trails are open to the public free of charge. Although they are not groomed or patrolled, these trails are appealing to many individuals, families, and groups because the high altitude regularly provides the most consistent natural snow in the region.

Belleayre offers approximately 4 miles of Nordic trails, ranging from easiest for beginners to the most difficult for experts. The trails are well designed with a series of loops and are appropriately identified with letters and DEC trail markers (yellow disks). The trails were originally designed for travel in a clockwise direction with signs and arrows pointing the way, but two-way travel is now permitted. A trail map specifying the degree of difficulty of the trails is available at the Discovery Lodge. The easiest trail is A Trail; J Trail is the most difficult. Those wishing to rent ski or snowshoe equipment or take cross-country ski lessons can do so at the Discovery Lodge, located adjacent to the Nordic ski trails. Because the Alpine teaching area is assisted by snowmaking, cross-country skiers may take lessons here even on days when there is no snow on the cross-country ski trails. Belleayre also offers an unusual opportunity for telemark ski lessons for those who want to improve their downhill skiing skills or become more proficient on the steeper cross-country ski trails and in the backcountry.

It is recommended that beginners and novices start off on the A Trail or AA Trail. These easiest trails can make trying the sport of cross-country skiing a positive experience for first-timers. Each trail is a loop of less than a mile, starting near and returning to the Nordic parking lot. Skiers can relax after each loop or combine the two novice loops. They can go to the nearby Discovery Lodge for food/drink or rest rooms returning to the Nordic trails in the afternoon. Experienced skiers may access the Discovery Lodge from the H Trail; others can walk or drive up the entrance road to the lodge. Belleayre's cross-country ski trails offer several optional trails for experienced and expert skiers and snowshoers, providing some very challenging skiing. The better your skills, the more of Belleayre's Nordic ski trails you can include. The H and J Trails are higher on the mountain, requiring better physical conditioning and a more advanced level of skill for both skiers and snowshoers. Expert Nordic skiers are welcome to use the Alpine ski trails, but must purchase a ticket to do so. While at Belleayre Mountain you may want to consider taking an advanced ski lesson from instructors at the Belleayre Mountain Ski School.

Beginners, novices, and others with limited time may begin the tour at Belleayre Cross-Country Ski Trail using the A Trail as a warm-up loop, then proceeding to the AA Trail, which is only a bit more difficult. Combining the A Trail and AA Trail before returning to the parking lot will give you a total of 1.5 miles of skiing or snowshoeing.

You may access Belleayre's cross-country ski trails just behind the large trail map marquee at the edge of the parking lot. Begin your tour of the A and AA Trails by skiing or snowshoeing straight ahead as the trail enters the woods. Pass the first junction on your right. This is a one-way return for the AA Trail. Continue a bit further turning at the first left junction and following the trail through a pretty mature forest of mixed hardwoods. The trail is mostly flat with a few undulations, gentle slopes, inclines, and gradual turns. There is a sharp left turn just before the trail reaches a fenced-in private home. Continuing along the trail you will exit the woods and cross an open field before arriving back at the parking lot. You may choose to quit here or enter the woods again to combine the AA Trail with your tour.

If you choose to continue, begin again at the trail map marquee skiing or snowshoeing straight-ahead passing a right junction and left junction. This trail is a little more challenging but quite enjoyable and safe for beginners and others. Here you will enjoy a nice long and gentle down-

Directions at a glance

0.0   Begin A Trail at parking lot.

0.1   Pass right junction.

0.12 Turn sharply left at sign for A Trail.

0.25 Pass HH Trail.

0.3   Pass Four Corner junction

0.5   Turn sharply left at private home.

0.7   Cross open field.

1.0   Return to parking lot and start of AA Trail.

1.0   Begin AA Trail.

1.1   Pass junction on right.

1.25 Pass junction and bridge of left for H Trail.

1.54 Turn left at entrance trail.

1.55 Return to parking lot.

hill run to the junction for the bridge and the H Trail. Snowshoers as well as intermediate and advanced skiers should turn here to access Belleayre's more advanced trails and the lower lodge.

After passing this junction you will begin a long steady climb until you reach a sharp swithback on your right. The trail flattens out and meanders through a forest of mixed hardwoods and evergreens. The terrain offers a few gentle slopes and climbs before passing an old cemetery and returning to the one-way entrance trail. Here you'll turn left for the short jaunt back to the parking lot.

How to get there

From the New York State Thruway (I–87) take exit 19 at Kingston. Travel west on Route 28 to Highmount. Follow signs to the ski center and cross-country parking lot.

From I–88 take exit 17 at Oneonta. Drive south on Main Street to Route 28. Turn right and follow Route 28 approximately 50 miles to Highmount. Follow signs to the ski center and cross-country parking lot.

Neversink and Sugar Shack Trails

Frost Valley YMCA Conference and Family Center, Claryville, New York

Type of trail:	▬▬ ◄
Also used by:	Hikers, walkers, equestrians
Distance:	3.2 miles
Terrain:	Flat to hilly
Trail difficulty:	Easiest to more difficult
Surface quality:	Packed and groomed
Food and facilities:	In winter Frost Valley's large horse barn is converted into a warm and friendly Frost Valley YMCA Nordic Center. The center offers modern ski and snowshoe equipment for guests as well as trail users who come for the day. Equipment rental, accessories, and lessons are available. Everyone is welcome to eat lunch at the Frost Valley Dining Hall; brown baggers are also welcome at the Nordic Center. Groceries and other supplies may be purchased at the Frost Valley store or at nearby Morra's Market and Deli at Big Indian (914–254–4649) and Belleayre Plaza Market in Pine Hill (914–254–4753). Other restaurants and lodging may be found in Big Indian and Pine Hill. Fast-food vendors, restaurants, chain stores, and other lodging may be found in New Paltz and Kingston. One of our favorite eateries is the Key West Cafe in Pine Hill, featuring traditional and vegetarian cuisine (914–254–4592). For lodging try Pine Hill Arms Hotel (800–932–2446).
Phone numbers:	Frost Valley YMCA, (914) 985–2291.
Fees:	There are fees for use of the trails and other facilities at the resort.
Caution:	Skiers and snowshoers must use caution when crossing roads.

The Frost Valley YMCA Conference and Family Center is located in a frosty valley in the heart of New York's Catskill Mountains. Pristine forests, rolling meadows, ponds, a lake, cascading waterfalls, and mountain streams make Frost Valley YMCA one of the most scenic conference and family centers in the country. It is indeed a snowy place, due to its location at the foothills of Slide Mountain, the highest peak in the Catskills. Frost Valley Nordic Center, 5 miles from the Slide Mountain trailhead, is part of the 6,500-acre Frost Valley YMCA.

Once the country estate and vacation home of Julius Forstman, the

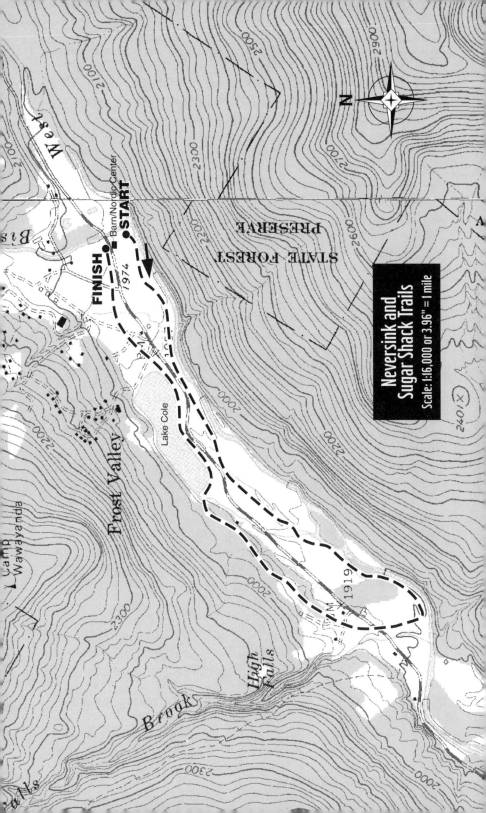

Neversink and
Sugar Shack Trails
Scale: 1:16,000 or 3.96" = 1 mile

START

FINISH

Barn/Nordic Center

1974

1919

State Forest
Preserve

West

Bi

Bi

Frost Valley

Lake Cole

Camp
Wawayanda

High
Falls

Brook

2400 X

N

2100
2500
2900
2300
2700
2700
2600
2200
2200
2000
2200
2000
2000
2300
2300
2000

property now serves as a year-round recreation and educational center. Like other YMCAs, Frost Valley Conference and Family Center prides itself on providing programs "to serve the needs of children, families, and communities while teaching respect, caring, honesty, and responsibility."

The public is welcome to participate in a wide variety of winter recreational activities, including snow tubing, tobogganing, ice-skating, snowshoeing, and cross-country skiing. Frost Valley boasts of nearly 35 kilometers of ski and snowshoe trails. Two trails, Devil's Hole and Sequoia Loop, are designated for snowshoeing.

The roots of the Frost Valley YMCA date to the first YMCA Camps in America. The Frost Valley Association and the Independent Frost Valley YMCA were created in 1958 when New Jersey's Camp Wawayanda moved to the Catskills and relocated on the Forstman Estate. As the camp proved successful, many buildings were winterized, allowing for year-round recreational and educational programs. Today Frost Valley comprises more than 6,500 acres of forest land and encompasses the two valleys of the east and west branches of the Neversink River. Innovative camping conferences and family and environmental programs serve more than 30,000 guests annually.

The trailhead for the Neversink Trail begins at the rear of the Nordic Center, which serves as a horse barn in summer. Cross-country ski equipment in children's and adult sizes is available for rent. A bulletin board displays daily postings of trail conditions, and the field in front of the barn serves as a teaching area for ski lessons. Castle Loop to the left of the barn is a practice trail for novices.

To access the Neversink Trail, turn right at the rear door of the Nordic Center and follow the trail signs through the corral to the first junction. The trail is generally wide enough for a groomed track on each side plus a rolled section in the center for snowshoeing or skate skiing. The Neversink Trail, marked with red blazes, meanders alongside the river through hardwood and evergreen groves with an occasional small stream crossing and flowing into the river. A small waterfall may be seen (or heard) in winter across the river. Many deer roam these trails and are often seen here by winter trail users.

As you follow the trail along the river you'll cross a culvert covered by an earthen bridge before reaching White Pond, a man-made fishing pond. You will also pass the maintenance buildings and trailside rest room (with a modern composting toilet). Here too is the Frost Valley Resource Management Center, where all of the resort's wastes are recycled. The center also serves as a research facility, providing a unique opportunity for studies by staff and guests.

The trail continues to be mostly flat, but it narrows here as it enters an evergreen grove. You will notice a stone wall on the left and the Red

A lone skier enjoys a sunny day on the trails at Frost Valley YMCA.

Bridge crossing the river ahead of you. The trail turns sharply to the right through a wetland as it follows the High Falls Stream. You will cross a wooden bridge, passing a small tree plantation before reaching the main road and barn used by the Claryville Fire Department. At this point novice and beginning skiers may wish to turn around and head back to the Nordic Center, reducing the length of the trip to 2.6 miles.

The next section presents a few hilly areas. Although there is nothing very difficult, it may require some sidestepping and herringbone ski techniques.

The Neversink River Trail crosses the road and joins the Sugar Shack Trail to complete the loop back to the Nordic Center. This trail is blazed with yellow markers and is slightly more difficult as it climbs the hills toward the Sugar Shack. The trail is rolling and undulating. This may be the place to try your ski-climbing techniques or remove skis and walk to the top. As you pass the Sugar Shack on your left you are likely to see some deer if the snow is not too deep. Bear right on the yellow trail and cross the bridge, keeping the Sugar Shack to your left. You will reach a small Christmas Tree Farm, planted and maintained by the Frost Valley staff. Keeping the tree farm to your left, follow the trail as it sweeps downhill and crosses another trail. Here you might wish to turn right to cross the road and return to the Neversink Trail and the Nordic Center.

Directions at a glance

0.0 Begin at Nordic Center.

0.1 Turn right on to Neversink Trail at the river.

0.3 Continue straight at intersection for shortcut to Lake Cole Trails.

1.0 Pass White Pond.

1.1 Trail turns before Red Bridge.

1.3 Cross road, or turn around and return to Nordic Center.

1.4 Pass Sugar Shack and bear right.

2.2 Stay right at the junction for upper and lower Lake Cole Trails.

3.2 Finish at Nordic Center.

Continuing straight ahead on the Sugar Shack Trail, you will cross a wooden bridge before reaching a private driveway. If snow conditions permit, you may ski along the driveway about 100 yards and continue on the trail to the junction for the Lake Cole Trails. Blazed with yellow markers, the upper trail (left) is the steeper of the two. Take the trail to the right, blazed with blue. This lower trail descends gradually to the lake outlet, crosses a bridge, and turns left to follow a ridge around the lake where the upper and lower trails meet again. The trail that circles the lake (portions of both Lake Cole and Sugar Shack Trails) is the Frost Valley Fitness Trail. Cole Lake is used for ice-skating and ice fishing when conditions permit, but, Frost Valley YMCA prohibits skiing and snowshoeing on the lake.

Continue past the lake, through a stone wall, and into a large field. In the middle of the field, the trail crosses the small Trickle Brook and returns to the Frost Valley Nordic Center.

How to get there

Take the New York State Thruway (I–87) to exit 19 (Kingston). Go 30 miles west on Route 28 to Big Indian. Turn left on County Road 47 and go 14 miles to Frost Valley.

Awosting and Castle Point Trail Loop
Minnewaska State Park Preserve, New Paltz, New York

Type of trail:	➡️ ◀
Distance:	9.2 miles
Terrain:	Hilly
Trail difficulty:	More difficult
Surface quality:	Machine groomed (double tracked)
Food and facilities:	A concessionaire operates a ski shop on weekends from the small Nature Center located near the winter parking lot. It provides rental equipment, some accessories, and instructors for ski lessons. Snacks and hot chocolate are also available. Portable toilets are located near the ski shop and a heated mobile home is installed in the parking lot as a warming hut for winter recreational users. Fast-food vendors, restaurants, grocery stores, and lodging may be found nearby in New Paltz (10 miles). For groceries try Family Farm Market at the New Paltz Plaza (914–255–4992) and Benson's Mountain Store & Deli near the park preserve entrance (914–255–2999).
Phone numbers:	Park Office, (914) 255–0752, Ski Shop, (914) 255–7059, McCoy Concessions, (914) 564–5858, Park Police (914) 786–2781 or dial 911 for emergencies.
Fees:	There is a fee for trail use.
Caution:	Carriageways, trails, and overlooks throughout the park are adjacent to steep descents and cliffs. Exercise extreme caution in all these areas.

Unique and sensitive environments, valuable for their many rare geological and vegetation features, characterize Minnewaska State Park Preserve. The preserve is situated in the dramatic Shawangunk Mountain Ridge, which rises more that 2,000 feet above sea level. The ridge dominates the Park Preserve and its immediate environs, as well as the rolling agricultural landscape of the surrounding towns and hamlets below. The Shawangunk and nearby Catskill Mountains have been attracting tourists and artists for more than a century, spurred by the completion of railroads linking the area to the Hudson River and New York City.

In winter Minnewaska Preserve opens about 20 miles of old carriage trails exclusively for cross-country skiing. Some of these are award-winning mountain bike trails. Walking, hiking, and snowshoeing are permitted on the hiking trails and trails off the Awosting parking lot and Peter's Kill area. The unusually wide ski trails are machine rolled and tracked for

Awosting and Castle
Point Trail Loop
Scale: 1:31,578 or 2" = 1 mile

START/
FINISH

Lake Minnewaska

Castle Point Trail

Upper Awosting Trail

Litchfield
Ledge

Castle

Castle
Point

Lake Minnewaska
Cliff House

ROCHESTER

Standens

Peters Kill

Widmer Run

Peters Kill

Camp
Laurel

Lake Awosting

SHAWANGUNK

N

classic (kick and glide) skiing, with most sections wide enough for skate skiing in the middle between two sets of tracks. The trails are blazed with color-coded trail markers and directional signs. Dogs are not allowed on the ski trails. Those who need to rent ski equipment (weekends only) will find a ski shop to the left of the winter parking lot.

The Minnewaska Park Preserve is open daily from 9:00 A.M. until 5:00 P.M. in winter. The gates are closed at other times. The parking lot is plowed and volunteers help to patrol the ski trails. Trail maps and other information are available at the park office. Ski lessons and equipment may be reserved in advance by calling (914) 564–5858.

To access Awosting and Castle Point Loop we recommend that all but the most experienced skiers carry their skis from the winter parking lot to the beach at Lake Minnewaska. Wedging and sidestepping techniques are also effective in negotiating this difficult initial section, but it is probably best to walk down to the beach area to start on this trail. The rest of the trail is easy until you return here to climb back to your car.

Skiers don "ole fashioned" ski wear for dress-up-day on the winter trails.

At the beach you will find the trail sign directing you to the Upper Awosting Trail. Follow the green markers as the trail begins a long and gradual climb through a hardwood forest with some plateaus for resting before continuing your uphill trek. At about 0.8 mile you will reach an open meadow and apple orchard, followed by more hardwood groves and a wide creek bed. The trail becomes slightly steeper and is crossed by a power line and a wooden bridge as it descends slightly before reaching a junction with the New York/New Jersey Long Path. Here you will find an imposing rock wall on the left and a view of the deep valley on your right. You will then be treated to one of the most spectacular views found anywhere as you reach the first outlook onto Lake Awosting surrounded by massive sections of the famous white Shawangunk conglomerate. This large flat ledge is an ideal stopping place for a rest. Don't go near the edge: It is a 200- to 300-foot drop to the bottom of these sheer cliffs.

The green markers end here and are replaced by blue markers as the trail continues to present great views of Lake Awosting, climbing for

Directions at a glance

0.0   Begin at the winter parking lot.

0.8   The apple orchard can be seen to the left.

2.3   Cross under power lines.

3.1   Pass junction for Awosting Lake Carriageway.

3.2   Pass junction for beach trail.

3.7   Pass junction for Hamilton Point Trail.

4.2   Reach Castle Point.

7.9   Reach Kempton Ledge.

9.2   Finish at winter parking lot.

some time along the top of the hill, meandering and twisting with some switchback turns along the top of the lake. At the junction for the Lake Awosting Beach (left), signs are posted giving distances and warning users to exercise extreme caution at the cliffs. From here it's a half mile to the junction for the Hamilton Point Carriageway (not groomed for skiing) and 1 mile to the Castle Point Carriageway.

You will encounter still more ledges and cliffs overlooking the lake and valley below as the trail continues to twist and turn toward Castle Point. The trail turns away from Lake Awosting and back toward Lake Minnewaska before reaching a sharp left at the junction for the Hamilton Point Carriageway. There is a very scenic view at Castle Point and others along the Castle Point Trail. Continuing east on the Castle Point Trail, you'll cross under the power line again before reaching the unique Kempton Ledge and a scenic view toward a medievel-looking wall.

The Awosting and Castle Point Loop now joins the western section of the Lake Minnewaska Carriageway (red markers). You'll ski on a gradual downhill run as the trail returns to the beach. Remember that the route from the beach to the parking lot ("Library Hill") is quite steep. It may be skied using sidestep and herringbone skiing techniques, but it's probably best to remove your skis here and walk to the parking lot.

How to get there

From exit 18 of the New York State Thruway (I–87) take Route 299 west. Travel through New Paltz 7.5 miles to Route 44/55. Turn right and travel 5 miles to the park entrance.

From the west take Route 209 to Rt. 44/55. Turn right and travel 6 miles to the park entrance.

Eagle Cliff Trail

Mohonk Mountain House, New Paltz, New York

Type of trail: ▬▬

Also used by: Walkers and hikers. Snowshoers may use the woods and open fields, but not the ski trails.

Distance: 1.9 miles

Terrain: Hilly

Trail difficulty: Easiest to more difficult

Surface quality: Groomed and double tracked

Food and facilities: Mohonk Mountain House offers first-class meals and accommodations for its guests. The dining room is open to the public and we highly recommend that you take time for lunch or dinner during your visit. Mohonk boasts of award-winning dining and lodging. Snack and beverage machines as well as rest rooms are available at the Gatehouse for those using the grounds only. Fast-food vendors, restaurants, grocery stores, and lodging may be found in nearby New Paltz. For groceries try the Family Farm Market at the New Paltz Plaza (914–255–4992). Stone Ridge Specialty Foods (914–471–6608) offers light fare.

Phone numbers: Mohonk Mountain House, (914) 255–1000, for reservations, (800) 772–6646. For ski conditions call (914) 256–2197.

Fees: There are trail fees, except for overnight guests.

Caution: Ski/snowshoe trails and footpaths are often adjacent to steep descents and cliffs, some without railings.Everyone must exercise extreme caution. Do not lean on railings or go around barriers. Stay away from cliff edges.

One of the last of America's great nineteenth-century mountain resorts, Mohonk Mountain House stands at the heart of a magnificent 26,000-acre natural area in the Shawangunk Mountains of New York. The sprawling Victorian castle stands guard at the edge of the beautiful Lake Mohonk near the top of the Shawangunk Ridge.

Mohonk Mountain House was founded more than 130 years ago by brothers Albert and Alfred Smiley. The establishment of the resort as a healthful retreat and the Smiley family's interest in conservation have had a significant influence on the architecture, flora, and fauna of the resort. The Smileys envisioned a peaceful retreat "where people and nature would exist in harmony." Albert purchased the property from John F. Stokes, and the brothers eventually turned the ten-room inn and tavern into the grand house it is today. They saw themselves as caretak-

START/FINISH

Mohonk Lake

Mohonk Lake

Eagle Cliff

434

N

Eagle Cliff Trail
Scale: 1:7,680 or 8.25" = 1 mile

ers rather than owners and sought to protect the land. Responsible stewardship has been a hallmark of Mohonk, according to members of the family who continue to manage the resort. In 1986 Mohonk Mountain House, including its complex and surrounding lands, was designated a National Historic Landmark.

Mohonk Mountain House today is a full-service resort, still operated by members of the Smiley family. With more than 260 guest rooms, four guest cottages, and three spacious dining rooms, the hotel is very impressive indeed. It also boasts of 150 working fireplaces, 200 balconies, a half dozen parlors, and three inviting verandas lined with wooden rockers for its many guests. The tranquil resort includes miles of trails and carriage roads well suited for walking and cross-country skiing. The grounds feature magnificent gardens with a Victorian maze, a greenhouse, picnic areas, a museum, stables, sports facilities (including a full-service ski shop), and an observation point known as Sky Top Tower. Once strictly a summer resort, Mohonk Mountain House now accommodates vacationers and conferences year-round. Day-use for cross-country skiing, snowshoeing, and other activities is welcome, provided a meal has been purchased in the dining room.

As you enter the grounds, a sign proclaims SLOWLY AND QUIETLY PLEASE as a reminder that Mohonk is indeed a place apart, a signal for guests and visitors to slow down to a more relaxed pace and to enjoy a serene perspective on life. Guests delight in Mohonk's nineteenth-century ambience and enjoy gourmet meals prepared by chefs who are graduates of the Culinary Institute of America and winners of national culinary competitions.

Winter trail users should stop at the ski shop for a trail map and information pertaining to the trail conditions. To access the Eagle Cliff Trail, skiers start at the main entrance of the Mountain House, turning left and taking the first trailhead. You will pass the beautiful Lake Mohonk, cross a bridge and pass a junction for the Granary and Underpath Trails. There are several switchbacks as the Eagle Cliff Trail turns and continues uphill toward the summit. To the left are wonderful vistas of Sky Top Mountain. After weaving through the wooded areas, you will emerge at Cuyler's Castle, one of the many gazebos constructed at outstanding scenic places along the trail and throughout the grounds of the resort. These unique structures, some appearing to hang over the cliffs, provide ideal spots for resting and savoring the views of the surrounding mountains and the picturesque valley below. A few of the gazebos and benches found along the Eagle Cliff Trail are designated in memory of departed loved ones.

At Cuyler's Castle you'll have a beautiful view of Sky Top Tower. The tower, now visible from the New York State Thruway and for miles around, was built as a memorial to Albert K. Smiley. It was funded by the

The Eagle Cliff Trail offers a spectacular view of Mohonk Mountain House and the Hudson River Valley.

community of Mohonk Mountain House guests in 1921. The stone used to construct the tower was quarried out of the Shawangunk Mountains. The reservoir to the north of the tower now fills the excavation site. As your eyes move from Sky Top Mountain to the snow-covered Mohonk Lake below, you may feel overwhelmed by the beauty and spaciousness of the castlelike Mountain House nestled at the far end of the lake.

The trail winds around to Schaff Chalet, a gazebo with eastern exposure views of the Wallkill Valley and the city of New Paltz. You will soon reach the apex of the Eagle Cliff Trail and find the Artist Rock Summerhouse and a spectacular southern panorama of the Shawangunk Mountains. An inscription here on one of the benches reads, "Beautiful vistas clear the mind and soothe the soul." On clear days the Catskill Mountains appear to be just a stone's throw away, and the turkey buzzards soar over your head on the wind currents.

From here it is all downhill as the Eagle Cliff Trail begins a long and gradual descent winding its way back to the Mountain House and the place you began your tour. The area contains mostly tall hemlocks and mixed hardwood groves, helping to make the return trip quiet and peaceful. Continuing downhill along the trail you will reach a steep rock wall (right) and a log hand railing (left) before emerging from the woods near the tennis courts. It's just a short glide from here to the finish of your ski tour and the entrance to Mohonk Mountain House, where you can stop to enjoy the wide variety of amenities at this fine mountain resort.

How to get there

From Exit 18 of the NYS Thruway (I–87) take Route 299 west. Travel through New Paltz. Immediately after crossing a bridge, turn right and follow the signs to Mohonk Mountain House.

From the west take Route 209 to Route 213 east. Continue through the light to Egg's Nest Restaurant. Turn right on Mountain Rest Road. Travel 5 miles to Mohonk Mountain House.

Rochester Hollow Trail
Catskill Forest Preserve, Big Indian, New York

Type of trail:	▬▬▬ ⬭
Also used by:	Hikers, bikers
Distance:	5.6 miles round-trip
Terrain:	Hilly
Surface quality:	Ungroomed, user tracked
Trail difficulty:	More difficult
Food and facilities:	There are no facilities at this wild forest preserve. Rest rooms and food may be found in the nearby villages of Big Indian and Pine Hill. Try Morra's Market and Deli (914–254–4649) in Big Indian, just over a mile from the trailhead, or Belleayre Plaza Grocery Store (914–254–4753) in Pine Hill (3 miles west). The area features a wide variety of restaurants and ski lodges associated with the Belleayre Mountain Ski Center. One of our favorite eateries is the Key West Cafe in Pine Hill, featuring traditional and vegetarian cuisine (914–254–4592). Call Belleayre's lodging service (914–254–5608) or Pine Hill Arms Hotel (800–932–2446).
Phone numbers:	Department of Environmental Conservation–New Paltz (914) 256–3111. For emergencies call 911.
Fees:	There are no fees to use the trail.
Caution:	This trail is in a wilderness area and is not patrolled.

Rochester Hollow is located on the edge of the Slide Mountain Wilderness in the Catskill Forest Preserve. New York's forest preserve is unique among all other wild public lands of the United States because it enjoys constitutional protection against sale or development. After it was determined that Slide Mountain is the highest peak in the Catskills, the region gained considerably more public attention. "Here the works of man dwindle, in the heart of the southern Catskills," wrote poet and naturalist John Burroughs. A plaque commemorating both the man and the mountain graces the face of the summit.

Situated so near the majestic Hudson River, the Catskills were often the subject of the early Hudson River painters whose pictures brought the mountains into museums and homes of thousands. Washington Irving introduced the world to Rip Van Winkle, the delightful Catskill character from Palenville who went off to South Mountain where he slept for twenty years.

The tough, rugged, and mountainous trails in the Catskills are gener-

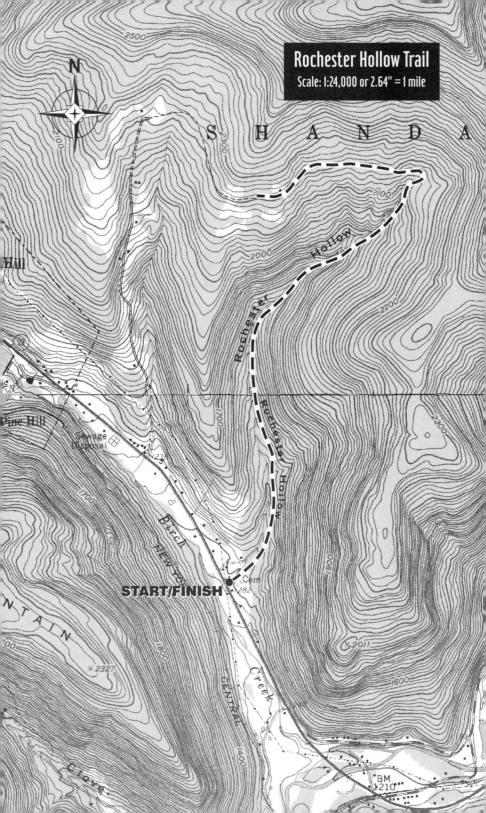

Rochester Hollow Trail
Scale: 1:24,000 or 2.64" = 1 mile

N

SHANDA

Hill

Rochester Hollow

Rochester Hollow

Pine Hill

Sewage Disposal

NEW YO

Birch

START/FINISH

Cem 282

NTAIN

x 2327

x 2011

CENTRAL

Creek

Clove

BM 1210

ally not suited for cross-country skiing. With elevations in the area from 1,100 to almost 4,200 feet, Rochester Hollow Trail is certainly not golf-course flat. It is, however, one of the few easier ski/snowshoe trails in the vicinity of Slide Mountain. As part of the Shandaken Wild Forest, it offers gentle climbs and gradual descents with no steep sections or dangerous downhill turns. This short, pleasant journey through a mostly deciduous forest can be taken at an easy pace or as an invigorating fitness workout, challenging the body on the way up the old woods road and providing a fast-paced slide on the way back. Many winter trail users consider such trails as a "destination tour," a self-paced ski or walk with a place to meet friends and fellow skiers/snowshoers for a trail breakfast or lunch before continuing a journey.

The name "Hill" is engraved in a marble plaque embedded in an old stone pillar at the entrance to the Rochester Hollow Trail. A small parking lot is located at the trailhead about 100 yards beyond the pillar. In winter, however, consider parking in the turnaround on the west side, or along the shoulder of the road because the final 100 yards is not plowed. There is a locked gate across the trail and posted signs identifying the trail as Forest Preserve property designated specifically as "Wild Forest Land." Although there is no register, rules and regulations are posted, advising that motor vehicles are prohibited.

Starting at the locked gate, skiers and snowshoers will begin a long but gradual climb on the old woods road following the Rochester Hollow Brook as it meanders alongside the mountain trail. Winter trail users will enjoy the often loud and cheerful bubbling and gurgling of the brook as they travel the trail, sometimes as close as 10 feet from the edge of the water. Several noisy tributaries also cross under the trail through culverts and stone tunnels originally constructed in the 1920s by the ancestors of local townsfolk. These tributaries join Rochester Hollow Brook on the left side of the trail as it tumbles downward along the woods road. A stone wall, made from the flat slate of the region, appears at about a half mile, followed by a short section of hemlock and other evergreens over-hanging the trail. These slate stones were also used extensively in the construction of the road built along the edge of the valley.

The trail continues on a fairly straight line curving slightly to the right while climbing gradually to a pair of uniquely designed stone pillars and a turnaround area. This is a nice spot for a rest or snack break. Some may choose to shorten the tour and return to the beginning from here (2.4 miles total).

Beyond the pillars the trail climbs steeply for about a half mile to a sharp left switchback. Just beyond the switchback on the right side of the trail you will find a plaque erected by the students of Raymond Riordon

Directions at a glance:

0.0   Begin at the parking lot and locked gate.

0.4   Pass stone wall.

0.7   Travel through hemlock grove.

1.2   Reach stone pillars.

1.7   Pass Burroughs plaque.

2.3   Pass former Colonel Rochester Estate.

2.8   Reach barrier at end of state land. Return via the same route.

School in 1921 in tribute to John Burroughs. The grade moderates as the trail heads west to arrive at the site of Colonel Rochester's estate. Although the house and most of the related structures have long since been removed, a garage foundation and the remains of a springhouse may be seen on the right side of the trail. Opposite the old foundation the road widens at what may have been a grand view overlooking the fields of this formerly farmed land. An attractive view of Slide Mountain can be seen through the trees to the south. You might look for the goldfish in the pond on the left just beyond the stone foundation. The trail continues for another half mile over moderate terrain to a barrier identifying the boundary of the state land. Signs are posted prohibiting public use of the trail (roadway) beyond this point. You might rest or enjoy a snack after your mostly uphill climb and before the downhill fun begins.

The downhill run can be as exhilarating as you wish, or as your ski skills will allow. The trail is straight enough to "let them run." There are no sharp turns or steep pitches and it is wide enough to make edging turns to slow your speed or stop if you wish. About halfway down the trail, a view of the Catskill Mountains appears on the horizon (just past the hemlock section). Here, on a sunny day, you may get a glimpse of a lake at the top of a distant mountain. You'll arrive back at the gate and parking lot, completing a 5.6-mile round-trip outing.

How to get there

From exit 19 of the New York State Thruway (I–87) take Route 28 west to Big Indian. Continue about a mile to Matyas Road. Turn right and travel .05 mile to trailhead.

From the west take I–88 to Oneonta exit. Take Route 28 southeast approximately 55 miles through Delhi and Margaretville to Pine Hill. Continue on Route 28 about a mile to Matyas Road in Big Indian. Turn left and travel .05 mile to trailhead.

Mountain Trail Loop
Williams Lake Resort, Rosendale, New York

Type of trail:	▬▬ ⬭
Also used by:	Hikers, bikers, walkers
Distance:	3.2 miles
Terrain:	Hilly
Trail difficulty:	More difficult
Surface quality:	Machine groomed
Food and facilities:	The Nordic ski center located in the main lodge offers ski, and snowshoe equipment rentals, accessories, and lessons when snow conditions permit. The lodge features a lounge area with rest rooms, a full-service restaurant, and a snack bar with space for brown baggers. Fast-food venues, restaurants, and grocery stores may be found in the village of Rosendale or nearby Stone Ridge, and in Kingston. For groceries try Rosendale Country Market (914–687–2214) or Emmanuel's Marketplace (914–658–3472).
Phone numbers:	Williams Lake Resort, (914) 658–3101.
Fees:	A fee is charged for use of the trails.

The beautiful year-round Williams Lake Resort is nestled among 600 acres of woodland overlooking a forty-acre spring-fed lake. The owners continue a third generation of warm hospitality, fine food, and friendly service at the conference center (main lodge) and guest houses. Winter activities include cross-country skiing, biathlon, hiking, ice-skating, and tobogganing.

The resort is located on property that in the 1800s was used by the Rosendale Cement Company for mining a portion of an 8-mile limestone vein that ran through the Rosendale region. Limestone was excavated from the caves and heated in lime kilns. The high quality limestone found here was used on such significant projects as the Brooklyn Bridge, the Empire State Building, and the New York State Thruway. Several kilns and a huge limestone cave can still be seen along the ski trails.

The Williams Lake Nordic Ski Club, established in 1963, was one of the earliest cross-country ski clubs in America, attracting hundreds of Scandinavian skiers and other European immigrants who had settled in the New York/New Jersey metropolitan area and were anxious to find places to ski. At Williams Lake, named for Finnish-born Gustav Williams, they found excellent skiing trails, friendly fellow Scandinavians, superb meals, and comfortable accommodations. Gustav's grandson, Edward

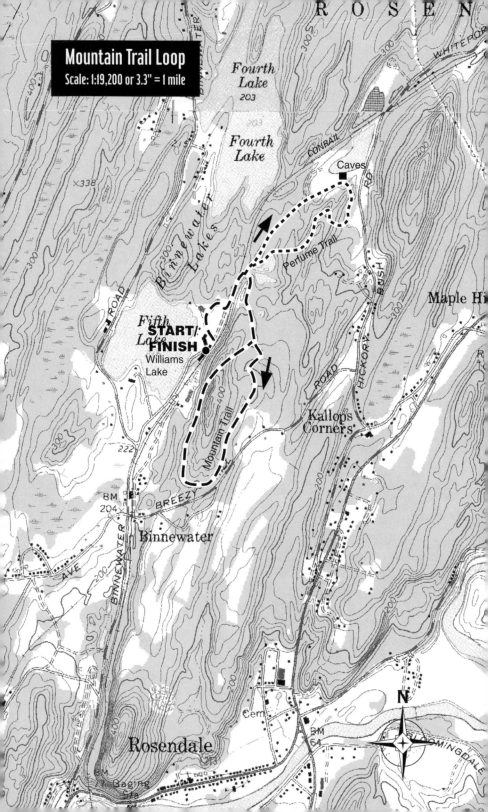

Williams, became one of America's best cross-country skiers. He was a member of the 1962 Olympic Biathlon Team, competing for the United States at Grenoble, France.

The Mountain Trail Loop is actually a combination of several trails, including the short Mountain Trail. All the trails at the resort are open for snowshoeing as well as skiing and are accessed from the Ski Shop and Nordic Center located in the main lodge. To reach the trails, cross the parking lot and travel along an abandoned rail trail past the tennis courts. The trail turns left and then right at the end of the courts. Continue bearing right for a few hundred yards, passing the Binnewater Trail junction on the left. Continue to the base of a 60-foot brick tower, an artifact of the famous Rosendale Cement Company.

For those interested in history, we suggest a quick side trip here (50 yards) to see the antique lime kilns built into a huge stone wall just beyond the tower. Here workmen dumped limestone rock into three waiting furnaces. Books available at the resort gift shop will explain Rosendale's famous cement-making process and the unique history of this region, only 90 miles from New York City.

Back on the route to the Mountain Trail Loop you will pass another trail junction on the left, the beginning of a 10-kilometer loop called The Long Trail. You will soon reach a large intersection (four corners) with well-marked trails emanating from here, including both right and left sections of the Perfume Trail as well as the Hickory Trail and the Mountain Trail. Following the signs for the Mountain Trail will bring you past the backside of the three kilns (right) and the entrance to a hiking trail called The Summit. Continue straight ahead on the Mountain Trail Loop for a

Skiers pose for a photo before ski touring at Williams Lake Resort.

fun-filled experience with lots of variation for snowshoers and intermediate to advanced skiers.

You will climb to the top of a gentle slope, then ski to the bottom only to climb again on the next hill. There are a few steeper slopes with gentle turns and easy out-runs at the bottom. Intermediate skiers will be able to let their skis run, as there are no sharp turns at the ends of steep hills or other tricky ski conditions to be considered.

Soon the Mountain Trail Loop splits and a directional sign indicates that you must stay left to travel the one-way loop. This is a wide multiuse trail, supporting hiking and biking in spring and summer as well as a NORBA mountain bike race each autumn. The trail offers mostly rolling terrain following an old stone wall through a forest of hardwoods interspersed with some large pine trees. You will encounter some moderate climbing to a plateau before reaching a slightly more difficult climb, offering a chance for some sidestepping or herringbone technique.

As you enter a large clearing, the trail makes a wide right turn and you begin to head back toward the finish of the loop. Here, a short path to the left offers an opportunity for a unique side trip to the summit overlooking the lake, the resort, and the foothills of the Catskill Mountains. We encourage you to take the time for this adventure. Turn right onto the narrow Summit Trail, which parallels the Mountain Trail at this point (within about 50 feet). Skiers may need to remove skis and walk the short distance to the overlook because the trail here is narrow and steep. Return to the Mountain Trail the same way. The spectacular views are well worth the trouble of reaching the summit.

Back on the Mountain Trail Loop, continue on the undulating terrain as you begin your descent to the end of the loop. The slope becomes fairly steep with a turn near the bottom. As earlier, straight running is possible because the trail ends on an uphill section, allowing for the natural slowing of speed. At the end of this short loop the trail returns to two-way traffic to the four-corner junction.

If time permits, you may take a unique side trip to see the huge limestone caves before returning to the Nordic Center. It is a short loop (1 mile) suitable for beginners and well worth the extra effort. Of course, you could elect to ski/snowshoe this section at another time. Enter the left section of the Perfume Trail at the four-corner junction and follow it for approximately a half mile. As the trail turns right, you'll see the cutoff for the caves on the left. You can ski to the edge of the enormous opening where you might remove your skis or snowshoes to observe and examine the huge sloping cave. It can be even more educational if you bring a flashlight. Stay as long as you wish before returning to the trail and continuing back to the four corners.

Directions at a glance

0.0 Begin at Nordic center, pass tennis courts.

0.2 Binnewater Trail enters at left.

0.4 Pass Long Trail junction on left to four corners.

0.5 Turn right on Mountain Trail.

1.2 Bear left on Mountain Trail.

2.0 Turn right on optional Summit Trail.

2.8 Return to four-corner junction; optional side trip to caves.

3.2 Finish at Nordic center and lodge.

From the four corners, retrace your tracks 0.4 mile back to the lodge, ski shop, and Nordic center.

How to get there

From the New York State Thruway (I–87) take exit 19 at Kingston. Follow Route 32 south to Route 213 west to Rosendale. Take Binnewater Road (County Route 50) just west of a high railroad trestle. Go 2 miles to Williams Lake Resort.

From the New York State Thruway (I–87) at the New Paltz exit, turn left onto 299W. Go into the village and make a right onto Route 32 travel north 7 miles and immediately after crossing second bridge take a left onto Route 213. Take Route 213 west about a mile to Binnewater Road (County Route 59) just west of a high railroad trestle. Turn right and go 2 miles to Williams Lake Resort.

Towpath Trail Loop
Chenango Valley State Park, Chenango Forks, New York

Type of trail:	▬▬ ⬤
Also used by:	Hikers, bikers, runners, walkers
Distance:	2.85 miles
Terrain:	Mostly flat
Trail difficulty:	Easiest
Surface quality:	Ungroomed, user packed/tracked
Food and facilities:	A fieldstone lodge overlooking the lake is open in winter, featuring a great room with beamed cathedral ceiling, two stone fireplaces, and several picnic tables. Downstairs are heated rest rooms, a cozy warm-up room, and a public telephone. There is also a large open-sided pavilion with fireplace for winter trail users. There are no food services at the park. Hess Mart and the Red Apple Convenient Store are located at I–88 exit 3 (3.5 miles). Fast-food vendors, restaurants, other grocery stores, and lodging may be found in nearby Binghamton (12 miles). There is a Days Inn in Binghamton, (607) 724–3297.
Phone numbers:	Park Office, (607) 648–5251. Park Police, (607) 648–3662. For emergencies call 911.
Fees:	There are no fees for winter trail use.
Caution:	Skiing and snowshoeing on the lakes and river are prohibited. This is a carry-in, carry-out facility. Dogs must be on a leash at all times.

Located on the edge of the great Chenango River, the 1,075-acre Chenango Valley State Park (CVSP) was once the property of lumberman Gideon Lounsberry. The state acquired the land from the Warner estate and opened it to the public in 1930. It is the southernmost park in central New York. Chenango Lake and Lily Lake, two glacially formed ponds whose names have been changed several times during the area's long history, are very busy in season for boating, fishing, and nature studies.

Another popular attraction at CVSP is the Chenango Canal, and the old Chenango Aqueduct, which carried the canal over the outflow from Chenango Lake. Skilled Irish stone masons built this and other structures along the canal between 1833 and 1836. The canal was in service from 1837 to 1878, running almost 100 miles from Binghamton to Utica. It was an important commerce route, promoting early growth in the Chenango Valley.

This pleasant scene is the view from the ski lodge at Chenango Valley State Park.

In 1933, intense construction activity began at the park when the Civilian Conservation Corps (CCC) undertook many projects, including dam construction to enlarge the lake and the introduction of electricity, a luxury in rural America at the time. The CCC constructed dozens of cabins and a nine-hole golf course, and planted many of the trees that we see today. In 1968 the golf course was enlarged to eighteen holes and new swimming facilities were constructed on Chenango Lake.

In 1996 the park received a gift of land from the estate of Dr. Willaim Bielecki, including the remnants of an original Chenango Canal lock, the only one remaining in Broome County. The Friends of Chenango Valley State Park helped to arrange for the acquisition.

Access to the Towpath Trail Loop begins at the historic Chenango Canal marker. The marker, located at the edge of the Chenango River, relates the history of the aqueduct. Head along the Chenango River, bearing left at the Interpretive Center and onto the Towpath Trail. The roadway that serves as the winter ski and snowshoe trail was constructed over the path once used by mules to tow barges along the canal, which appears on your left. In winter the roadway is partially plowed, leaving plenty of space for cross-country skiing and snowshoeing.

This mostly flat roadway offers one of the most picturesque winter trails in the state. There is a real likelihood that you will have the good fortune to observe some of nature's inhabitants along this riverbank trail. Deer, rabbits, black bears, squirrels, woodchucks, chipmunks, raccoons,

red foxes, coyotes, and beavers have been spotted here. The river is also home to many waterfowl, including geese, ducks, herons, and kingfishers. Other birds such as woodpeckers, nuthatches, warblers, tanagers, orioles, and thrushes may also be seen in the area. The New York State bluebird, a threatened species, frequents the golf course where nest boxes have been placed.

About a half mile from the start, you will reach a crossing used by golf carts in season. The historic park golf course was constructed partially by workers at the CCC camp in the 1930s. At this point the river bends away from the roadway and trail, allowing room for several fairways and golf tees on the left. At 1 mile the trail comes to a second golf course crossing. Turn left here and continue past the small pond to the stone house at the edge of the river. This old structure is a pump house used to irrigate the farmland along the river. This is a great spot for a rest, snack, or bag lunch at one of the picnic tables. You may catch a glimpse of a freight train passing along the other side of the river. Continuing along the river you will pass the number 6 tee and follow the trail across the fairway to tee 7. The trail, though mostly flat, has some undulating and rolling sections. Bear left and ski/snowshoe to the raised tee (8) and return to the Towpath Trail. Turning right, you may then follow your tracks along the river and back to the winter lodge and parking lot.

You may, however, wish to ski/snowshoe on the golf course for more fun in the snow. Just be sure to stay away from the roped-off golf greens.

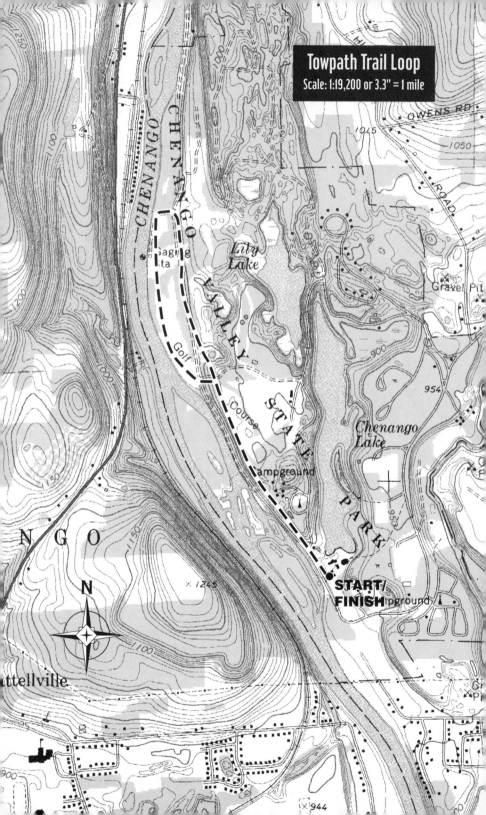

Directions at a glance

0.0   Begin at historic marker.

0.2   Pass Interpretive Center on your right.

0.75 Reach golf cart crossing.

1.0   Pass path on right to golf course.

1.3   Turn left at second golf cart crossing.

1.4   Pass stone pump house.

2.1   Return to Towpath Trail at tee 8.

2.85 Return to parking lot and lodge.

Ski or snowshoe tracks on the greens may severely damage the special grasses.

Before we leave this chapter we want to mention another of our favorite winter trails at CVSP, the Chenango Lake Trail. This intermediate trail offers a wide variety of terrain, including paths along the lake, the river, and the golf course, as well as Cabin Colony Road and the hilly route between the two lakes.

How to get there

Take I–88 to exit 3 in Port Crane. Drive north on Route 369, about 35 miles to the park.

Lakes Trail

Green Lakes State Park, Fayetteville, New York

Type of trail:	━━━ ⬭
Also used by:	Hikers, walkers, bikers
Distance:	2.3 miles (3.1 miles including Round Lake Loop)
Terrain:	Flat, gentle, rolling
Trail difficulty:	Easiest
Surface quality:	Ungroomed, user packed
Food and facilities:	Green Lakes State Park is open every day from dawn until dusk year-round. In winter the park office remains open during daylight hours on weekdays. It may be open weekends, depending on staff availability. Visitors may use the heated rest rooms and pay phones, and obtain trail maps and other winter trail information from office personnel or rangers. Trail maps may also be found at trailhead sign-in boxes. Portable toilets are located in the parking lot near Green Lake. There are no eating facilities in the park, but several stores are located in nearby Fayetteville and Minoa. A wide variety of restaurants and lodging facilities may be found in Syracuse, about 20 minutes away. The Craftman Inn in Fayetteville is highly recommended (315–637–8000). Smith's Grocery Store, Minoa (315–656–7239). Friendly's Restaurant, Fayetteville (315–637–9518).
Phone numbers:	Park Office, (315) 637–6111. Park Police, (315) 492–6422. For emergencies call 911.
Fees:	There are no fees to use the winter trails.
Caution:	Skiing or snow shoeing on the lakes is illegal. This is a carry-in, carry-out facility.

Two unique and rare glacial lakes with a decidedly green color are a major attraction of the Green Lakes State Park, located in Onondaga County just east of Syracuse. Extending over 1,800 acres of forested rolling hills and open meadows, the park draws almost a million visitors per year. Visitors to the lakes (Green Lake and Round Lake) will notice deposits of marl (reeflike structures) in many places around the shoreline. Several species of algae and small shells are found in the composition of these interesting reefs. Upon microscopic examination, it was determined that the green color of the glacial lakes is due to a combination of factors, including the algae, purple bacteria, and calcium carbonate. Light waves reflected in a special way through the very deep water and the

Lakes Trail
Scale: 1:21,818 or 2.9" = 1 mile

START/FINISH

Winter Parking
Picnic Area

Green Lake
418

Round Lake
421

GREEN LAKES STATE PARK

M A N L I U S

PIERSON ROAD

ROAD

ROAD

TAYLOR ROAD

Golf Course

Gravel Pits

Gravel Pit

Lake

Footbridge

ERIE CANAL

Park Office

Campgrounds

Route 290

OLD

Reservoir

Manlius Center

×772

×668

×597

N

tiny suspended materials produce the characteristic green color.

Both Green and Round Lakes are meromictic lakes, which means that surface waters do not mix with the bottom water. Round Lake has been designated a National Natural Landmark by the U.S. Department of the Interior. Surrounded by a virgin forest of white cedar trees, Round Lake is cut into a steep circular basin, which Native Americans believed to be bottomless. It has been measured and found to be 150 feet deep; Green Lake is 195 feet deep.

All the land now known as Green Lakes State Park was part of the so-called Military Track that was surveyed in 1792 and divided into lots for compensation to the soldiers of the Revolutionary War. Much of the land surrounding the two glacial lakes was settled by David Collin III in 1817 and later divided among his seven children. The surrounding lands known as the "Indian Ovens" were donated to the park by the Betsy Knapp estate.

The park has nine different trails identified by color and letters. With more than 17 miles of winter trails, you are certain to find one to suit your ability and interest. Because the trails around Green Lake (2.3 miles) and the adjacent Round Lake (0.8 mile) are wide and mostly flat with a few rolling hills, they are quite suitable for beginner and novice skiers, as well as snowshoers. The trail to Round Lake can be reached only by skiing or snowshoeing about halfway around Green Lake to the connecting trail. Both trails hold the snow well, due to a thick base cover of bark chips. Snowshoers are welcome to use the winter trails but must be careful not to damage the ski tracks. Although there are no machine-groomed tracks, those made by other skiers are usually better than none.

Follow the entrance road to the winter parking lot adjacent to Green Lake. All cross-country ski and snowshoe trails begin at the trailhead here. Visitors are encouraged to obtain a trail map and sign in at the registration box in the parking lot.

From the parking lot, travel about 0.2 mile to the boathouse. Here you'll find a sign for the Lakes Trail with a description and explanation of the two lakes. At this point you are at the edge of Green Lake, with Round Lake about three quarters of a mile further south along the Lakes Trail.

This is the park's most popular trail year-round. In winter the green lakes, when not frozen, contrast beautifully with the white snow. Northern white cedars and a collection of mixed hardwoods shade most of the trail, giving a deep-forest feeling even though you are gliding only a few feet from the open lake. Wooden benches are scattered around both lakes. Blue blaze marks appear on the trees along this trail. You will also see some wooden trail markers designating certain features on the inter-

*Ski and snowshoe trails circle both Round Lake and Green Lake
at Green Lakes State Park.*

pretive nature trail. The terrain rolls gently as you follow the path around
the lake.

After passing a long, steep staircase from the top of the hill, you'll find
a handrail where the trail climbs above the lake. As you descend gradually the lake comes right up to meet the trail at this point. There are more
wooden trail markers here identifying items of interest in season. We
also noticed some wooden benches at this junction for those who choose
to sit for a while. Some of these have plaques dedicating the benches in
the memory of special people. Additional benches are scattered along the
trail for resting and enjoying the pleasant surroundings.

Straight ahead is the junction for the trail to the Round Lake section
of the Lakes Trail. Those wishing to complete the entire Lakes Trail will
bear right here, following the white markers. The short Round Lake loop
(0.8 mile) is marked with red markers and signs leading you back to the
main Lakes Trail. The Lakes Trail, however, turns left at this junction and
crosses a small footbridge over the outlet, bringing you to a trail junction
marked with yellow blazes. This is the return trail where those who
complete the Round Lake section will rejoin the main Lakes Trail. It also
leads to the more challenging trails that traverse the golf course and provide spectacular views of Green Lake and the surrounding park.

Continuing to bear left while following the blue blazes, you'll travel alongside the lake. The hills, covered with evergreens and hardwoods, will be on your right. You will be tempted to ski on the lake at various openings along this trail, but you must remember that it is strictly forbidden! If snow conditions permit you will note a variety of driftwood and an old foundation.

As you approach the beach area you'll pass a large stone building, formerly the administration building, that has been abandoned and closed at the time of this publication. Coming out of the forested area, you'll cross the beach area and arrive back at the bathhouse and parking lot where you began.

How to get there

From Syracuse, take I–690 east to Route 290 at exit 17. Follow the signs to the park.

From the New York State Thruway (I–90) take exit 34A to I–481. Take I–481 south to exit 5E. Take Kirkville Road east to Fremont Road. Turn right on Fremont Road and then left on Route 290 and follow the signs to the park.

Note: Parking for the winter trails is at the first parking lot past the park office, identified as "Trailhead Parking," although visitors are welcome to park at the park office.

Oquaga Creek Winter Trail
Oquaga Creek State Park, Masonville, New York

Type of trail:	▬▬▬ ▭▭▭
Also used by:	Hikers, hunters, bikers, walkers
Distance:	2.0 miles
Terrain:	Hilly
Trail difficulty:	Easiest to more difficult
Surface quality:	Groomed
Food and facilities:	In winter the Oquaga Creek parking lot is plowed for winter trail users. There are toilets in the park office, which is open weekdays during regular work hours. Portable toilets are available on the weekends. Trail maps may be obtained at the park office. There are no eating facilities in the park, but a cozy warming room in the bathhouse may be opened on request. Pack a bag lunch and some snacks. Fast-food vendors, restaurants, groceries, and lodging may be found in nearby Bainbridge, Sydney, and Deposit. Grand Union for groceries (607–563–2733). For lodging try the Deposit Motel (607–467–2998). Toddies is a popular local restaurant (607–563–8465).
Phone numbers:	Oquaga Creek State Park, (607) 467–4160. For emergencies call 911.
Fees:	There are no fees to use the winter trails.
Caution:	The lake may be unsafe for skiing and snowshoeing. This is a carry-in, carry-out facility.

The history of the land at Oquaga Creek State Park dates back to land grants issued to veterans of the Revolutionary War. The farms established by these veterans were not very successful, due to the short growing season and high elevation. Most were abandoned and the land returned to its natural state. In the 1930s ownership of the land reverted back to the state and remained as state forest land until the 1960s when the New York State Office of Parks and Recreation obtained it. The park was opened to the public in July 1979.

Oquaga is an Indian word meaning "land of the wild grape," and may have been derived from the abundance of wild grapes, blueberries, raspberries, and blackberries that dot the landscape in this region. Although the 1,450 acres at Oquaga Creek are tucked away in a fairly rural area of Broome and Delaware Counties, it is a perfect vacation spot in a beautiful setting for year-round recreational activities. Winter activities in the

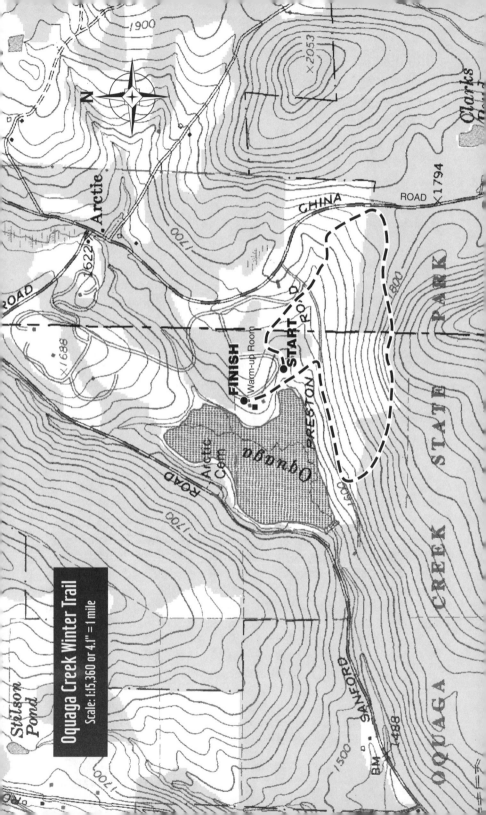

park include cross-country skiing, snowshoeing, sledding, ice-skating, and guided moonlight ski/snowshoe tours. It is not unusual for the park to receive 4 to 4.5 feet of snow per season due to its elevation (about 2,300 feet) and its location in a mountain trough at the foothills of New York's Catskill Mountains.

Entering Oquaga Creek State Park in Masonville at East Afton Road (County Route 20), winter trail users may stop at the park office to obtain a trail map, brochure, and general information.

Visitors to the park will surely notice the bluebird nesting boxes placed here to attract New York State's eastern bluebird. A successful conservation effort on the part of the staff and volunteers has resulted in a significantly increased population of this beautiful bird.

Oquaga Creek State Park offers 6 miles of trails for skiing and snowshoeing. Access to the multiuse trails at Oquaga Creek is either from the winter parking lot near the office, or from the larger winter parking lot near the bathhouse. In winter the bathhouse has a warming room. We recommend that you begin near the bathhouse at the trailhead designated on the trail map as the starting point for skiing and snowshoeing. This southern loop begins with a short climb from the winter parking lot through a tree-covered picnic grove and out into an open meadow. Bearing right, you will pass rest room facilities and a nice open picnic shelter. You will pass the park's maintenance buildings and a playground with a swing set at the end of the meadow, then cross a service road and enter a hemlock forest.

The trail begins a nice gradual climb with several turns. You will notice the changing vegetation as you leave the hemlock grove. At the first junction you'll find a sign identifying an optional side trip or additional loop. A few yards further is the junction of a section of the Finger Lakes Trail. (See Trail 26 for a description of the Finger Lakes Trail System.)

The trail continues to climb to an elevation of 2,200 feet before reaching the summit, then it gradually descends toward the lake. It passes through several old rock walls and through pine groves and mature hardwoods, including yellow birch, red maple, and black cherry. You may encounter some of the many birds and animals that inhabit these restoration plantations, including deer, rabbit, black bear, coyote, and red fox.

Soon you will find a spectacular view of the lake through the trees to the right. Here too is the junction for a trail known to locals as "Suicide Hill," a short, steep cutoff to the road below. You may dare to ski this steep trail or continue to the wooden bridge. Here the trial turns sharply right, bringing you out of the woods and onto a wide park road. This is Lake Road, which travels along the man-made Arctic Lake.

Watch for a sign on the left for a turn that will take you from Lake

Directions at a glance

0.0 Begin at the winter parking lot across from the bathhouse.

0.2 Cross through picnic grove.

0.3 Pass maintenance building and cross the road.

0.8 Pass junction for Finger Lakes Trail (left).

1.3 "Suicide Hill" trail goes right.

1.4 Cross bridge to Lake Road.

1.5 Pass lower junction for Suicide Hill.

1.7 Turn off Lake Road (left).

2.0 Finish at bathhouse and parking lot.

Road downhill to the lake and across the lawn back to the bathhouse. You will also pass through posts identifying the unique Frisbee Disk Golf Course. You may end your tour at the bathhouse or continue on the northern loop as designated on the trail map. You may wish to stop at one of the several park benches near the bathhouse for a rest and to enjoy the picturesque surroundings. The warming room may be opened by request.

How to get there

From I–88 take exit 8 (Bainbridge). Follow Route 206 approximately 5 miles. Turn right onto County Route 20 (Beech Hill Road), then go 5 miles. Turn right onto East Afton Road and proceed a half-mile to the Oquaga State Park entrance.

From Route 17 take exit 82. Follow Route 8 for approximately 2 miles. Turn left on County Route 20 and go approximately 8 miles. Turn left onto East Afton Road, then drive a half-mile to the park entrance.

The Nature Trail

Rogers Environmental Education Center, Sherburne, New York

Type of trail:	▬▬ ⬤
Also used by:	Walkers, hikers
Distance:	2.0 miles
Terrain:	Mostly flat
Trail difficulty:	Easiest
Surface quality:	Ungroomed, user packed
Food and facilities:	Heated rest rooms are available at the Visitor Center, but there are no eating facilities. Bring snacks or a bag lunch. Fast-food vendors, grocery stores, restaurants, and lodging may be found in nearby Sherburne and Norwich. For groceries try Skip's Market (607–674–9058), Sherburne Big N (607–674–4128), or the Great American (607–874–9008). For lodging call the Sherburne Motel (607–674–5511). Local restaurants are Bull Thistle Inn, (607–674–6900), Gilligan's (607–674–4397), and Joe's Pizzeria (607–675–2495).
Phone numbers:	Rogers Center, (607) 674–4017. For emergencies dial 911.
Fees:	There are no fees for use of the trails.
Caution:	No pets or alcoholic beverages are permitted on the property. Trial users are asked not to feed the waterfowl.

The 600-acre Rogers Environmental Education Center is operated by the Department of Environmental Conservation (DEC) in conjunction with the Friends of Rogers. The DEC is responsible for the protection of the state's natural resources; Rogers Environmental Education Center is devoted to teaching people about these resources and their wise use. The Visitor Center offers a wide variety of activities throughout the year, including winter skiing and snowshoeing. The trails traverse woodlands, meadows, wetlands, tree plantations, and farm fields, as well as traveling along the edge of a swift river.

Six miles of well-marked and labeled interpretive trails have been developed at the environmental education center, covering a wide variety of flora and fauna throughout the ponds and wetlands that border the Chenango River. Trail guide booklets explain various aspects of the natural resources found along the trails. A 2-mile section of the Nature Trail consisting of four distinct loops begins at the Visitor Center just off Route 80. Another mile of interpretive trail, located just across the street from the Visitor Center, winds its way up the hill to the Farm Tower where you can enjoy a wonderful panoramic view of the Chenango Valley.

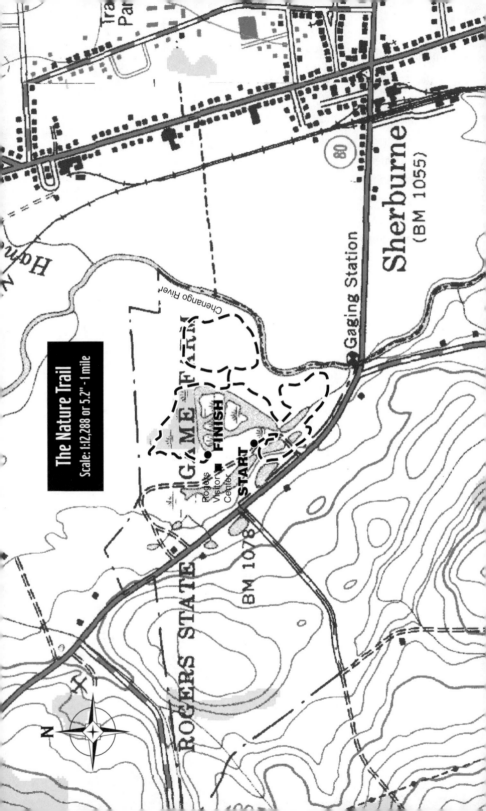

The Nature Trail
Scale: 1:12,288 or 5.2" - 1 mile

Sherburne
(BM 1055)

80

Gaging Station

Chenango River

GAME FARM

ROGERS STATE

Rogers
Visitor
Center

FINISH

START

BM 1078

N

Skiers and snowshoers are likely to spot ducks and other wildlife at Rogers Environmental Education Center.

The trails at the Rogers Center are open to the public daily from sunrise to sunset. The Visitor Center, featuring exhibits focusing on natural resources, is open year-round, six days a week in winter and seven days during the summer. The Center has rest rooms, a library, and staff offices in addition to program and classroom spaces. The upper gallery of the Visitor Center offers a view of the marsh, enabling visitors to see geese, ducks, muskrats, great blue herons, and ospreys.

To access the 2-mile Nature Trail, begin at the Visitor Center, where you may obtain a trail map and brochure describing observations to be made at each labeled station along four loops. Take along a copy of the *Winter Field Guide to Animal Tracks*—as you are sure to see many tracks along the Nature Trail.

From the front steps of the Visitor Center, bear left and head across the lawn to the directional sign and map at the edge of the lawn. Enter the woods just beyond the trail map. Cross the bridge and continue to the first junction at the top of a short rise; bear slightly right to start on the Spruce Ridge Trail (green markers), rather than turning left to stay on the Channels Trail (red). Follow the winding Spruce Ridge path through the thicket and then climb as the trail overlooks the pond (on your right). At the top of this rise take a left and follow the trail as it crosses over a service roadway. Continue over the bridge that crosses the Minnow Pond Inlet until you join the junction with the South Trail (yellow).

To stay on the South Trail, make a sharp right. You will pass through a thicket area where there will likely be many animal tracks. The South Trail goes along the Chenango River for a while and then heads away from the river and eventually leads to a T intersection where you will meet up with the Channels Trail again. Turn right and follow the red markers along the Channels Trail. On your left is a channel of water that eventually leads to the Chenango River. You'll pass through mostly thicket areas. Farther along the trail follow the sign that points left to "The Blind." This is a great spot to view the marsh and not be seen by any wildlife that may be there. From your side trip to The Blind, return to the Channels Trail and continue (left) along the path to the junction with the Boundary Trail (blue). This goes off to the right, while the Channels Trail takes a sharp left across another bridge.

The Boundary Trail has a variety of habitats to traverse, including a thicket, open fields, river edge, and a hardwood forest. This is the trail least traveled by people and perhaps the most traveled by wildlife. Many people take this one for a more solitary visit and nice views along the Chenango River. Here you may also see some of the very interesting ice formations the river makes during winter. Follow the blue markers as the trail undulates with a few small ups and downs until you return again to the Channels Trail; cross the bridge and turn right to continue your tour. For another interesting side trip take a left just after the bridge to reach a teaching platform over the marsh.

Directions at a glance

0.0	Cross the lawn at the Visitor Center to the start of the Nature Trail.
0.2	Turn right onto Spruce Ridge Loop.
0.4	Join South Loop.
0.8	Turn right at T intersection.
1.1	Turn right onto the Boundary Loop.
1.7	Turn right at T intersection.
1.8	Cross bridge over Channels Marsh.
2.0	Complete Channels Loop at Visitor Center.

Return to the Channels Trail and turn left onto a narrow bridge of land with the larger marsh on the left and a smaller channel on the right. Canada geese and other types of waterfowl may often be seen here. Continue along the trail, following the red markers. Cross the channel over another bridge and through an area called the Swamp Forest. You will come to a second land bridge across the marsh. After passing the water on both sides of the path, you can take a left turn at the junction for the shortest route back to the Visitor Center. We recommend following the path straight ahead, continuing on a short loop. The trail rises up and then gradually winds down to end near the amphitheater area with the Visitor Center in sight.

Be sure to stop at the Visitor Center to warm up before bidding farewell to the Nature Trail and Rogers Environmental Education Center. Make plans to return for the Winter Living Celebration, held annually on the first Saturday of January.

How to get there

From Utica take Route 12 south to Sherburne. Turn right on Route 80 and travel 1 mile west to the Rogers Center.

From Binghamton take I–81 north to Route 12. Take Route 12 north to Sherburne. Turn left on Route 80 and travel 1 mile west to the Rogers Center.

Nature Trail

Verona Beach State Park, Verona Beach, New York

Type of trail:	▬▬ 🔘
Also used by:	Hikers, hunters, equestrians, snowmobilers
Distance:	3.0 miles, with option of 7 miles
Terrain:	Mostly flat
Trail difficulty:	Easiest
Surface quality:	Skier tracked
Food and facilities:	The parking lot at Verona Beach State Park is plowed daily for winter trail users. Portable toilets are located there. Trail maps may be found at the ticket booth and the registration kiosk at the beginning of the trail, or at the park office (open weekdays). There are no eating facilities in the park. Pack a bag lunch and some snacks. Grocery stores, restaurants, and lodging will be found in nearby Sylvan Beach: Nice-n-Easy (315–762–4600) Cinderella Restaurant and Motel (315–762–4280). Fast-food vendors, other restaurants, and lodging may be found in nearby Canastota (6 miles): P&C grocery store (315–697–2700), Days Inn (315–697–3309).
Phone numbers:	Verona Beach State Park, (315) 762–4463. Park Police, (315) 492–6422, or call 911.
Fees:	There are no fees to use the winter trails.
Caution:	The winter trails are shared partially with snowmobilers and hunters (in season). Be cautious when crossing Route 13.

The land utilized today by Verona Beach State Park for recreational pursuits was the site of many battles during the French and Indian War of the 1750s. The region was highly attractive to the Native Americans in the seventeenth and eighteenth centuries. The region's fine transportation routes, such as Wood Creek, allowed the Oneidas and Onandagas to transfer needed supplies from the Mohawk Valley. Later glass-making industries utilized sands from beds along Oneida Lake's shore, shipping them via Ontario, Western, and Lehigh Railroads. Until 1888 a ferry ran from Sylvan Beach to Verona Beach.

The State Department of Parks and Recreation initiated a program of development at Verona Beach in 1947, but the state park wasn't completed until 1958. Today only 300 of more than 1,700 acres of park land are developed. The remaining land has been left in its natural state, providing excellent opportunities for a wide variety of outdoor activities, including cross-country skiing and snowshoeing.

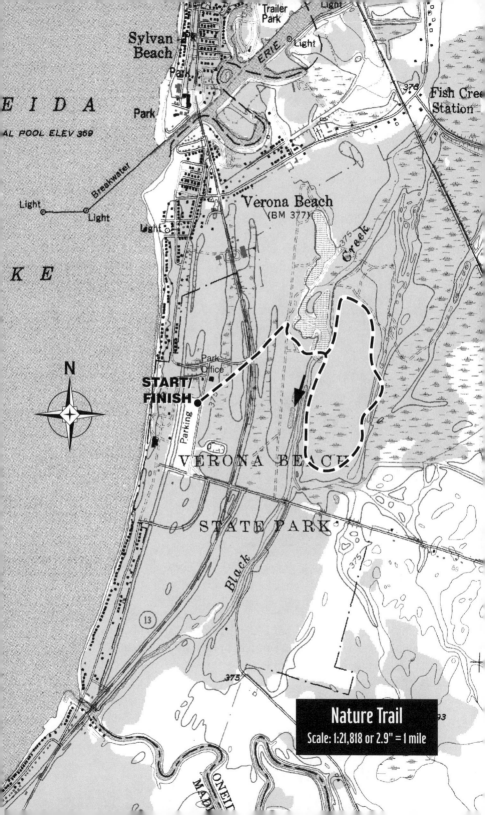

The trails at VBSP are well marked, identifying and separating (for the most part) the ski/snowshoe trails and the equestrian/snowmobile trails. The sections of winter trails used for snowmobiling are the same as those used by horseback riders in other seasons. The trail map shows 7 miles designated for skiing, hiking, and snowshoeing, including the 3-mile Nature Trail. A small section of the 8-mile snowmobile trail is shared in winter.

The park's multiuse trails have been in operation for more than 20 years. The ski/snowshoe trails are fairly easy. They are mostly flat with a few gently rolling sections and gradual downhills, but nothing very steep. The winter trails are generally wide roadways or woodland hiking paths.

To access the trails, park at the winter parking lot, which is cleared daily and well maintained for winter use. The trail begins at the registration kiosk at the north end of the parking lot, not far from the park office.

Snowshoe competitors follow a wooded trail at Verona Beach State Park.

The trail winds gently through the woods to the edge of Route 13. You will need to remove your skis or snowshoes before crossing the busy highway. Be very cautious: There are no pedestrian crossing signs or painted crosswalks.

After crossing the highway, winter trail users will proceed along the roadway to the beginning of a wooded area. The ski and snowshoe trail starts on the same path as the ten-station Verona Beach Nature Trail. The first junction is a T intersection. Here the shorter Nature Trail turns right while the longer cross-country ski trail turns left and follows a woods road north along a small man-made pond. Continuing on the Nature Trail, you'll turn right for a short stretch on the woods road then left before passing interpretive station 3, an area used by birders intent on observing some of the park's feathered inhabitants. Soon you will cross Black River Creek at station 4.

After crossing the earth bridge, the Nature Trail bears right and passes the junction (left) for the snowmobile/equestrian trail. Passing station 5,

Directions at a glance

0.0   Begin at the parking lot.

0.4   Cross Route 13 carefully.

0.8   Turn right at first T junction.

1.0   Cross bridge over Black Creek.

1.3   Pass junction for bridge to Poppleton/Sterling Loop.

1.6   Travel to wetland overlook.

2.0   Join the shared-trail section between stations 8 and 9.

2.2   Turn left at second T junction.

2.5   Turn right at bridge over Black Creek

3.0   Cross Route 13 (be cautious) and return to parking lot.

you'll travel through a hardwood grove of maple and eastern hemlock. You may notice some Department of Environmental Education (DEC) trail markers posted along this path. You will surely notice how picturesque the Black Creek is as it meanders through the quiet woods.

When you reach Station 6 you may be able to observe the beaver houses in the snow. Soon the junction for the outer loop of the skiing/snowshoeing trail appears on your right. From here you can see the bridge for the new Poppleton/Sterling Loop, which is shared partially with snowmobiles and returns to the beginning of the trail. You will bear left at this junction as the Nature Trail continues, circling through the forest to a Y junction.

Consulting your trail map, you'll see that turning right at this junction will lead you on a short loop to an overlook. Here is the park's vast wetland, where you may also observe some of the wildlife native to the 1,700-acre state park. The trail reconnects with the Nature Trail and continues to another junction, the place where snowmobilers share this corridor with other winter trail users.

Turn left at this junction and pass station 9 before arriving at another T in the trail. Make a sharp left turn and continue to station 10 and the bridge crossing, which returns you to the entrance road and Route 13. Carefully cross the highway and return to the parking lot.

How to get there

Take the New York State Thruway (I–90) to exit 34. Take Route 13 north about 6 miles to Verona Beach State Trail. The park entrance is at the stoplight on Route 13.

The Red Trail Loop

Bear Swamp State Forest, Sempronius, New York

Type of trail:	▬▬ 🔘
Also used by:	Hikers, bikers, equestrians
Distance:	3.0 miles (plus options)
Terrain:	Hilly
Trail difficulty:	More difficult
Surface quality:	Ungroomed, user packed
Food and facilities:	There are no facilities at Bear Swamp State Forest. The Colonial Lodge Restaurant off Route 41A at the west entrance serves lunch and dinner (315–496–9401). The Sempronius Diner (about 2 miles) is open daily for breakfast and lunch. Grocery stores, fast-food vendors, and lodging may be found in nearby Moravia and Skaneateles. Try the Glen Haven Hotel at the southwest end of Skaneateles Lake for fine dining (607–749–3779).
Phone numbers:	New York State Department of Environmental Conservation Office of Lands and Forests, (607) 753–3095.
Fees:	There are no fees to use the trails.
Caution:	The trails are in a wilderness area with no patrols.

Bear Swamp State Forest is part of two state forests containing more than 3,000 acres near the south end of Skaneateles Lake in Cayuga County. It is a multiple-use area known for the large wetlands and creek that bisect the forests. More than 13 miles of trails meander through mixed hardwood forests and softwood plantations.

The forest and the surrounding area were dramatically affected by glaciation about 10,000 years ago. Skaneateles Lake, the steep valley walls, and the flattop ridges are the result of this geologic event. Native Americans used the area sparingly to hunt and travel through. After the Revolutionary War, veterans and their families cleared and settled the area. One famous son of the area is Millard Fillmore, our thirteenth president, who was born and raised nearby.

Farm settlement peaked around the Civil War, and slowly declined after that until the Great Depression of 1929 hastened farm abandonment. Most of the state forest comprises deserted farmland bought in the 1930s. The large amount of open land was planted with coniferous trees—red pine, Norway spruce, and larch. Very little old-growth forest is present today. The steep valley slopes leading to Skaneateles Lake have some, as well as small pockets around the creek.

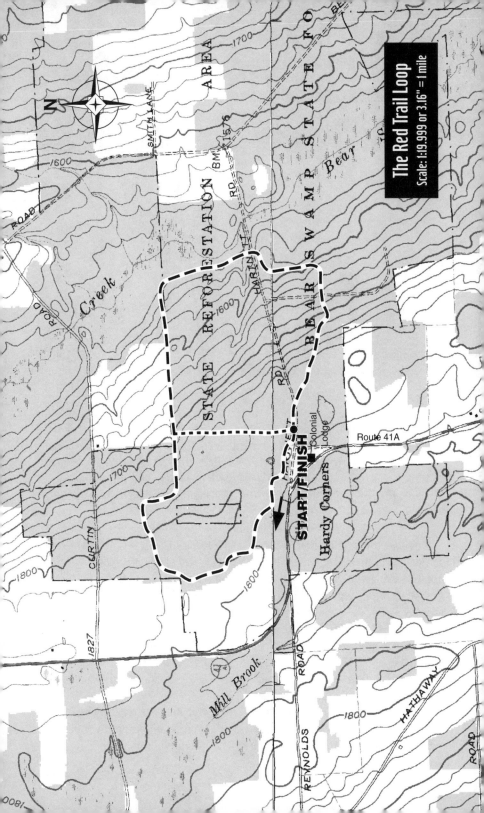

The Red Trail Loop
Scale: 1:19,999 or 3.16" = 1 mile

N

SMITH LANE

ROAD

BM 1576

1576

1700

1700

1600

STATE REFORESTATION AREA

HARIN TR

1600

BEAR SWAMP STATE FO

Bear Sw

Creek

ROAD

1700

START/FINISH

Colonial Lodge

Route 41A

Hardy Corners

CURTIN

1800

1827

1800

1800

Mill Brook

REYNOLDS ROAD

1800

HATHAWAY ROAD

0081

Man's best friend waits patiently along the trail while his master takes a break.

The Bear Swamp State Forest trail system was developed with volunteer help in the 1980s. Improvements were made in the 1990s and continue today, with work crews provided by the New York State Department of Environmental Conservation (DEC). The improvements include the construction of a fine kiosk for the registration logbook at the west entrance (Hartnett Road).

The Bear Swamp Trails have become increasingly popular, providing enjoyable tours with lovely views of Bear Swamp Creek, Skaneateles Lake, Grout Brook, and the Glen Haven Valley. It is a favorite destination of knowledgeable winter trail users of the region, as these trails often are snow-covered when other trails are bare. There are three parking areas for accessing the winter trails. We have selected the west entrance just off Route 41A at Hartnett Road, a few hundred yards from the Colonial Lodge, a popular meeting place. Here you will find the parking area and the covered kiosk with the registration logbook and copies of the trail map. It is important that you sign in and sign out. The map also shows the location of other parking areas.

Although the winter trails are blazed and marked with paint (red, blue, and yellow), it is wise to take a map along with you on the trail. As always, carry a compass and check the trail map when in doubt.

The Red Trail Loop is marked with numbers from 1 to 5, beginning at the kiosk near the Hartnett Road entrance. Be careful to turn left at the trailhead (entry point); the path heading straight ahead is the cut-off trail for those wishing to complete only the first 1.5-mile loop. The left trail (R1) goes westerly through flat terrain and conifer plantations of Norway spruce, white pine, and red pine, which were planted by the Dresserville Civilian Conservation Corp (CCC) in 1932.

The trail crosses several corduroy areas and wooden bridges over wet trail sections and passes through large areas of managed forest. The Red Trail turns north along a logging road, where you will see stumps and the tops of trees cut for firewood and pulpwood. Continue north through a forest of red oak and red pine until you reach an old fire lane. Follow the lane as it continues north to the forest boundary line (blazed yellow) where it turns east then northeast along a red pine plantation. You'll reach another woods road, where the trail turns south. Note the contrast between a thinned, managed hardwood forest on your right and the crowded, unmanaged red pine forest on the left.

The trail soon turns east and continues along the woods road and fire lane to the first junction. You may turn south here and return to the parking lot, having traveled 1.5 miles. We recommend continuing east on Red Trail 2 to complete the 3-mile Red Trail.

Continue straight ahead on the Red Trail (R2), traveling along a fire lane down a long but gradual hill. At the bottom the trail turns south, then takes you on a skid road through a Norway spruce forest to a four-way junction at Hartnett Road. (If you turn left on Hartnett Road you can ski or snowshoe to the entrance for the Blue and Yellow trail systems, which cover an additional 10 miles. Turning right, you can return to your car, completing about 2.3 miles.)

Cross Hartnett Road, continuing on the Red Trail (R4). Travel south on this trail until it turns right (west) and climbs uphill through a Norway spruce forest. After a short while the trail merges with R5 at a forest access road. Traveling straight ahead, you'll climb gradually, first through a Norway spruce plantation and then through a hardwood forest of native maple, ash, and cherry. When you reach the hilltop, continue west along Hartnett Road for a few hundred yards back to the parking lot, completing the 3-mile tour.

Everyone using the Bear Swamp State Forest trails is encouraged to take the time to visit the Blue Trail (B5) for a look at the Great Bear Swamp, "a spectacular view in any season." This is one of the highlights of Bear Swamp Multiple Use Area. According to DEC officials, "The swamp has an Adirondack-like quality with balsam fir, swamp meadow grass, and alder patches."

Directions at a glance

0.0 Begin at registration kiosk. Go left on Red Trail (R1).

0.2 Continue through intersection of R1 and R2.

2.0 Continue through intersection of R2 and R4; cross at Hartnett Road.

2.3 Continue through intersection of R4 and R5 at access road.

2.6 Turn left at intersection R5 with Hartnett Road.

3.0 Finish at parking lot.

How to get there

From I–81, take exit 12 and travel north through Homer on Route 281. Turn left on Route 41 and travel 2.5 miles to a left on Route 41A. Continue north about 10 miles to Hartnett Road. Turn right at Colonial Lodge Restaurant. Parking area is behind the restaurant.

From Route 20 in Skaneateles, take Route 41A south through New Hope to Hartnett Road, approximately 16 miles. Turn left at Colonial Lodge Restaurant. Parking is behind the restaurant.

The Yellow Trail

Hammond Hill State Forest, Ithaca, New York

Type of trail:	▬▬▬ ⬭
Also used by:	Hikers, bikers, backcountry skiers
Distance:	5.6 miles (with shorter options)
Terrain:	Hilly
Trail difficulty:	Easiest to more difficult
Surface quality:	Ungroomed, skier tracked
Food and facilities:	There is a small and modest warming hut at the trailhead parking lot, providing a warm room with a picnic table for snacks or bag lunch. Although referred to as the "Hammond Hill Hilton," there are no rest rooms. Fast-food vendors, grocery stores, restaurants, and lodging may be found in nearby Dryden, Ithaca, and the Greater Ithaca Area. One of our favorite eating places is the famed Moosewood Restaurant in Ithaca (607–273–9610). For groceries try P&C Grocers in East Hill (607–272–5838) or Dryden Food Market (607–844–4251). For lodging, Best Western Hotel (607–272–6100) or Ramada Inn (607–257–3100).
Phone numbers:	Cayuga Nordic Ski Club, (716) 257–7252. Department of Environmental Conservation, (607) 753–3095. For emergencies call 911.
Fees:	There are no fees to use these trails.
Caution:	It is important that you stick to the DEC marked trail. Many trails crisscross the main trail, making it quite easy to become lost in this area. There is no ski patrol.

The land now called Hammond Hill was Native American tribal land for centuries before the white man arrived. Most recently it belonged to the Cayugas, one of the six nations that made up the Iroquois Confederacy. Through treaties signed in 1789 and 1795, the Cayugas sold most of their land to New York State.

Immediately after the American Revolution, much of central New York was surveyed and divided into military lots, which were given to Revolutionary War soldiers as partial payment for their military service. A number of drywall foundations on Hammond Hill are reminders of the early white settlers.

During the Great Depression of the 1930s, the government of Franklin D. Roosevelt created the Resettlement Administration (RA), which hired agronomists to classify farmland as either suitable or unsuit-

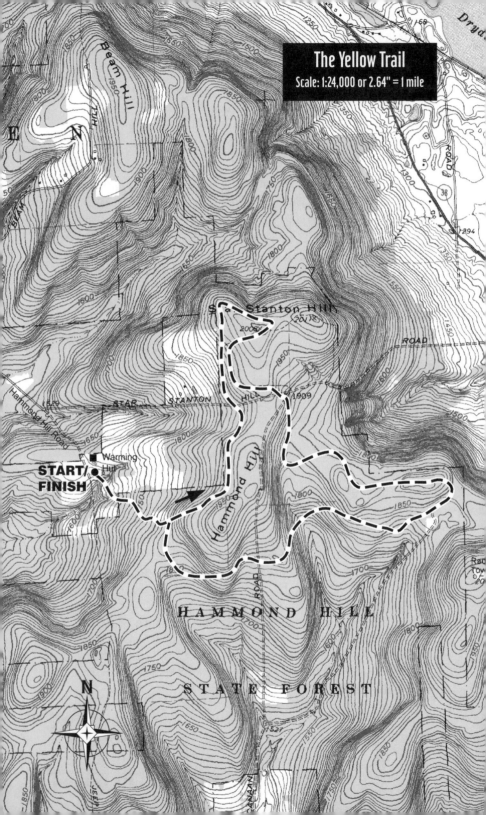

The Yellow Trail
Scale: 1:24,000 or 2.64" = 1 mile

START/
FINISH

Warming
Hut

Beam Hill

Stanton Hill

STANTON HILL

Hammond Hill

Hammond Hill Road

STAR

HAMMOND HILL

STATE FOREST

ROAD

ROAD

38

Dryd.

able for farming. To help the farm families on land that was classified as unsuitable, the RA purchased the farms and assisted these families in resettling on land that was more productive. The RA purchased six million acres of poor farmland in New York State, most of it in large tracts.

In the 1930s men from the Slaterville Camp of the Civilian Conservation Corps (CCC) reforested or developed these large tracts of land for wildlife preserves before they were ceded to New York and other states. Some of New York's unproductive farmland was purchased with funds made available by the New York State Reforestation Act. About half of Hammond Hill State Forest (HHSF) was acquired under this act and planted with thousands of pine, spruce, larch, maple, cherry, ash, and oak seedlings. Today the 3,600-acre forest is managed under the New York State Department of Environmental Conservation (DEC) Division of Lands and Forests. According to the DEC, "Almost one hundred percent of the area is now forested and the harvesting of forest products supports all the management activities including the recreation trails."

An 11-mile multiuse trail system has been developed at HHSF through cooperative efforts between the DEC, Cayuga Nordic Ski Club, Cayuga Nature Center, Friends of HH, and the Town of Dryden. The Yellow Trail System is the central loop from which other trails depart (blue, red, and green). The Yellow Trail Loop is divided into six sections (Y1–Y6), offering mostly easy skiing with some intermediate level hills. It provides a long ski/snowshoe loop (5.6 miles) that can be shortened by using unplowed forest roads to various distances of about 2 miles to 3.8 miles. In addition to the DEC trails, there are unmarked trails that are used by many local skiers, including members of the Cayuga Nordic Ski Club and the Cornell University Ski Team. The DEC has prepared a Hammond Hill State Forest trail map and installed circular trail signs (in colors) to indicate the difficulty. Green markers designate snowmobile trails. It is very important to stick to the trails marked by the DEC except where noted, as it is quite easy to become disoriented or lost in this area.

To access the Yellow Trail System, begin at the warming hut located near the parking lot on Hammond Hill Road. The small building on private land is referred to as the "Hammond Hill Hilton" by local skiers and is maintained by the Cayuga Nordic Ski Club. It is unlocked and contains a woodstove and picnic table. Nearby is a kiosk with trail maps and a registration book. Be sure to sign in and out and get a copy of the trail map.

From the warming hut the trail immediately crosses a ravine along a sweeping S-curve, then skirts an open field, arriving at the DEC property line and a split in the trail. Here two options are available. To the right is the DEC trail (Y1) marked by yellow disks and the numeral 1. We recommend that you bear left instead, taking an alternate route. Both trails

Baby rides piggyback as mom and dad go snowshoeing at Hammond Hill State Forest.

lead through a recently logged area to the main trail a few hundred yards apart and both climb most of the way. The alternate trail is somewhat steeper and shorter, but is wider and easier to ski. The main trail can be skied in either direction, but is described here as a clockwise loop (see map).

Turning left, the Yellow Trail Loop (Y1) begins with a moderate upward grade through a logged conifer plantation. Several other trails intersect this section and should be avoided. Soon the trail makes a sharp left turn and leads into a pleasant mixed forest with undulating but generally downhill slopes. At just over 0.5 mile, the trail reaches Star Stanton Road, which at that point slopes rather steeply westward. A shortened tour can be made by turning right here and skiing uphill on this unplowed roadway to the junction with Canaan Road (see trail map) and returning to the warming hut following Canaan Road and sections Y5 and Y6 of the Yellow Trail.

The Yellow Trail Loop crosses Star Stanton Road and travels along a gentle side hill through a mature oak and maple grove. It joins an old farm road, climbing gently uphill along the edge of old farm fields. The trail levels off and continues northward through a deciduous forest, then turns sharply right at about 1 mile from the beginning. This easterly section roughly follows the contour of the steep north slope of Hammond Hill, providing pleasant skiing with nice views of the valley. You will come to a junction marking the end of Y1 and the start of Y2 and Y3. Here you must take a hard right turn on Y2 as the Yellow Trail Loop switches back and continues its gentle climb nearly to the top of Star Stanton Hill at an elevation of more than 2,000 feet.

The trail then descends gradually along an old road and via a DEC cutoff, reaching the intersection of Star Stanton and Canaan Roads at about 2 miles from the beginning. This section, through mixed forest, provides very easy going. Yellow Trail Loop continues diagonally across the road junction, where it is marked Y4. The next mile of trail traverses mature forest with beautiful scenery and views of the lowlands to the north. This section is easy to moderate, but there are several unmarked trails that should be avoided. White trail blazes signify that here the 800-mile Finger Lakes Trail (FLT) has joined the Yellow Trail for about a half mile before continuing south along the eastern property line of the state forest.

As you reach an old shale pit, the trail number changes to Y5, climbing steeply and awkwardly out of the pit. After traversing about a half mile of planted conifers, the trail enters mature woods and descends on a moderate slope to a creek crossing. This recently constructed downhill trail is rather narrow; care should be taken on the descent.

Beyond the creek the trail climbs moderately along an old logging road and crosses the unplowed Canaan Road. It descends slightly at first but then climbs along a newly cut side-hill trail. At about 4.5 miles the trail descends moderately to steeply. Caution is definitely needed over this stretch, especially near the bottom. The last 0.2 mile (Y6) is along a moderate uphill grade through the logged area to the two entrance trails. The first trail reached is the Y1 return trail, but, a downhill traverse of this is not advised. Continue about 200 yards to the clearing, turning left and returning along the alternate entrance trail to the warming hut.

Directions at a glance

0.0   Begin at the warming hut.

0.2   Stay left for alternate trail (DEC Trail System).

0.3   Turn left onto Y1.

0.6   Cross Star Stanton Road or return on cutoff trail.

1.1   Turn right at north slope.

1.4   Turn right at junction for Y1, Y2, and Y3.

2.0   Cross Star Stanton and Canaan Roads to Y4.

3.0   Connect with Y5 at shale pit.

4.0   Cross the creek.

4.2   Cross Canaan Road.

4.7   Pass junction of the Y1 return trail.

4.9   Turn left on entrance trail.

5.3   Finish at warming hut.

How to get there

From Cortland take Route 13 about 9.5 miles south to Dryden. Drive west about a half mile to Irish Settlement Road. Turn left and drive south for 3.5 miles to Hammond Hill Road (left). Drive east about a half mile to the end of the road and the parking lot.

From the south take Route 79 to the west end of Slaterville Springs. Turn right (north) onto Midline Road, which forks right onto Irish Settlement Road (about 2 miles). Turn left and drive south for 3.5 miles to Hammond Hill Road (left). Drive east about a half mile to the end of the road and the parking lot.

Sidewinder Trail Loop

Harriet Hollister Spencer Memorial State Recreation Area, Honeoye, New York

Type of trail:	▬▬▬ ⬤
Also used by:	Hikers, bikers, hunters, and in part by snowmobilers
Distance:	3.5 miles
Terrain:	Hilly with some steep sections
Trail difficulty:	Most difficult
Surface quality:	Machine groomed and tracked
Food and facilities:	There is no park office or warming room at Harriet H. Spencer Memorial Park. A large barnlike building open on one side (similar to a lean-to) provides the only "indoor facility." Toilets are available near the open lodge. Fast-food vendors, restaurants, grocery stores, and lodging may be found in the tiny hamlet of Honeoye (7 miles) and in Honeoye Falls (15 miles). For groceries: Sure Fine (716–229–2122) and Honeoye Falls Market (716–624–1190). The Valley Inn at Honeoye serves good food (716–229–5400).
Phone numbers:	No phone at site. For information call Park Police, (716) 335–8111 or (800) 255–3577. For emergencies call 911.
Fees:	There are no fees to use the trails.
Caution:	The trails are not patrolled. Some trails have steep downhill runs and sharp turns. The south side of the entrance road is shared with snowmobiles. This is a carry-in, carry-out facility.

During the 1930s and early '40s Thomas and Harriet Hollister Spencer bought six properties of farmland and woodland adjoining their cottage on the top of Canadice Hill overlooking Honeoye Lake in Canadice, Ontario County. The location, Harriet wrote, " has a breathtaking view of the sweep of Honeoye Lake and Valley. On a clear day Rochester skyline appears like a miniature city in a mirage." Harriet became famous for her garden, modeled after a sixteenth century Elizabethan garden. It included eight varieties of herbs and was renowned for its rose collection.

In 1958 Harriet H. Spencer was awarded a fellowship at the Rochester Museum of Science for "her contributions to the knowledge of rose history, herb lore, landscaping design, and various phases of horticulture." She designed and planted the kitchen herb garden at the Eastman House, birthplace of George Eastman, and served as an adviser on the landscape design for the Genesee Hospital.

In 1963 Thomas Spencer gave almost 700 acres of their property to

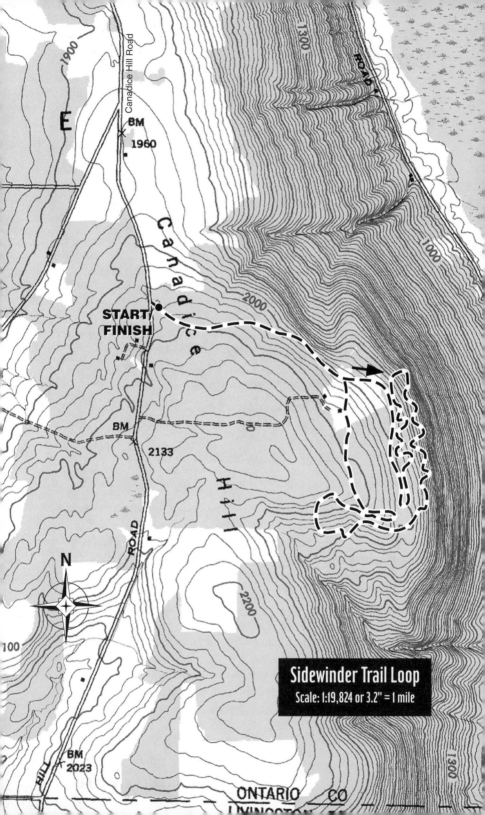

Sidewinder Trail Loop
Scale: 1:19,824 or 3.2" = 1 mile

the people of the state of New York as a memorial to his wife. He requested that the property be used as a recreational area with the stipulation that hunting be prohibited. The park is now known as the H.H. Spencer Memorial Recreation Area. Roads have been built by the state and trails have been cut in the dense woods.

The Harriet Hollister Spencer Memorial Park is now administered by New York State Office of Parks, Recreation, and Historic Preservation. It is situated in a high elevation area and is "blessed"—according to diehard Nordic skiers—with the wind and snow off Lake Erie. Skiers, snowshoers, and other winter trails users are almost guaranteed to find suitable snow conditions throughout the winter, when other local trails are often snowless. About 30 miles south of Rochester in the town of Canadice, this small recreation area has contributed significantly to the successful ski racing programs of several area high schools, largely due to its location, altitude, and snowfall. Because the park is heavily wooded, the snow remains throughout the winter months and well into spring. Area skiers and snowshoers are usually able to enjoy good conditions from early December through March. It has been a well-kept secret by avid Nordic skiers.

Development of the Harriet Hollister Spencer trail system began in 1988 and now offers approximately 9 miles of winter trails for beginners, novices, and experienced skiers and snowshoers. The trail system has become a primary training area for high school and college Nordic ski teams, at the same time serving as a popular recreational center for other skiers, snowshoers, hikers, and bikers. These trails are used as an access corridor by snowmobilers to area snowmobile trails and occasionally by dogsledders. The Nordic ski trails at Harriet Hollister Spencer Memorial Recreation Area were constructed and are now maintained and groomed by volunteers of the New York State Section 5 Ski League, under the

Directions at a glance

0.0 Begin at the parking lot.

0.5 Reach Overlook Trail.

0.7 Pass junction for Little Whiteface Trail.

0.75 Bear left onto Raccoon Run.

1.25 Turn sharply left onto Sidewinder Trail.

2.4 Re-enter Raccoon Run.

2.8 Stop at Lodge for snacks, lunch, or a rest.

3.55 Return to parking lot.

guidance and direction of leaders of the Public High School Athletic Association.

For those cross-country skiers looking for a real challenge, we have included an advanced ski trail at Harriet Hollister Spencer Memorial Recreation Area. This loop is a combination of trails, with access from the parking lot. The main winter trail, called Overlook Trail, is the park's entrance road in other seasons. The roadway, about three quarters of a mile long, leads to the picnic area and Lodge where there is a circular drive that leads you back downhill to the entrance.

To reach the Sidewinder Trail, follow the Overlook Trail, passing two junctions for the gentle ¾-mile Bear Cub Trail, which winds through a wooded area. The Overlook Trail continues east for a quarter mile of gradual downhill skiing to the spectacular overview of beautiful Honeoye Lake far below you. This must-see spot, a real photo opportunity, is often used as a takeoff point for hang gliders.

Several loops have been developed off of the main Overlook Trail. One of these, Raccoon Run, will lead you to the Sidewinder Trail. About 500 yards beyond the lake overlook, the trail turns right, leading uphill to the Meadows and the Lodge. You will bear left onto Raccoon Run and continue toward the Sidewinder Trail for about 100 yards where you'll arrive at a fork in the trail. Keep to the right as Fox Run goes left. Fox Run is a half-mile loop with a very challenging downhill run called Bear Trap Hill, followed by a difficult uphill called Thumper.

Continuing on Raccoon Run, there is a gentle climb for the next half mile until you reach an intersection. At this junction you may shorten the trip by continuing on Raccoon Run, which will take you downhill in the direction of the Meadows and the Lodge and toilet facilities.

Advanced skiers will surely want to challenge themselves on the Sidewinder Trail, designed especially for ski racing. It has some of the most challenging and demanding cross-country skiing in the state. "In just 1.5 miles there are three fast and technical downhill runs with banked turns and a major uphill that winds back and forth through huge red oak trees," according to the local high school coach. The steepest downhill section is called Viper; Kodiak is the toughest uphill climb. Upper Sidewinder begins at the top of Kodiak and continues to twist and turn nicely before it reconnects with Raccoon Run. After another 0.4 mile you'll reach the Lodge, where some winter trail users stop to make a fire in the fireplace, have lunch, or just take a break before completing the 0.75-mile climb back to the parking lot.

For a stirring view as the winter day ends, you may decide to take a 1.1-mile side trip on Blue Spruce Way to see the lights of Hunt Hollow Ski Center from the top of a ridge. Otherwise, continue on Raccoon Run to the Overlook Trail and retrace your route back to the parking lot.

How to get there

From the New York State Thruway (I–90) take Route 15A south through Honeoye Falls to Route 20A at Hemlock. Take 20A east to Honeoye. Turn right at the Valley Inn onto Canadice Hill Road (County Route 37). Travel about 7 miles to the park.

From the Genesee Expressway (I–390) take exit 3 to Route 21. Travel north through Wayland to County Route 37 and then to the park.

From the east take Routes 5 and 20 west to Route 64. Go south to Route 20A then west to County Route 37. Turn left and continue 7 miles to the park.

From the west take Routes 5 and 20 east to Route 15A and south to Route 20A. Go east on Route 20A to County Route 37. Turn right and continue 7 miles to the park.

Finger Lakes Trail

Letchworth State Park, Castile, New York

Type of trail:	═══ ⬭
Also used by:	Hikers, bikers, walkers
Distance:	3.1 miles
Trail difficulty:	Easiest
Surface quality:	Ungroomed, skier packed and tracked
Food and facilities:	There are no facilities on the Finger Lakes Trail System, but may be found nearby. Letchworth State Park is open year-round with warming rooms and rest room facilities. Fast-food vendors, grocery stores, restaurants, and lodging are available in several towns and villages surrounding the park. For groceries try Shur Save Market in Castile (315–493–5494). Lorraine's Place in Castile is a local favorite for home cooking (716–493–3060). Lodging nearby includes the Colonial Motel in Portageville (716–493–5700), Country Inn and Suites in Mt. Morris (716–658–4080), and the Genesee Falls Inn at Portageville (716–493–2484).
Fees:	There are no fees to use the Finger Lakes Trail.
Caution:	Letchworth Park has many dangerous cliffs. Obey the caution signs and do not venture near the edges.

The Finger Lakes Trail System (FLT) consists of the 560-mile main trail and several branches totaling an additional 250 miles. The Finger Lakes Trail begins at the Pennsylvania border and extends east to the Long Path in the Catskill Mountains. The Trail System is marked with white blazes on trees and posts. White trail identifier disks are also placed at intervals along the trail. Branches of the Finger Lakes Trail are marked with orange; in Letchworth Park, yellow is used. Side trails from either the main trail or branch trails are marked in blue. Double blazes, one above each other, are used to alert users to a turn or a trail condition requiring closer attention to avoid straying off the trail. The trails are kept clear of brush and are marked by volunteers.

Although there are many sections of the main trail and its branches suitable for skiing and snowshoeing, we have selected a small section of the Finger Lakes Trail for inclusion in this guidebook: the portion that passes through Letchworth State Park. This part of the trail is also known as Park Trail 7. Access to the Finger Lakes Trail is from the Parade Grounds Entrance on Route 436. Because this entrance is officially closed in winter, park your car just outside the entrance and along the highway.

Finger Lakes Trail

Scale: 1:38,160 or 1.66" = 1 mile

N

Option 2

Option 1

Option 3

START/FINISH

START/FINISH

The Finger Lakes Trail crosses under this historic railroad bridge at Letchworth State Park.

The Parade Grounds area of the park offers some of the best winter trail locations for beginners and novices, including several spectacular views of the Genesee River Gorge, "The Grand Canyon of the East." The Parade Grounds are dedicated to the 130th New York Regiment that served in the Civil War. Later called the New York Dragoons, the regiment gathered and practiced here from 1862 to 1865.

Beginning your tour at the Route 436 Parade Grounds Entrance can be great fun as the trail descends rapidly from here to the summer parking lot. You may enjoy the adrenaline rush associated with this easy downhill run. On your right is a pull-off where you might stop to catch a distant view of the Genesee Valley. Continuing downhill to the summer parking lot, you'll find a covered pavilion with a stone fireplace and several picnic tables. This is a nice gathering place to enjoy lunch, a snack, or rest before continuing to the entrance to the Finger Lakes Trail. Some winter trail users build fires in the large stone fireplace. There is a public telephone at the entrance to this area.

About 100 yards downhill from the pavilion, you will leave the service road (left) and enter the Finger Lakes Trail at a gated entrance. Here the FLT blazes are yellow as noted above. This flat section of trail follows the old Genesee Canal and the rail bed of the Pennsylvania Railroad, where you will find several observation points overlooking the magnificent Genesee River Gorge. Seeing and hearing the wonderfully thunderous 107-foot Middle Falls may take your breath away, as it did ours.

As you continue along the trail you may notice the mouth of the famed "cave-in" (left) where men and horses tragically lost their lives while attempting to construct a tunnel. Another stop along the trail provides a direct view across the gorge to the slim Deh-ga-ya-soa waterfalls. A short distance beyond, you will come to an even closer view of the Middle Falls and the incredible ice spectacle created in winter by the splash and spray of the powerful river. Here too is a turnaround in the trail for those wishing to return to the park entrance and their cars.

Die-hard skiers and snowshoers may choose to continue on the trail (left) over the difficult "slide area" to the Upper Falls and the Portageville Bridge Trailhead. However, we strongly encourage you to turn around here. Regretfully, the base of the trail continues to slide into the river, gradually destroying the path at this point. The area has been and continues to be a major problem for park and FLT officials as well as trail users. Moreover, the slide area is known to be dangerously coated with ice in the winter, making it most difficult and risky. *Consequently, we don't recommend it.*

There are three options if you choose to turn around at this point. (1) The first is to return to your car, completing 1.5 miles of the Finger Lakes Trail. (2) The second is to continue on the former canal/railbed on the opposite side of the entrance road. This 3.6-mile side-trip on the FLT will lead you to the edge of the park property near Oakland, where it continues as the Genesee Valley Greenway. Retracing your tracks back to the Parade Grounds Entrance provides a tour of approximately 8 miles.

(3) However, we recommend a third option, requiring that you return to your car and drive west on Route 436 less than 1 mile to the FLT parking lot at the edge of the Portageville Bridge. To complete the FLT, you must now climb the short hill from the trailhead behind the parking lot and travel along the abandoned roadway, skirting the private property on your right. Descending to the pathway along the river, you'll follow the old canal/railbed to the spectacular High Bridge. This 235-foot railroad trestle over the gorge was originally constructed of wood. You may be fortunate to get here in time to see the daily train crossing the famous bridge. Here too is our reconnection to the first section of the FLT. From the concrete base of the present iron bridge, reconstructed in 1875, you will marvel at this great wonder and the wintry show put on by the splashing and rumbling Upper Falls. Then, retracing your tracks, you will once again pass under the High Bridge and continue along the gorge back toward the Portageville Bridge.

You may choose to take a short side trip to the gorge overlooking the village of Portageville. To do this travel straight ahead to the edge of the river where there is an informational plaque explaining the history of this crossing.

Directions at a glance

Option 1

0.0   Start at the Parade Grounds Entrance.

0.1   Pass the covered pavilion.

0.3   Reach gated entrance to Finger Lakes Trail.

0.7   Reach overlook and turn around.

1.2   Pass gated entrance at service road.

1.5   Return to park entrance, partially completing the trail.

Option 3

0.0   Begin remaining section of Finger Lakes Trail at Portageville Bridge.

0.8   Reach High Bridge and turn around.

1.25 Take a side trip to former aqueduct over river.

1.6   Finish at second parking lot (totaling 3.1 miles).

In the mid-1800s the Genesee Valley Canal continued across the river at this point. The water was carried in a wooden aqueduct, a photo of which can be seen at the Letchworth Museum. The photo shows ten pillars supporting the aqueduct, with water squirting out of the cracks in the boards. Today you will see only the remains of two concrete pillars, which supported the railroad bridge that replaced the aqueduct.

After the side trip to the river's edge, follow your own ski tracks back to the first junction. Turn right, retracing your earlier travels along the park boundary and return to the parking lot. You may wish to end your day with a walk across the Portageville Bridge and a stop at the Genesee Falls Inn for a cup of soup, hot chocolate, or other beverage. We recommend it.

To learn more about the winter trail opportunities on the Finger Lakes Trail contact the Finger Lakes Trail Conference (see appendix).

How to get there

From the north take I–390 south to exit 7. Take Route 408 south through Mt. Morris to Route 436. Turn right and follow Route 436 west to the Parade Grounds Entrance to the park.

From the south take I–390 to exit 4 at Dansville. Take Route 436 west to the Parade Grounds Entrance to the park.

Gravel Trail Loop
Letchworth State Park, Castile, New York

Type of trail:	▬▬▶
Also used by:	Hikers, walkers
Distance:	1.75 miles
Terrain:	Flat, rolling
Trail difficulty:	Easiest
Food and facilities:	Letchworth State Park offers winter trail users the rustic Trailside Lodge at the edge of the cross-country ski trail system. The log building, constructed in the 1960s, features a central open-pit fireplace, picnic tables, and toilet facilities. A concessionaire provides rental equipment and food services, or you can bring your favorite brown bag lunch or snacks. A warm, glowing fire is usually kept alive by helpful park staff. Other heated rest rooms are provided at Inspiration Point and the Visitor Center. The park offers year-round cabins for rent with woodstoves or electric heat. For groceries try Shur Save Market in nearby Castile (315–493–5494). Lorraine's Place in Castile is a favorite of the locals for home cooking (716–493–3060). Lodging nearby includes the Colonial Motel in Portageville (716–493–5700), Country Inn and Suites in Mt. Morris (716–658–4080), and the Genesee Falls Inn at Portageville (716–493–2484).
Phone numbers:	Park Office, (716) 493–3600. Park Police, (716) 658–4692. Call 911 for emergencies.
Fees:	There is a parking fee on weekends when there are snow conditions.
Caution:	Letchworth Park has many dangerous cliffs. Obey the caution signs and do not venture near the edges.

Letchworth State Park, just 45 miles south of Rochester, comprises 14,300 acres of scenic magnificence. The precipitous walls of the gorge, the Genesee River winding below, the plunge and spray of dramatic waterfalls, and the lush forest all contribute to make this park one of the most notable examples of waterfalls and scenery in the United States. Within the park the Genesee River roars over three major waterfalls, cutting into the dramatic cliffs that approach 600 feet in height. The middle waterfall is 107 feet high. Carved by the river, the majestic gorge snakes through the 17-mile-long park, providing awesome views at many overlooks.

In winter, cross-country skiing, snowshoeing, snowmobiling, ice-skating, horse-drawn sleigh rides, and tubing are fun activities held near Trailside Lodge. Skiers and snowshoers are urged to stop at the lodge to pick up a copy of the trail map and to learn about any recent changes as noted on the park's colorful display board. Classifying and describing all the multiuse trails within the vast trail system might be considered a work in progress. Letchworth State Park has developed a complex network of cross-country ski trails within its narrow borders. In fact, there are five specific trail zones: Lower Falls, Pond, Tower, Inspiration Woods, and Bishop's Woods. Trail names, totaling almost four dozen, have been given to each trail within the zones.

Some of the winter trails at Letchworth State Park are shared with other trail users, including snowmobilers. We have selected the Gravel Trail Loop, a 1.75-mile "ski only" trail in the Tower Zone. It is a fun trail for beginners and novices, with nice variations, gradual climbs, and gentle slopes. The Gravel Trail Loop utilizes a network of many other trails with many different names. The two-way loop joins or crosses other trails and meets about a dozen different intersections on its way to and from the gravel pit. Although it is a well-defined ski loop, it is wise to check your trail map from time to time.

To access the Gravel Trail Loop, park at the Trailside Lodge and begin your tour at the teaching area in front of the tubing hill. Cross-country ski lessons are taught here on weekends throughout the season (conditions permitting). The tubing hill, formerly the 1960s downhill ski area associated with the park's winter recreational facilities, is also used in connection with the ski lessons.

Cross the lawn and turn right onto the Gravel Trail Loop, identified with trail markers. You will travel through an evergreen grove to the first intersection, the Tower Trail. Turn left onto this wide woods road and ski uphill almost to the base of the hill ahead of you, on which the radio tower is located. Turn left and continue around the base of tower hill, cross the dirt road between the tubing hill and the radio tower, and ski to the power line. Follow underneath the power line a short distance. Take Tower Trail (left) over a short rise and turn right. The trail continues to descend onto the Swamp Crossing Trail, avoiding the wetland.

You will then come back to the power line and follow underneath it for a short distance before turning right and skiing to the southern edge of Denton Woods. Passing through a grove of mixed hardwoods, including beech, red oak, a 200-year-old tulip tree, and a 150-foot-tall pine tree, the terrain is gentle and undulating with a few gradual climbs. You'll ski through an evergreen planting between Denton Woods and the gravel pit.

Continuing on the Gravel Trail Loop, you'll come into the gravel pit

Directions at a glance

0.0   Begin at the base of the tubing hill on right side of hill.

0.1   Turn left at intersection with Tower Trail.

0.2   Turn left at base of radio tower.

0.4   Ski under power line.

0.5   Turn right, ski to Swamp Crossing Trail.

0.7   Return to the power line.

0.9   Reach the edge of Denton Woods.

1.0   Enter west side of park's gravel pit.

1.2   Switchback on south side of pit.

1.5   Ski through the pine meadows around the hill.

1.7   Recross the Tower Trail.

1.75 Finish at Trailside Lodge.

on the west side and ski to the wide, unplowed maintenance road. Traveling around the pit, down the road on the east side and then leaving the road, you'll make a sharp right turn, beginning a switchback on the south side of the gravel pit. You are about halfway around the loop. After another switchback you'll reach pine meadows, offering very flat trails where herds of deer are often observed. Follow along the pine meadows around the hill and through various snow-covered paths. The radio tower will appear ahead of you as you ski through the woods before arriving back at your original connection to Tower Trail. Cross the trail and return to the Trailside Lodge.

How to get there

From I–390 take exit 7 to Route 408. Drive east 2 miles to Route 36. Take Route 36 north to Route 39. Travel south on Route 39 to Route 19A. Follow Route 19A south to the Castile entrance.

From Buffalo take Route 400 south to Route 20A. Drive east to Route 19 at Warsaw. Take Route 19 south to Route 19A. Follow Route 19A south to the Castile entrance.

North Meadow Trail Loop

Mendon Ponds County Park, Mendon, New York

Type of trail: ▬▬ ⬭

Distance: 3.0 miles

Trail difficulty: Easiest to more difficult

Terrain: Hilly, rolling

Food and facilities: There are several heated rest rooms at the park, but no facilities for food in winter. Bring snacks or pack a lunch. Monroe County parks provide year-round lodges and shelters for rent, including several at Mendon Ponds Park. Fast-food vendors, grocery stores, restaurants, and lodging may be found in nearby Pittsford, Honeoye Falls, and Rochester. For groceries try the Market Place & Deli (716–624–1560) and for great bread, the Montana Mills Bread Company (716–248–2280). For day-use lodging at Mendon Ponds Park call (716–256–4951) or (800–662–1220). Other lodging includes the Hampton Inn and Suites (716–914–4400) and Super 8 (716–359–1638).

Phone numbers: Park Office, (716) 359–1433. For emergencies dial 911.

Fees: There are no fees to use the trails

Caution: The ponds are off-limits to skiers and snowshoers. Do not remove any plants or glacial material from the park.

Mendon Ponds Park, established in 1929, is one of the gems in a system of municipal parks operated and maintained by the Monroe County Parks Department. Totaling 2,550 acres, it is the largest in the diverse park system. In 1969 it was designated a National Natural Landmark by the United States Department of Interior because of its unique geological glacial landforms. The park lends itself to wildlife watching and photography, as well as more active recreational pursuits, including hiking, cross-country skiing, and horseback riding. Various waterfowl and songbird populations are plentiful, as are the deer, beaver, and turkey. Some meadows in the park are maintained specifically to enable populations of bluebirds, grassland birds, and butterflies to flourish. Several turf grass trails are mowed throughout these areas for bird-watching and cross-country skiing. The ponds are enjoyed by many fishermen and canoeists. Any habitat imaginable is found in this diverse and unique municipal park.

As a result of geological activities in the Ice Age, vast lakes formed at the edge of the ice sheet. It was the transport of sand, gravel, and rocks

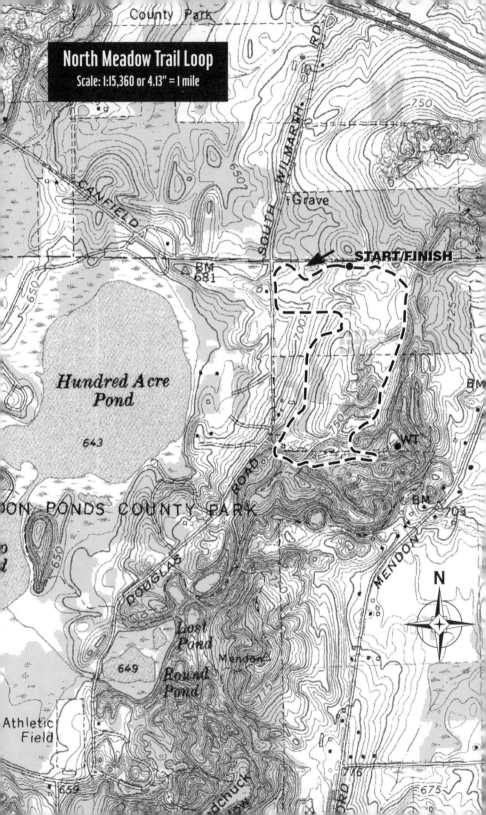

North Meadow Trail Loop
Scale: 1:15,360 or 4.13" = 1 mile

County Park

SOUTH WILMARTH RD

CANFIELD

Grave

START/FINISH

BM 681

Hundred Acre Pond

643

650

700

725

BM

WT

ON PONDS COUNTY PARK

BM 703

Douglas Road

MENDON

Lost Pond

Mendon

649

Round Pond

Athletic Field

659

675

N

from the melting ice sheet into the glacial lake that accounts for the unique geologic features—kettles, kames, and eskers—now seen in Mendon Ponds Park. The five beautiful ponds from which the park gets its name are from kettle holes left by the glacier. As the ice sheet retreated past what is now the Mendon area, it often broke apart at its edge. The ice blocks would melt, leaving behind roughly circular depressions called kettle holes, or kettles. There are many kettles in Mendon Ponds Park, some dry, some filled with water. Round Pond and Lost Pond are water-filled kettles.

Mounds of rubble left behind when the glacial rivers receded can be seen today as small conical hills called kames. Although they occur throughout the park, the best examples can be found to the east of Douglas Road behind Round Pond and Lost Pond. Several of these conical hills are traversed by Mendon Ponds' ski and snowshoe trails. Sometimes the rivers on the ice sheet would bore a hole in the sheet and flow under it in a winding tunnel. Rocky material carried by the streams would accumulate on the streambeds, and when the ice sheet and lake were gone, these streambeds remained as eskers—low, snaking ridges of rubble. Trail users will certainly marvel at these geological wonders as they "snake their way along" on the ridge trails, noticing cliffs on both sides of them. For additional information about these glacial features, stop at the Nature Center in the park for a map and to see the displays. Guests may hand feed the chickadees on Birdsong Trail for a memorable experience. The park is open year-round and cabins may be reserved year-round for day use.

Mendon Ponds Park has approximately 30 miles of multiuse trails. Most are open to cross-country skiers; the exceptions are Birdsong and Swamp Trails, which are accessible from the Nature Center. Many of the park's trails are also open to horseback riders. During the ski season, Mendon Ponds Park grooms 6 miles of trails, which are open to the public free of charge. The East Esker Trails south of Mendon and the North Meadow Trails combine to make a 6-mile loop. In addition, several large field areas west of Douglas Road have groomed loops. When conditions permit, the Quaker Pond Trail Loop is also groomed. The cross-country ski trails are very popular with local fitness enthusiasts as well as recreation seekers.

The winter trails at Mendon Ponds Park are among the most varied in the state, providing a highly rewarding experience for beginning skiers through experts. The trails bring skiers and snowshoers to the top of several hills with spectacular views of the surrounding farmland, villages, and towns, as well as rolling hills and valleys, flatland, meadows, and tree-covered forests. The trails are very well designed and meticulously maintained throughout the year. Wide grass-covered trails are mowed in the off-season and carefully groomed in winter. The hills and steeper areas are covered with bark and wood chips, which help to hold the snow during winter. The ski trails attract 10,000 to 15,000 skiers and snowshoers each year. Many use the facilities to train year-round, including high school and college ski teams. Snowshoers are permitted on all trails with the caution that they stay to the side and avoid damaging the machine-made ski tracks. Warm rest rooms with flush toilets may be found in several locations in the park.

Winter trail users should enter Mendon Ponds Park at the Canfield Road entrance off Route 65 (Clover Street). Stop at the Park Office (on Douglas Road) to obtain a trail map and other information.

To access the North Meadow Ski Trails, the northernmost (and easiest) of the 6 miles of trails, begin at the fire hydrant and look for the North Meadow Loop sign with the arrow near the trail map box. All ski trails are one-way and marked with arrows. Bear right at the start, following the wide trail that runs parallel to the road. After climbing a few gradual hills as the trail bears left, you'll come to a T intersection. Turn right on a very wide trail, going gradually downhill. You'll snake through a right, left, right section while passing some young trees and shrubbery. Turn left at the natural barriers of bushes and hedgerow, skiing parallel to Douglas Road. Continue for about 1,200 feet and you will see a large century-old cobblestone house on the opposite side of the road.

At the next intersection take a sharp left onto the wide roadway leading up the long and gradual hill toward an evergreen forest. Continuing

Competitors gather at Mendon Ponds Park for a high school cross-country ski race.

Directions at a glance

0.0 Begin at fire hydrant at North Meadow.

0.1 Turn right at T intersection.

0.3 Pass stone building, turn left at junction.

0.5 Turn right at marker 27.

0.6 Cross four-way junction, pass park office.

1.0 Bear left at Y intersection.

1.5 Switchback at marker 25.

2.2 Jog right at marker 26.

2.8 Turn left at North Meadow.

2.9 Cross four-way intersection.

3.0 Finish at trail map box and fire hydrant.

around a wide turn to the right you'll arrive at a four-way intersection identified with the blue (27) marker.

North Meadow Trail now turns sharply right and begins a gradual downhill while passing under a grove of evergreens. The trail continues to descend, making a series of turns and continuing around the bend to another four-way intersection. Directly ahead, the trail meanders through mixed hardwoods to an open meadow behind the park office. Continue across the meadow and ski up a little hill, entering a locust grove. Turn left at the Y marked with North Meadow Loop Trail sign, then climb a long, gradual uphill about 1,200 feet toward the water tower. When you reach the blue (25) marker make a sharp left turn (marked with a directional arrow) for the North Meadow Loop Trail and head downhill on a long straightaway before a large banked turn. Turn left through an open meadow, passing a huge oak tree. At the blue (26) marker the trail turns right and continues on a straight run toward the road. At the intersection, bear left just before the road and proceed through a final four-way intersection, then back to the trail map box, fire hydrant, and your car.

How to get there

Take State Route 65 (Clover Street) to Canfield Road, the first entrance to Mendon Ponds County Park. Turn into the park and drive about a mile to the cobblestone building on the right. Turn right on Douglas Road and continue to the park office.

Old Pasture Trail Loop

Fahnestock Winter Park, Cold Spring, New York

Type of trail:	━━━ ⬡
Also used by:	Hikers, hunters, walkers
Distance:	7.2 miles
Terrain:	Hilly
Trail difficulty:	More difficult
Surface quality:	Machine groomed and tracked
Food and facilities:	The Fahnestock Winter Lodge features a cozy lounge, cafeteria, rest rooms, and changing rooms. The ski shop offers both ski and snowshoe rentals, accessories, and lessons. Soup, sandwiches, snacks, and drinks are available. Tables are provided for brown baggers and those who purchase food at the lodge. Ample parking is available for cars and buses. Winterized cabins near the park are available for rent by groups. Fast-food vendors, grocery stores, restaurants, and lodging may be found in nearby Cold Spring, Peekskill, Fishkill, and Beacon. For groceries try Grand Union (914–265–7826) or T & L Deli (914–265–3007).
Phone numbers:	Fahnestock Winter Park, (914) 225–3998 or (914) 265–3773.
Fees:	There is a fee to use the trails.
Caution:	The wilderness trails are not patrolled. This is a carry-in, carry-out facility.

At the center of the Clarence Fahnestock Memorial State Park in the heart of the Hudson River Valley is Fahnestock Winter Park. Located near Cold Spring, about 12 miles northeast of Peekskill and only an hour's drive from Manhattan, the park is a very popular winter recreation destination. Offering miles of winter trails for skiing and snowshoeing, its diverse terrain appeals to both beginner and expert skiers as well as snowshoers and winter hikers.

Fahnestock's winter trails are groomed by machine for both classic and skate-style cross-country skiing. Many more miles of wilderness trails may be accessed from the park. The wilderness trails are not groomed or maintained by park staff, but are used by many winter enthusiasts interested in exploring the vast woods on their own. The park provides a picturesque setting for winter adventures throughout its 10,000 acres, including tubing on the park's sledding hill.

The beauty and winter splendor of the trails at Fahnestock are breathtaking as you glide through hemlock and hardwood groves, passing

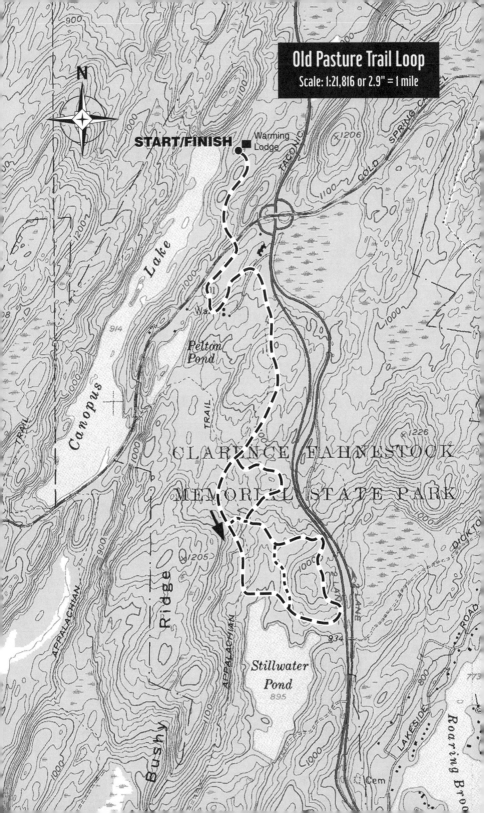

Old Pasture Trail Loop
Scale: 1:21,816 or 2.9" = 1 mile

START/FINISH

Warming Lodge

Canopus Lake

Pelton Pond

CLARENCE FAHNESTOCK MEMORIAL STATE PARK

Bushy Ridge

Stillwater Pond
895

Roaring Brook

Skiers appreciate the machine-made tracks at Fahnstock Winter Park.

lakes, streams, and meadows dotted with rock outcroppings. Winter trail users may notice old stone walls, foundations, and stone chimneys. These are remains of a Civilian Conservation Corps (CCC) camp from the 1930s. This camp, like others throughout the nation, housed young unemployed men whose work projects provided the momentum in creating a system of state and national parks. At Fahnestock, the CCC crew built many park structures, including the campground, stone shelters, dams, and some of the trails used today for year-round recreation. The original tract of land for the park (2,000 acres) was given to the state in 1929 by Dr. Earnest Fahnestock as a memorial to his brother, Major Clarence Fahnestock.

A variety of linked ski trails for beginners to experts originates from the Fahnestock Warming Lodge just off County Route 301. The highway divides the winter park into two sections. Winter trails north of the highway comprise the Canopus Lake Trail System; those to the south are part of the Stillwater Lake Trail System. The most popular trails are the CCC, Hemlock Grove, Old Pasture, and Mt. Laurel Loop.

We have selected the Old Pasture Trail, which is a favorite trek for experienced skiers. Beginning at the Fahnestock Warming Lodge, you will travel about a mile along the entrance road to the highway (Route 301). This can be a busy thoroughfare, so take extra precautions as you cross the highway to the park campground and the Stillwater Lake Trail System. Follow the trail signs and begin your journey on the Stillwater Trail, passing through a hemlock forest. Within a quarter mile you will see a stone bathhouse (used by summer visitors). At the southern end of this trail, about a half mile from the bathhouse, is the access point to the Old Pasture Loop. After another quarter mile, you will pass the end of the Mt. Laurel Trail at "The Corners." Here you are whisked downhill for 1.5 miles on a moderately descending hill to Stillwater Lake. The trail bears left and heads uphill in an easterly direction.

At the Stillwater Lake intersection, you may take the first path on the left (Maple Lane), which cuts off the most challenging uphill and downhill terrain on the Old Pasture Trail Loop, or continue straight along on the most challenging route. The two trails will meet again in approximately 1 mile, where the Old Pasture Trail begins a gradual ascent for a quarter mile. At this point you can take another cutoff to eliminate the more challenging uphill section or continue until the trails meet within a half mile at "The Corners" intersection. Here you will turn right and retrace your tracks back to the campground, across the highway and then back to the Warming Lodge.

How to get there

Exit the Taconic State Parkway at Cold Spring (Route 301). Travel west 0.25 mile to the park (right).

From Route 9 take Route 301 east 5.5 miles to the park (left).

By rail from Grand Central Station in New York City, take the MetroNorth Commuter Train to Cold Spring and taxi to the park.

Eagle Hill Trail Loop

Rockefeller State Park Preserve, Tarrytown, New York

Type of trail:	▬▬▬ ⬭
Also used by:	Hikers, carriage drivers, dog walkers, runners, nature enthusiasts, equestrians
Distance:	4.8 miles
Terrain:	Hilly
Trail difficulty:	More difficult
Surface quality:	Ungroomed, skier tracked
Food and facilities:	The Visitor Center, open year-round, has rest rooms. There are no facilities for food. Bring snacks or bag lunches. Fast-food vendors, restaurants, grocery stores, and lodging may be found in Tarrytown and other nearby villages. For groceries: Town Groceries (914–631–3960), Grand Union (914–747–1104). Restaurants include Pleasantville Diner (914–769–8585) and Horseman's Diner (914–631–2984). For lodging try the Marriot Hotel (914–631–2200) or Hilton (914–631–5700).
Phone numbers:	Rockefeller Preserve, (914) 631–1470. Park Police, (914) 889–4100. For emergencies dial 911.
Fees:	Parking fees are collected on weekends and holidays from December through March.
Caution:	Dogs are welcome on the trails, but must be leashed. This is a carry-in, carry-out facility.

Rockefeller State Park Preserve was made possible through the generous gifts of the Rockefeller family. More than 850 acres of their estate at Pocantico Hills have been deeded to New York State since 1983. A handsome visitor center opened in 1994. Operated by the New York State Office of Parks, Recreation, and Historic Preservation, the Preserve "will safeguard the natural environment and wildlife of these lands for present and future generations." The trails at the Rockefeller Preserve, which were designed by the Rockefellers for horseback riding and carriage driving, are ideal for cross-country skiing and snowshoeing. When there is snow, the ultra-wide carriage roads offer a unique experience for cross-country skiers and snowshoers.

The Rockefeller Preserve is characterized by a variety of wildlife habitats, woodlands, wetlands, meadows, and a twenty-four-acre lake. Twenty miles of carriage roads take visitors on intimate wooded lanes and paths along the Pocantico River and lead to wonderful panoramic

Eagle Hill Trail Loop

Scale: 1:15,024 or 4.22" = 1 mile

START

FINISH

Visitor Center

Swan Lake

Reservoir

Reservoir

Route 117

Pumping S

Rockefeller

HOLLOW

BROOK

Pocantico S

N

River

ROAD

Gory

ROAD

Pocantico

GORY

ALBANY

ROAD

Pocantico

d Pond

219

*Children enjoy
the freedom and fun
of snowshoeing.*

vistas. As with other preserves, bicycles and motorized vehicles are prohibited. Camping, open fires, swimming, hunting, and trapping are also prohibited at Rockefeller Preserve. The Rockefeller Preserve is a carry-in, carry-out facility. You must carry out (bring home) all trash because receptacles are no longer provided. There are no provisions for picnicking, although trail users may find places to enjoy snacks or bag lunches while on the trail.

The ski and snowshoe trails at Rockefeller Preserve serve for walking, running, and nature study during other seasons. They were designed expressly as carriage roads with the unique style of road construction of the day (1890) known as broken-stone roads. The winter trails here are among the widest ski and snowshoe trails found anywhere in New York State. They are fully described in Anne Rockefeller Robert's book *Mr. Rockefeller's Roads*.

Access to the Eagle Hill area may be gained by following the Old Sleepy Hollow Road Trail from the parking lot, but we suggest a more historic and scenic route, beginning at the magnificent Visitor Center. Here you'll find trail maps, some park literature, and a cozy room for getting warm on a cold winter day. A few hundred yards downhill from the Visitor Center toward the lake is a kiosk with an information board and enlarged trail map. Here too is the entrance to the Overlook Trail. Turn right and follow the Overlook Trail to the marker at the first junction, the Ash Tree Loop. From here you'll continue straight ahead down a moderate and winding road to a four-way junction at Old Sleepy Hollow Road Trail and Nature's Way. Turning left, follow the moderately sloping grade to the town road that cuts through the park, Sleepy Hollow Road.

Check for traffic before crossing the road to enter the Eagle Hill area of the Preserve. A large wooden information board with a trail map is located on the other side of the roadway. Continuing ahead, you will cross the Pocantico River via a bridge and arrive at a T intersection. Take a left, then the first right up to Eagle Hill. Continue straight up the hill to a three-way intersection. The 13 Bridges Loop Trail will be on your right. Turn left at this intersection onto Eagle Hill Trail. This is a moderately steep climb leading to the summit of Eagle Hill and the spectacular views of the Hudson River below. Kykuit, the historic estate of John D. Rockefeller at Pocantico Hills, can also be seen clearly in the distance.

After spending some time at the summit enjoying the views and the peaceful environs, continue around the loop and retrace your route back downhill to the junction of Pocantico River Trail and Sleepy Hollow Road. Cross the road and continue uphill on the Sleepy Hollow Road Trail. At the four-way intersection, turn left onto Nature's Way. This trail will be a welcome treat before completing your tour of the winter trails

Directions at a glance

0.0   Begin at Visitor Center.

0.1   Turn right onto Overlook Trail at the lake.

0.7   Turn right at intersection with Ash Tree Loop.

1.1   Turn left at four-way intersection.

1.5   Cross to Sleepy Hollow Road.

1.8   Turn left at T junction.

2.2   Turn left at three-way intersection.

3.0   Reach Eagle Hill Summit.

3.2   Turn right at three-way intersection and retrace your route to Sleepy Hollow Road.

4.3   Turn left onto Nature's Way at four-way intersection.

4.8   Finish at parking lot and Visitor Center.

at Rockefeller Preserve. It is a delightfully narrow trail through a forested section of the Preserve, following a ridge and overlooking the surrounding valley. It offers a pleasant change of scenery after following the extra-wide carriage roads. Continue on Nature's Way back to the parking lot and Visitor Center.

How to get there

From the New York State Thruway (I–87) take exit 9 in Tarrytown. Follow Route 9 north 3.5 miles to Route 117. Turn right and travel about a half mile east to the Preserve entrance.

Yellow-Red Trail Loop

Connetquot River State Park Preserve, Oakdale, New York

Type of trail:	▬▬▬ ⬤
Also used by:	Walkers, hikers, equestrians
Distance:	2.35 miles
Terrain:	Flat, gentle, and rolling
Trail difficulty:	Easiest
Surface quality:	Ungroomed, user tracked
Food and facilities:	The park office, with rest rooms and warming facilities, is open year-round except Monday and Tuesday from October 1 through March 31. No food is available and picnicking is not permitted except for "through hikers and other trail users." There is a picnic table near the parking lot at the entrance gate for hiker/skier use. Fast-food vendors, grocery stores, restaurants, and lodging may be found in surrounding villages and towns. Grocery stores include Walbaums in Oakdale and King Kullens on Waverly Avenue. For lodging try Holiday Inn (631–585–9500) or Summit Lodge (631–666–6000). The nearby Snapper Inn overlooking the confluence of the Connetquot River serves great food and offers lunch and dinner specials (516–589–0248). Other nearby restaurants include Oakdale House (631–218–0111) and Applebee's (631–224–1912).
Phone numbers:	Connetquot River State Park and Preserve, (516) 581–1005.
Fees:	There is a vehicle use fee, but no fee for use of the trails.
Caution:	Access to the State Park and Preserve is by permit only. Requests should be made in writing to Connetquot River State Park and Preserve, Box 505, Oakdale, NY 11769. This is a carry-in, carry-out trail. Visitors must refrain from feeding the wildlife.

Connetquot River Preserve is unique among the more than twenty state parks in the Long Island Region of New York State. The majority of the 3,400+ acre refuge is located in the pine barrens in the town of Islip between the Veterans Memorial Highway and the Sunrise Highway, with its main entrance located at Oakdale. As in all state preserves, motorized vehicles, bicycles, and other wheeled conveyances are strictly prohibited, giving the trails at Connetquot River State Park Preserve a special air of peace and tranquility.

The records indicate that William Nicoll, the founder of the town,

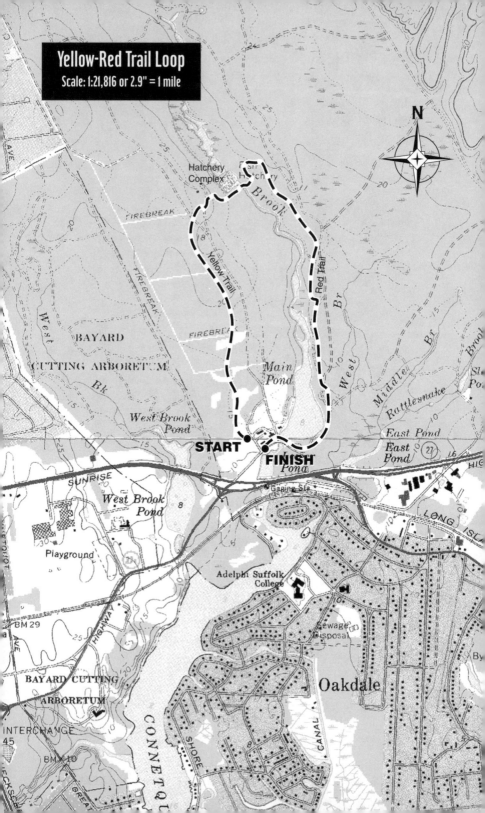

A winter enthusiast hurries to enjoy a rare snowfall at Connetquot River State Park Preserve on Long Island.

bought the land from the Connetquot Indians. A gristmill located on the property at the edge of the river dates to the mid-1700s. Part of what is now the park headquarters was originally Snedecor's Inn. Located on the old Montauk Highway, the Inn served as a stagecoach stop for travelers from New York City to the Long Island countryside.

Eliphalet Snedecor had operated another inn at Jamaica, New York, and brought many of his customers east to enjoy hunting, fishing, and horseback riding among the aromatic pines of his popular resort. In 1866, a hundred wealthy men joined in a venture to purchase the Inn and the land, forming the South Side Sportsmen's Club. This exclusive, generally undeveloped sportsman's retreat catered to such notable men as Daniel Webster and Generals Grant and Sherman. The land was sold in 1963 to the state and was opened as a park in 1973.

Traces of the preserve's past still survive in the complex of old wooden buildings at the southern end of the park. In the northern section, above Collins Crossing, raised mounds mark the remains of a carriage road that took club members and other travelers to the railroad station in the 1800s. Still visible in some sections of the Preserve are patches of crushed oyster shells used as paving material when Long Island oyster industry was at its zenith.

The Connetquot River, one of Long Island's four major rivers, is the focal point of this regional park. Arising from several underground springs, artesian wells, and freshwater streams, its source is about midway between the north and south shores of Long Island. The river flows south for miles through the region's flat pine plains before reaching the Great South Bay and the Atlantic Ocean. It is stocked with trout from a hatchery located in the center of the Preserve. Thousands of fishermen come here to enjoy their favorite sport. Owls and hawks take refuge at this vast Preserve. According to a park booklet, great blue herons, ospreys or, on rare occasions, bald eagles may be spotted. The fresh water of the river mixes daily with the saltwater tides at the estuary near Dowling College where (in season) the rowing crews may be seen practicing for intercollegiate competition.

Featuring more than 50 miles of trails dedicated entirely to foot traffic, visitors with permits may hike year-round at Connetquot River Preserve or ski and snowshoe when snow covers the trails. Horses and their riders are permitted on trails designated for equestrian use. Although the number of skiing days is minimal in this most southern region of New York State "area residents flock to the trails as soon as it is blessed with snow," according to Preserve officials. The trails are well covered with fine wood chips and sawdust, making it possible to ski on a few inches of the "white gold from heaven."

All access to Connetquot River State Park and Preserve is by permit. Although free of charge, the permits must be obtained in advance of your visit. Visitors must check in at the park entrance booth. You will receive a trail map and general information about the Preserve. A visit to the Interpretive Center, museum, and gift shop is highly recommended. Here you may obtain literature and information about guided walks (year-round) and educational programs regularly sponsored by the Environmental Education Office of State Parks, located at Connetquot Preserve.

To access the Yellow/Red Trail Loop, park in the lot near the entrance booth. After leaving the Interpretive Center, turn left at the eastern end of the Main House and walk to the end of the horse paddock where you'll make another left turn. The Yellow Trail can be entered just before reaching the park's horse barn. The trail is identified with yellow markers (directional arrows). You will also observe white painted blazes on trees and fence posts, as this section of the trail is also part of Long Island's Greenbelt Trail, a 34-mile National Recreation Trail.

The Yellow Trail will lead you in a northerly direction on a fairly straight path through a young oak and pine forest. Primarily a pine barren, the terrain here is mostly flat, making for easy skiing and snowshoeing. With snow covering the shrubs and trees, the trail turns into a winter wonderland. Wildlife is plentiful in the Preserve; you may be able to observe some of the many deer and fox that inhabit these woods.

After passing a couple of open meadows, you will cross Hatchery Road and arrive at the park's Hatchery Complex. You may decide to stop here for a closer examination of the fish pools and the exteriors of the old buildings. Although some park programs include a tour of the hatchery buildings, they are generally not open to the public. Various size fish may be seen in the hatching pools and ponds that are fed by water from the river.

At the hatchery, the Red Trail section of the loop can be entered. Follow the red arrows across the river via two wooden bridges and an elevated walkway. At the end of the walkway the trail turns left and continues a few hundred yards to a junction. The Red Trail turns right at this point. The smaller trail (straight ahead) is a popular secondary loop around the Hatchery Complex. Continue on the Red Trail to a small pond fed by artesian wells. After passing the pond, make a right and continue in a southerly direction (parallel to Brook Road) along the east side of the river.

Here the forest is older; tall oak trees are interspersed with large pitch pines. The Red Trail is very pretty as it meanders through the woodland parallel to the Connetquot River. It offers at least a couple of side trips to the river's edge (numbered fishing sites) before continuing south toward the office area. The trail is a bit more enjoyable on this side of the river, thanks to some nicely undulating terrain. At the junction for Brook Road the Red Trail joins the Blue Trail and continues around Main Pond to the park office.

Directions at a glance

0.0   Begin at the Main House.

0.1   Pass stable and turn onto Yellow Trail.

0.9   Cross Hatchery Road.

1.0   Reach Hatchery Complex. Follow Red Trail across the river.

1.2   Follow red markers as trail turns left near the artesian wells.

1.3   Pass four-way junction (smaller trails).

1.5   Continue on Red Trail as two trails go left to Brook Road.

1.8   Red Trail joins the Blue Trail at Brook Road.

2.1   Reach wooden pillars and junction for Old Montauk Highway.

2.2   Pass Grist Mill.

2.35 Finish at Main Building Complex.

After passing Slade Pond Road, you will pass through reproductions of the original wooden gateposts for the old South Side Sportsmen's Club and travel past the roadway that was the original Montauk Highway. As the trail (Red/Blue at this point) turns right, you will have a magnificent view of Main Pond, a favorite wintering place for a wide variety of ducks and Canada geese. Continue past the famed Oakdale Grist Mill (1701–1751) and arrive at the front lawn of the Main Building Complex. Here you will most likely find yourself among hundreds of friendly ducks and geese. Just remember: Don't feed the wildlife.

How to get there

From points west, take Grand Central Parkway to Northern State Parkway (east) to Sagtikos Parkway (south), then to Southern State Parkway (east) to Exit 44. Take Sunrise Highway (Route 27) east to the Connetquot River State Park Preserve in Oakdale.

From the east, take Sunrise Highway (Route 27) west to the Preserve in Oakdale.

Rusty Nail Ski Trail Loop

Byrncliff Resort & Conference Center, Varysburg, New York

Type of trail:	══ ◁
Also used by:	Hikers, backcountry skiers
Distance:	2.5 miles
Terrain:	Hilly
Difficulty:	Easiest
Surface quality:	Machine groomed and tracked
Food and facilities:	Byrncliff Resort & Conference Center offers fine food and lodging, a warm and cozy clubhouse, and a full-service ski shop. The ski shop provides rental equipment and instruction for both day and night skiing. All the facilities are open to the public, with optional ski packages available for meals and lodging. Fast-food vendors, restaurants, and lodging may be found in nearby East Aurora and Buffalo. For groceries: C&G Praller in Varysburg (716–535–7155) or Oasis Gas Shop in Varysburg (716–535–7877). For homemade soups try Byrncliff or Mary's Place in Varysburg (716–535–7542).
Phone numbers:	Byrncliff Resort, (716) 535–7300.
Fees:	There is a fee for use of the trails.

Nestled in the beautiful rolling hills of Wyoming County in western New York State, Byrncliff is a full-service resort catering to golfers in season and cross-country skiers in winter. Byrncliff Resort & Conference Center offers first-class accommodations for overnight guests as well as for those who come for a day of golfing, enjoying the heated pool and hot tub, or skiing on the well-groomed trails. Only 35 miles from Buffalo and 50 miles from Rochester, the family-owned and -managed resort provides for the varied recreational needs of many outdoor enthusiasts, including nighttime skiers who enjoy the pleasures of skiing on the well-lighted trails.

The cross-country ski trails at Byrncliff Resort & Conference Center are groomed and tracked with state-of-the-art equipment for skiers of all abilities, providing some of the best cross-country skiing in the state. The 12-mile ski trail system is uniquely situated on two sides of the picturesque Tonawanda Creek Valley, offering two distinct skiing areas: the West and East Trail Systems. About 6 miles of the West Hill trails, generally considered to be the easier area, are lighted for nighttime skiing. The East Trail System offers more varied terrain for all levels of skiing ability.

Byrncliff's ski trails, named for famous drinks, are well marked and

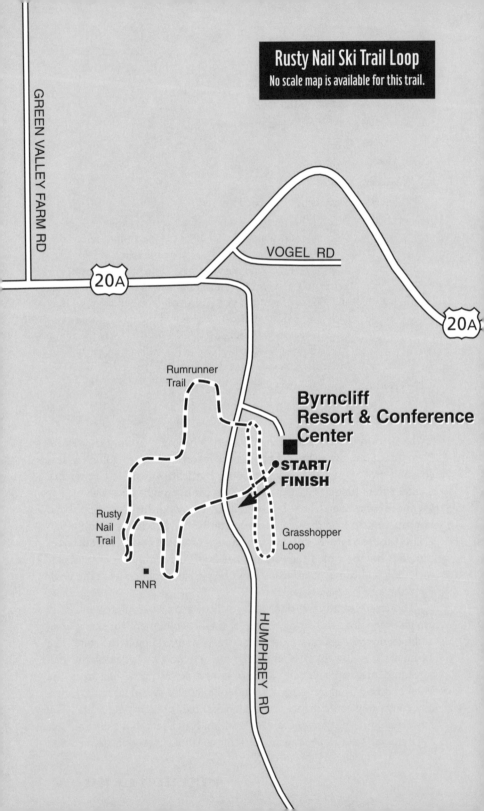

noted on a large full-color trail map posted in the clubhouse near the ski shop. Full-color trail maps are also available for users to take along on their trail tours. Trails marked with arrows are one-way trails. All others are for two-way traffic. The winter trails are open to the public for competitive as well as recreational skiing. Ski clubs and schools often choose these trails for their competitive ski events. The resort offers a variety of weekday and weekend ski packages including meals and lodging.

For *Winter Trails: New York* we have selected the Rusty Nail Trail on the West Hill of the Byrncliff Resort. Beginning at the ski center, follow the signs for the Rusty Nail Trail across Humphrey Road, passing the Grasshopper skate-skiing loop. Soon you begin to climb a gradual uphill to an open slope where the trail turns sharply left and enters the woods. Following the trail signs and groomed tracks, cross the Swizzler Trail, continuing your gradual climb toward the resort's summit. Soon the trail makes a sweeping turn, bringing you to a lean-to-style hut on the side of the trail. The hut, called Rusty Nail Rendezvous, is a great spot for a rest, or to meet friends for a snack or cup of hot cocoa. Local skiers love to gather at the Rendevous, especially in the evening to enjoy the pleasures of night skiing.

Shortly after the Rusty Nail Rendezvous the trail crosses the Swizzler again as you continue to ski through the woods toward the summit of the west hill. The trail turns through an open field, paralleling the Manhattan Lane Trail for approximately a quarter mile. When you leave the field you'll turn right to begin a long and gradual descent. This is a nicely undulating section with some sweeping turns before it whizzes you downhill through a hardwood grove.

After crossing Mahogany Ridge Trail and heading toward the pond, you'll come back out onto the open fields overlooking the magnificent

Directions at a glance

0.0   Start at the ski shop.

0.1   Continue straight at intersection with the Grasshopper Loop.

0.2   Cross Humphrey Road.

0.3   Enter the woods at top of the hill.

0.4   Trail intersects Swizzler.

1.0   Reach Rendezvous Hut.

2.0   Cross Mahogany Ridge Trail and continue on Rusty Nail to the Rumrunner Trail.

2.5   Finish at the ski shop.

valley. The views are spectacular—a panorama of the resort and the ski trails on the other side of the resort (East Hill). From here skiers have several choices of other trails to experience, if desired.

The Rusty Nail Trail eventually connects with the Rumrunner Trail, which will take you back across Humphrey Road. If you still have energy for some more skiing (there's plenty of it at Byrncliff), try a few turns around the Grasshopper Loop before returning to the ski shop and clubhouse.

How to get there

From Buffalo take Route 400 east to Route 20A. Head east on Route 20A approximately12 miles to Byrncliff Resort.

From Rochester and the east take I–90 west to Pembrook exit. Take Route 77 south to Route 20A. Turn left and travel about a half mile to Byrncliff Resort.

Spruce Bog Trail Loop

Grafton Lakes State Park, Grafton, New York

Type of trail:	▬▬ ⬬
Also used by:	Hikers, bikers, equestrians, hunters, snowmobilers
Distance:	6 miles
Terrain:	Flat, hilly
Trail difficulty:	More difficult
Surface quality:	Ungroomed, skier tracked and backcountry
Food and facilities:	Grafton Lakes State Park is open year-round with warming room, toilets, and tables for bag lunches. Fast-food vendors, restaurants, and lodging may be found in nearby Troy and Albany. For a local restaurant try Lena's Kitchen on Route 2 (518–279–3842). Grafton General Store (518–279–9663) has groceries and supplies. Local lodging includes Grafton Inn (518–279–9489) and Grafton Mountain House (518–279–1465).
Phone numbers:	Park Office, (518) 279–1155. Park Police, (518) 584–2004. For emergencies call 911.
Fees:	There are no fees for use of the trails.
Caution:	The lake may be unsafe for skiing and snowshoeing. During limited snow years there may be rock exposures on the trails. Stop at the park office for a trail map and current trail and ice conditions. Dogs with proper rabies shots are permitted on the winter trails, and must be on a leash. This is a carry-in, carry-out facility.

With 2,357 acres, Grafton Lakes is one of New York's largest state parks, featuring four ponds, many old roads that wind through the area, and the Martin-Durham Reservoir. The city of Troy used the ponds for its water supply until 1960 when the land was acquired for a park. Open year-round, Grafton Lakes State Park is located on a 1,500-foot forested plateau between the Taconic Mountain Valley in Massachusetts and the Hudson River Valley in New York. Only twenty minutes from Troy and forty minutes from downtown Albany, the park offers a wide variety of year-round activities for residents of the large metropolitan region, including day and night cross-country skiing, snowshoeing, and sledding. A comprehensive Winter Festival is held annually to promote winter activities in the park.

Twenty miles of multiuse trails have been developed throughout the park, including several for handicapped participants. A self-guided nature

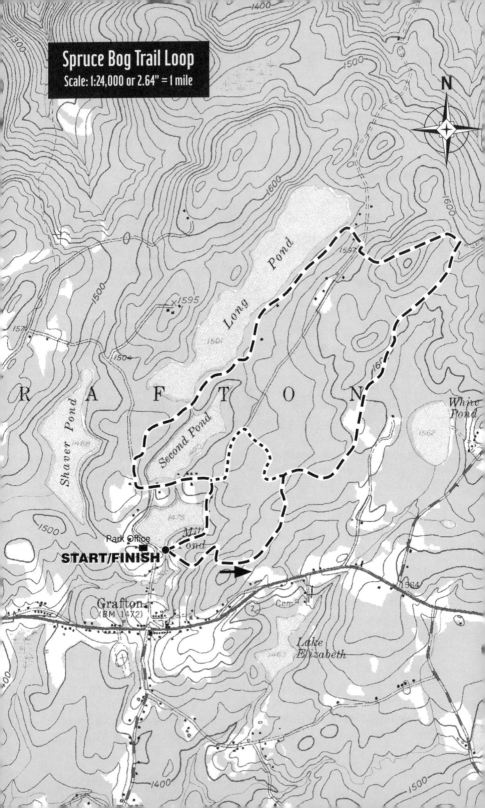

Spruce Bog Trail Loop
Scale: 1:24,000 or 2.64" = 1 mile

N

Long Pond

1595

1501

1504

1557

1600

1500

1571

R A F T O N

White Pond

1562

Shaver Pond

1468

Second Pond

1480

1475

Mill Pond

Park Office
START/FINISH

Grafton
(BM 1472)

Cem

Lake Elizabeth

1463

1500

1400

1300

1400

1500

1600

This is one of several bridges enjoyed by winter trail users at Grafton Lakes State Park.

trail was created as a cooperative environmental program between Hudson Valley Community College and the park. Skiers, snowshoers, and snowmobilers share most winter trails; a few are dedicated for skier use only. Ice fishing and skating on Mill Pond are popular winter activities when conditions permit. Winter trail users are requested to park vehicles at the Mill Pond parking lot just off Long Pond Road. All trailheads have standardized signage and are blazed with blue trail markers.

The Spruce Bog Loop is actually a combination of trails. To access this loop travel over the short footbridge that spans the outlet of Mill Pond. After climbing the first short hill you may choose to stop and view the old headstones at the Snyder-Williams Cemetery, one of four cemeteries within the park. The land was originally part of the Van Rensselaer Patroonship and these burial sites are from the former landowners. During that time it was customary to bury deceased relations on your own private property. The Francis West family burial ground is of particular interest for its inclusion of two notable local authors. Granville Hicks was a free thinking professor at Rensselaer Polytechnic Institute (RPI) who wrote the book, *Small Town* (1946) based on his impressions of the town of Grafton. The other is Henry Christman, author of *Tin Horns and Calico* (1945) a fascinating historical account of the anti rent wars which occurred in the region in the 1840s.

Continuing the gradual climb on a series of small hills, you will soon reach the top of the plateau. Travel about 0.75 mile through a grove of

Directions at a glance

0.0   Cross over wooden bridge.

0.1   Pass cemetery.

0.25 Reach plateau.

1.0   Turn right at intersection.

1.5   Cross open field (picnic table on trail).

2.5   Turn left at Fire Tower Trail.

3.5   Turn left onto Long Pond Trail.

5.0   Pass boathouse and continue to Main Park Road.

6.0   Finish at parking lot.

old-time hardwoods such as oak, maple, ash and beech, until you reach the first intersection. At this point you have two options. You may go left and ski a shorter loop (2 miles) through thick hemlocks, returning alongside Mill Pond and arriving back at the cemetery where you began. Or you can turn right and travel through other hardwoods, following the trail for another half-mile through an open field, abundant with wild blueberries in the summer.

If you stay on the longer loop, you'll reenter the woods and pass by large stands of spruce, hemlock, and white pine trees. This is the spruce bog section from whence the trail gets its name. There are a few wet spots on this section but they are usually frozen in winter. Once you reach Fire Tower Trail you will turn left and descend a series of fairly steep hills until you reach the Long Pond Trail. In some of these areas you may see stone walls, which were built by early settlers to divide farmland or mark property boundaries. Turn left on Long Pond Trail and ski or snowshoe adjacent to the largest pond on the property to the Long Pond trailhead near the boathouse. From the boathouse continue through Rabbit Run picnic area and intersect with Main Park Road. Take a left and ski to the office sign at the managers' house, then uphill to the Mill Pond parking lot.

How to get there

The park is located 12 miles east of Troy on Route 2. The park's winter entrance is located adjacent to the Grafton General Store. It is approximately one mile east of the main entrance. Turn left onto North Long Pond Road at the village green, just after the store. Follow the road past the driveway for the maintenance building, and uphill to Mill Pond (also known as First Pond).

Sisu-Karhu Trail Loop

Lapland Lake Cross-Country Ski & Vacation Center, Northville, New York

Type of trail:	━━ ◤
Also used by:	Hikers, bikers
Distance:	6.3 miles (with optional shortcuts)
Terrain:	Hilly, mountainous
Trail difficulty:	More difficult to most difficult
Surface quality:	Groomed and tracked for both techniques
Food and facilities:	Lapland Lake resort offers a modern full-service ski lodge with tables for brown bag lunches or light fare from the snack bar. Couches in front of the large woodstove provide additional seating and winter ambience. The resort's Tuulen Tupa Restaurant is open for lunch and dinner. A full service sales and rental shop provides a complete line of skis, snowshoes, ice skates, snow tubes, kicksleds, pulks, and accessories. Lapland Lake offers on-site lodging in several unique cottages. Fast-food venues, other restaurants, grocery stores, and lodging may be found in nearby Northville (5 miles). Grand Union has groceries (518–863–6776). Other restaurants include Lanzi's on the Lake (518–661–7711). For additional lodging try the Inn at the Bridge (518–863–2240) or Trailhead Lodge (518–863–2198).
Phone numbers:	Lapland Lake Center, (518) 863–4974. For conditions call (800) 453–SNOW.
Fees:	A fee is charged for use of the trails.
Caution:	Sisu-Karhu is a long and difficult trail. Be prepared to turn around or take one of the shortcuts. The Sisu- Karhu Trail is for cross-country skiing only. There are 12.5 kilometers of ungroomed trails designated for snowshoeing.

Tucked away in the southern corner of New York's six-million-acre Adirondack Park, Lapland Lake Cross-Country Ski & Vacation Center offers a wide variety of winter activities in the natural beauty of the surrounding forever-wild forest land. The resort features European-style hospitality in a country setting with Finnish names on all the ski trails, cottages, and the restaurant. The Finnish Line Lodge is as modern and comfortable as the facilities at any of today's Alpine ski resorts. The beautiful knotty pine lodge lends real charm to its schedule of lively wintertime activities for youngsters of every age. The separate Tuulen Tupa Restaurant offers fine dining featuring mouthwatering Finnish and

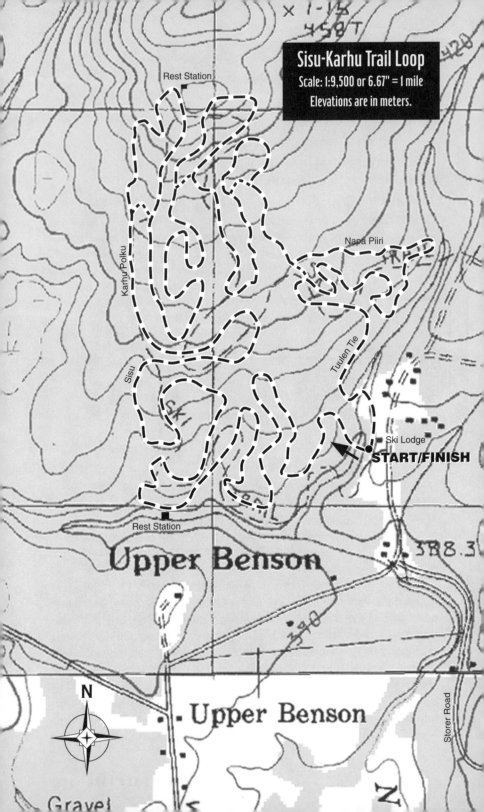

Sisu-Karhu Trail Loop
Scale: 1:9,500 or 6.67" = 1 mile
Elevations are in meters.

Rest Station

Napa Piiri

Karhu-Polku

Tuulen Tie

Sisu

Ski Lodge

START/FINISH

Rest Station

Upper Benson

388.3

Upper Benson

Storer Road

N

Gravel

Reindeer are popular residents at Lapland Lake Resort.

American dishes for health-conscious patrons. Overnight accommodations are available in the resort's quaint and charming housekeeping cottages called Tupas. Overnight guests have use of the popular wood-burning sauna.

The Finnish names at Lapland Lake are in honor of the homeland of its owner, Olavi Hirvonen, who grew up in a small European town where everybody learned to cross-country ski almost as early as walking. After his family settled in America, Olavi competed on the U.S. Ski Team in the 1960 Olympics at Squaw Valley, California. Olavi has trained several reindeer for the entertainment of the resort's guests, providing demonstrations of the skill of skiing behind a harnessed reindeer.

Skiers and snowshoers have many trail choices for an hour, a day, or more at Lapland Lake. There is night skiing on lighted trails. Two separate trails have been designated for snowshoeing only. Here we describe a long trail for intermediate and advanced skiers, although there are many miles of trails at Lapland for beginners and novice skiers.

The Sisu-Karhu Trail Loop is a combination of trails providing a 6.3-

mile loop. There are several options along the way for shorter trips, depending upon your skiing skill and time available. Access to the Sisu-Karhu Trail (blue) is from the Finnish Line Lodge via a bridge over Grant Stream to Honka Tie Trail. Turn left and follow the signs to the Sisu Loop. The trail meanders alongside the noisy West Stoney Creek before arriving at the 200-year-old giant pine. About 150 feet tall, the pine tree is so wide that the hands of two adults with outstretched arms cannot meet.

Continuing along the creek you will arrive at a "resting station" with a hanging seat, a nice place to relax and enjoy the peaceful environs of the creekside trail. A little further you may notice the remains of an old stone bridge bulkhead just over the creek leading to a farm. The stone walls to the left of the trail are most likely the remains of a carriage shed. At about 1.5 miles is a trailside fire pit used by the resort for such special events as moonlight tours with bonfires. Just beyond you will find the foundation of an old farm homestead, a fieldstone circular well, and an old apple orchard. The old homestead was reportedly destroyed by fire during the late 1800s.

To this point you have experienced gently rolling hills through a lush pine forest. At the junction of the Sisu and Karhu Trails (5) skiers may elect to return via a shortcut to the lodge for a total distance of 2.5 miles, or continue further by taking a left turn onto Karhu Polku Trail. If you choose to continue, you will soon approach a junction (6) where you have another choice: to remain on the Karhu Trail, or return via the Leilan Latu Trail for a distance of about 3 miles.

At the first shortcut on the Karhu Trail (2.7 mi.) you have another choice: to continue on the more difficult section of the trail (blue) or turn left to enter the most difficult section (black markers). Those electing to enter the most difficult section will begin a climb through the resort's hardwood forest to the highest elevation of the trail system, a total climb of 250 feet to the highest point. Here you will find another resting station with a hanging swing seat. It's a good place for a rest, taking time to enjoy the great views and the peaceful surroundings.

The Karhu Trail then takes you on a long, straight downhill run, about 0.25 mile, returning to the rolling hills of the pine forest and the terrain of the "blue" section. You will approach a junction where you will bear right to remain on the blue trail. Skilled cross-country skiers may continue straight ahead on the "black diamond" section of the Karhu Trail. About 75 yards beyond this junction is a stone fortification that legend suggests may have been used as a firing position during the Civil War. Another short distance beyond the fortification, skiers will note a sign indicating the foundation of a former sugarhouse. Just beyond is the start of the steepest climb on the trail. You'll most likely need to use the

Directions at a glance

0.0   Cross bridge to Honka Tie Trail.

1.2.   Pass the giant pine tree.

1.5   Pass trailside fire pit.

2.1   Sisu Trail junction (5) offers a shortcut back to lodge (2.5 miles total).

2.4   Karhu Polku junction (6) offers a shortcut (3.1 miles total).

2.7   Leilan Latu junction offers a shortcut (3.9 miles total).

3.8   Another shortcut off Karhu Trail (avoiding Black Diamond section).

4.4   Reach junction (8) for Napa Piiri.

5.6   Reach intersection (9) of Tuulen Tie and Leilan Latu Trails.

6.3   Return to Finnish Line Lodge.

herringbone or other climbing techniques to reach Lapland's highest point and a spectacular overlook to Little Cathead Mountain and the surrounding valley.

Upon leaving the overlook, advanced skiers will delight in a long roller-coaster downhill ride back into the evergreen forest to the junction of the Karhu and Tuulen Tie Trails. You may elect to take a shortcut (7) via Tuulen Tie back to the lodge (about 4 miles), or continue on the remainder of the Karhu Trail with its steep hills and "most difficult" terrain. Note that there is still one more shortcut before the steepest downhill section and prior to reaching the Napa Piiri Trail (8).

Those preferring to complete the entire 6.3-mile loop should follow the Napa Piiri Trail along the Grant Stream and through the evergreen trees to a short, steep climb nicknamed "The Wall." It is the steepest section in the entire Lapland Lake trail system, followed by a long, gentle roller-coaster downhill run on Tuulen Tie Trail, to the bridge and back to the Finnish Line Ski Lodge.

How to get there

From Route 30 in Northville, drive east on County Route 6 (toward Benson). Travel 5.2 miles to Storer Road. Turn right and continue (bearing right) for 0.75 mile to the Ski Lodge.

The Long Path

Cole Hill State Forest, East Berne, New York

Type of trail:	▬▬▬ ⬤
Also used by:	Hikers, equestrians
Distance:	2.57 miles
Terrain:	Flat to hilly
Trail difficulty:	More difficult
Surface quality:	Ungroomed, skier tracked
Food and facilities:	There are no facilities at this trail. Light fare and groceries may be found at Clarksville Stewart's (518–768–8023), Settler's General Store and Deli in Berne (518–872–2472), and Price Chopper in Slingerlands (518–479–0688). There is a convenience store in East Berne. Fast-food vendors, restaurants, and lodging may be found in and around Albany (14 miles).
Phone numbers:	Long Path Coordinator Mike Willsey, (518) 872–1044. State Forest information, (518) 943–5040 or 357–2066.
Fees:	There are no fees to use the trails.
Caution:	Be careful crossing the stream. There are no ski patrols on these trails. Sign in and out at the state register.

The Long Path, similar to Vermont's Long Trail, was proposed in the 1930s for hikers and skiers to travel on a trail from New York City north to the Adirondack Mountains and the Canadian border. The Long Path now extends from the George Washington Bridge in New York City to Schenectady, about 350 miles. The route is along wooded trails as much as possible, but also travels along paved roads and streets in several sections out of necessity. There are hundreds of access points along the trail. For this guidebook, we have chosen a ski trail near the northern end of the Long Path.

The Long Path is marked with aqua blue blazes. In some sections the route is maintained by the Department of Environmental Conservation (DEC) and the trail may have additional markings, including yellow or red DEC markers. Side trails may be marked differently. The Long Path also follows the Appalachian Trail (AT) at some points, with white blazes identifying the Appalachian Trail. Round, blue plastic markers bearing the Long Path (LP) logo may be found at trail junctions, but these are often removed by vandals.

Commercial maps of all sections of the Long Path are available from the New York/New Jersey Trails Conference, a trails organization com-

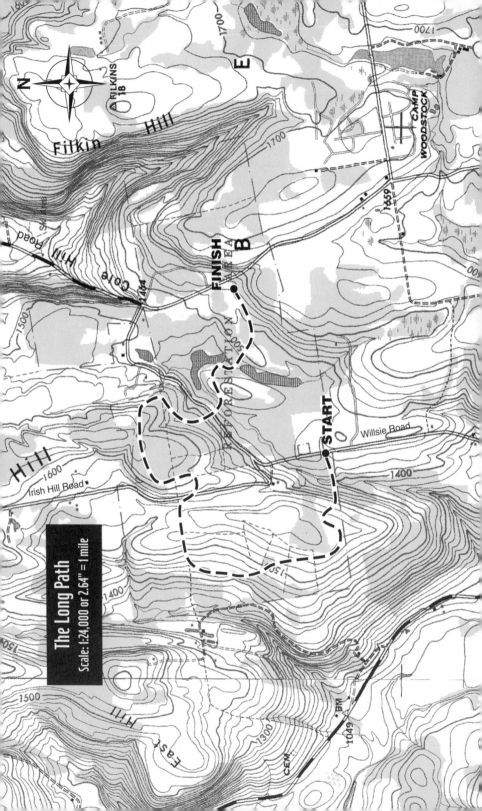

The Long Path
Scale: 1:24,000 or 2.64" = 1mile

posed of many hiking clubs (see appendix). The Trails Conference publishes books and other useful materials for its multiple-use trail systems.

Although many sections of the Long Path are not suitable for skiing, most of it can be navigated in winter on snowshoes (conditions permitting). In some sections skiers and snowshoers share the winter trail with snowmobilers. Some sections use old logging roads or the wide carriageways at state parks and forest preserves. Other sections are more like deer paths, too narrow and steep for skiing.

The Cole Hill section of the Long Path in the Capital Region is a pleasant blend of ski/snowshoe trail and road walking; in winter you may avoid the road walking by beginning and ending your ski loop at a designated parking area. You may also consider leaving a vehicle at one end of the trail to avoid retracing your tracks.

Access to the trail is at the Cole Hill State Forest designated trailhead on Willsie Road. It is identified with markings for both the Long Path and the DEC Ski Trail System. There is a sign here describing the state's "Adopt a Natural Resource" program, dedicated to the Long Path North Hiking Club. This trail is also designated as an "ATV Access Route" for handicapped users with a permit.

Enter the trail and follow the aqua blue paint marks of the Long Path, ascending gradually to a ridge where the trail turns right and descends to a stream. A bridge is planned for this area, but for now you will cross over corduroy, rocks, and other natural materials. After crossing the stream, pass through a stone fence and ascend a fairly steep hill. You'll pass through another stone fence before reaching a plateau on Irish Hill and a nice panoramic view of Cole Hill and the valley below.

Continuing along the trail, you'll climb again for a bit before turning left through a stone wall to an open field. Follow the markings for the Long Path, traversing the edge of a farm field and turning left to descend along a stand of white birch trees. Turning right, the trail then takes you through several pine groves separated by stone fences. The trail descends gradually with some undulating terrain before entering a mixed hardwood grove. It twists and turns through additional stone walls before reaching a fire control access road, formerly a town road. After turning right, the trail is crossed by another trail, identified as the DEC #2 Trail. You will continue straight about 200 yards and cross Irish Hill Road, reentering the Long Path on the other side.

Here the trail through the Cole Hill State Forest is identified as "State Forest Nordic Ski Trails." There is a parking lot at this trailhead, a DEC registration box, and a posted trail map indicating the ski/snowshoe trail with dotted lines. The trail is marked with the standard DEC yellow ski trail markers as well as the aqua blue paint marks of the Long Path. After

A lone skier leaves a trail across the bridge on the Long Path.

a gradual climb the trail enters a red pine reforestation area, coming out at an open meadow where the Long Path turns left at an intersection with a DEC ski trail. The Long Path now follows a long, flat logging road before turning right and traveling along the top of an escarpment. This wide path soon reaches an overlook of the escarpment, with great views west of Switz Kill Valley and Partridge Run Wildlife Management Area

(5,400 acres). Just past the overlook the trail crosses another stone wall and turns left on an old woods road leading to the edge of the state land.

At the PRIVATE PROPERTY signs a woods road goes off to the left, leading into the private property. The ski/snowshoe trail continues straight ahead and begins a long, gradual descent on an old logging road. Here is a good place to let your skis run, as there is an incline at the bottom to slow your speed. This is followed by another long escarpment, this one edged by a stone wall about 10 feet to the left of the trail. Although the trail becomes a little steeper, it is wide enough for skiers to traverse the slope with several turns as they head downhill. A logging road intersects the trail just before an old family cemetery with headstones dating to the mid-1800s. After a stop at this historic landmark, continue left about 50 yards where the trail turns sharply right and down a short slope to Willsie Road and the parking area. Some trail users leave a second vehicle here, completing a 3-mile tour. We chose to continue to the next road and parking area.

Here the ski/snowshoe trail is designated as DEC Trail #4 with yellow DEC markers. You will continue to follow the aqua blue Long Path markers as the trail crosses the road and heads back into the forest. You will soon reach a beaver pond and follow along its edge before crossing the stream. This Cole Hill Bridge was constructed in 1995 "with the combined efforts of the DEC and the NYS Department of Correctional Services. All the lumber used for the erection of the bridge was harvested from state forest land and prepared at the nearby Summit Shock Sawmill," according to the dedication plaque posted here.

After crossing the bridge the trail begins to ascend gently while switching back and forth to the top of a ridge. Following the aqua blue blazes you will enter a deep evergreen forest known locally as the Avenue of the Pines. Local resident Bruce Smith is credited with developing this section of the trail in the Cole Hill State Forest. At the far end of the Avenue of the Pines, the trail opens to a wide view of an abandoned beaver pond, now a vast wetland filled with marsh grasses. The trail soon reaches another beaver pond and a second bridge, constructed in 1996. "The scene here is reminiscent of the Adirondacks," according to the Long Path Guide for Section 32. The beaver dam has been unplugged, leaving a deep plunge hole in the streambed. A hitching rail for equestrians is also located here. This is a nice spot to stop and rest.

After crossing the bridge, the trail climbs a fairly steep section and enters a hardwood grove with several large black cherry trees. You will pass through still another stone fence before traversing a hemlock grove. You'll then make a left-hand jog and arrive at Cole Hill Road and the parking area. If you have not parked a second vehicle here you may now

Directions at a glance

0.0 Begin at parking area on Willsie Road.

0.1 Cross stream.

0.3 Reach plateau on Irish Hill.

1.0 Turn right onto fire control access road.

1.2 Cross Irish Hill Road and parking lot.

2.0 Reach escarpment and overlook of Switz Kill Valley.

2.15 Reach old family cemetery.

2.2 Cross Willsie Road, head into woods.

2.3 Cross 1995 Cole Hill Bridge.

2.4 Reach abandoned beaver pond (wetland).

2.5 Cross 1996 Cole Hill Bridge.

2.57 Reach Cole Hill Road and parking area.

retrace your tracks and return to the starting point. An alternative, of course, is to walk back to your car along Willsie Road.

How to get there

From the New York State Thruway (I–87), take exit 22 at Selkirk. Take Route 144 south to Route 396. Turn right on Route 396 and drive 6 miles to South Bethlehem. Route 396 becomes County Route 301. Follow County Route 301 west 6 miles to Route 443 in Clarksville. Turn left and travel 9 miles on Route 443 (Helderberg Trail) to the Berne Post Office. Travel 1 mile west of Berne to Cole Hill Road (County Route 2). Turn left at the Helderberg Ambulance Building and travel to Willsie Road. Park in the off-road parking area opposite the entrance to the Long Path Trailhead.

From I–90 in Albany take Route 85 south (exit 4) through Slingerlands to Route 443 at Clarksville. Turn right and travel about 4 miles to Cole Hill Road. Turn left and continue just over a mile to a right turn on to Willsie Road. Park in the off-road parking area opposite the entrance to the Long Path trailhead.

From I–88 at Schoharie follow Route 33 south (3 miles) to Route 443. Travel east 9 miles to Switz Kill Road. Turn right and travel 5 miles to a left onto Willsie Road (County Route 3). Continue 4.5 miles to the off-road parking area opposite the entrance to the Long Path trailhead.

Nature Trail Ski Loop
Moreau Lake State Park, Gansevoort, New York

Type of trail:	▬▬▬
Also used by:	Hikers, walkers, equestrians
Distance:	2.7 miles
Terrain:	Hilly
Trail difficulty:	Easiest to more difficult
Surface quality:	Ungroomed, skier tracked
Food and facilities:	Open-air pavilions and portable toilets are the only winter facilities. Fast-food vendors, restaurants, lodging, and grocery stores may be found in nearby Glens Falls and South Glens Falls: Nice & Easy Grocery Shop (518–743–0081), Queensbury Hotel (518–793–3471).
Phone numbers:	Park Office, (518) 793–0511. Park Police, (518) 584–2004. For emergencies call 911.
Fees:	There are no fees to use the winter trails.
Caution:	The lake may be unsafe for skiing and snowshoeing. This is a carry-in, carry-out facility. Dogs are permitted on the winter trails, but must have rabies shots and be on a leash.

The centerpiece of Moreau Lake State Park is the lake, a 120-acre bowl-shaped kettle reaching depths of 50 feet. The park lies along the Palmertown Range in both Saratoga and Warren Counties at the foothills of the magnificent Adirondack Mountains. With the acquisition of an additional 3,200 acres of land in 1998, the park totals nearly 4,100 acres, making it the ninth largest park in New York State's park system. The Hudson River bisects the park in the area known as Spier Falls and Sherman Island in the towns of Corinth and Lake Luzerne. The river flows through the park for 3.5 miles. The park also boasts of several small ponds, including Lake Ann.

The topography within Moreau Lake State Park varies widely, from flat areas adjacent to Moreau Lake to steep and rocky outcroppings associated with the mountainous ridges of the upland sections. Skiers and other winter trail users may enjoy several loops of campsite roads, which are maintained in season, but unplowed in the winter. As with most New York State parks, motorized vehicles are not permitted on the trails in the winter. However, some of the newly acquired sections near Spier Falls may be allowed to remain as snowmobile trails.

Winter trail users may observe a variety of fauna here, including white-tailed deer, turkeys, and small mammals such as raccoons, squir-

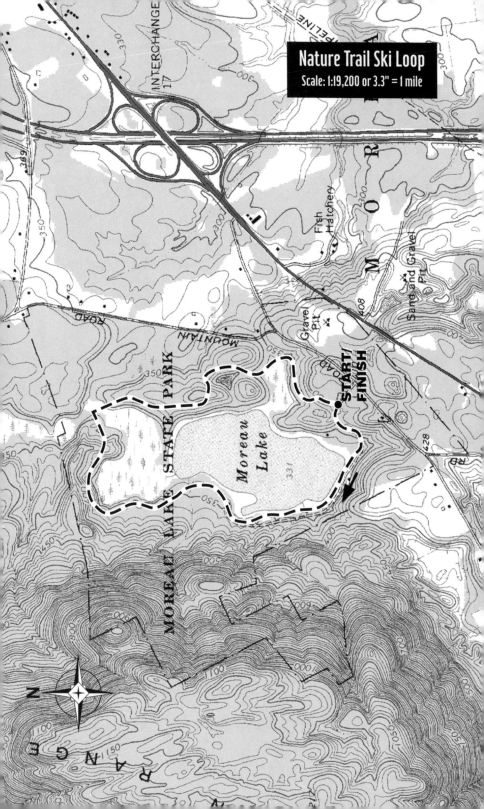

Nature Trail Ski Loop
Scale: 1:19,200 or 3.3" = 1 mile

INTERCHANGE 17

Fish Hatchery

Sand and Gravel

Gravel Pit

MOUNTAIN ROAD

START/FINISH

Moreau Lake

331

MOREAU LAKE STATE PARK

RANGE

rels, chipmunks, and muskrats. Numerous bird species are also found in the park, including owls and an occasional sighting of the pileated woodpecker. Mallard ducks and Canada geese rest in the ponds in the spring and fall. Ice fishing for trout and pickerel is a popular winter activity at Moreau Lake State Park. Ice-skating and the annual ice-fishing contest bring many local families back to the park to enjoy the lake in winter. The forest cover can be generally characterized as mixed upland hardwoods and softwoods typical of northeast New York. Common species include red and white oak, white pine, American beech, hemlock, red and sugar maple, white birch, and cherry. The small Nature Center, housed in the boathouse, serves as a focal point for numerous nature programs in season.

Uphill from Moreau Lake is Congdon Pond. Called Mud Pond by area residents, it is steadily evolving to a marsh and is the subject of much study by students. Skiers and other winter trail users are able to follow the trail around the marsh. The Wetland Trail also receives much year-round attention as visitors follow a series of interpretive stations using a self-guided brochure. In addition, the park supports a short self-guided nature trail, which is mostly skiable in winters with good snow cover.

Skiers and snowshoers access the winter trails at Moreau Lake State Park from the main entrance off Old Saratoga Road. A variety of routes offered to winter trail users of all abilities can be reached from the winter parking lot. All the winter trails are suitable for two-way skiing and snowshoeing. Snowshoers generally do not use the ski trails, but trek off into the woods on the fresh, ungroomed and untracked snow. Guided snowshoe tours are conducted at the park throughout the season. These trips often end with a picnic and social gathering around one of the many campground fireplaces.

To access the Nature Trail Ski Loop, actually a combination of trails, begin at the winter parking lot and follow the left route around the lake. Pass the winter gate and ski downhill, following the path beside the roadway and enter the woods between the park road and the lake. You will soon reach an open meadow at the edge of the lake, providing a breathtaking view of the lake, beach, boathouse, and the impressive Palmertown Mountains behind. There are several benches here to rest while enjoying some of nature's finest scenery. Continue along the ski trail as it circles to the right, bringing you to a wide clearing, a sloping boat ramp, and the edge of the lake. A caution is in order about skiing on the lake. If conditions permit, people do ski or snowshoe on the lake. In fact, ice-skating and ice fishing are very popular activities here. However, it is wise to check at the office before venturing out onto the ice.

If the ice is safe, you might cross the lake from here to the beach and beach parking lot where you'll rejoin the winter trail. Otherwise, play it

Snowshoers climb to the top of a snowy pasture.

safe and continue on the Lake Trail to the bathhouse, beach, and play area. Here you'll find a large picnic shelter (pavilion) where you might stop for a rest or to meet friends. This is a popular gathering place in winter for a snack, bag lunch, or hot beverage.

Past the picnic area, the Lake Trail goes right, crossing the footbridge and causeway to the other side of the lake. Some skiers follow the causeway to complete the unique "Figure Eight Loop," at the park. In this guidebook, however, we will describe the more direct and shorter Nature Trail Ski Loop.

Turning left at the open shelter, ski across the beach parking lot to the entrance to the Nature Trail. You will note a sign at the west end of the parking lot identifying the trailhead to the park's more difficult trails, including the trail to the "Overlook" and miles of multiuse trails. Here too is an entrance to sections of the 3,200 acres of land added to the park in 1998. Pass the entrance sign to the Nature Trail and begin the long climb to the top where the views of the lake and surrounding hills are indeed magnificent. You will note some interpretive signs as you proceed along this section of the Nature Trail. The climb is gradual with a few undulations. On the right you'll pass the southern end of a small loop off the Nature Trail. This steep, narrow section is not skiable. The trail becomes steeper, curving left and right as it continues to present beautiful views of the lake while meandering through the forested hills. Passing the water tower, the trail is joined on the right by the northern section of Nature Trail's small loop, which is great for summer hikes, but not skiable. Beyond the water tower is another intersection, a trailhead to the Mud Pond Trail, a loop of about a mile.

The Nature Trail Ski Loop now begins a long descent to the lake with some nice downhill runs. The trail is wide enough here to hang-on for a quick downhill tuck as the trail dips and turns gradually. After a gentle climb and another long downhill section, the trail reaches the edge of the lake and crosses over a culvert and earthen bridge between two wetlands. Here is another trailhead (left) for the Mud Pond Trail and the western end of the wetland trail with its interpretive stations. The trail soon splits: The Nature Trail Ski Loop and the Lake Trail turn to the right, and the Campground Trail continues straight ahead to one of the park's seven campground loops. Following to the right you will join the service road in Campground-D at site 69. After about a hundred yards along the roadway you will find the trail leading back to the causeway (right).

Follow the unplowed park roadways for about a mile, returning to the winter parking lot.

How to get there

From the Adirondack Northway (I–87) take exit 17S. Travel south on Route 9, just over the Northway and turn right onto Old Saratoga Road (first right turn). Travel 1 mile to park entrance.

Round Top Trail

Pineridge Cross-Country Ski Area, East Poestenkill, New York

Type of trail:	▬ ◄
Also used by:	Hikers
Distance:	2.4 miles
Terrain:	Hilly, mountainous
Trail difficulty:	Most difficult
Surface quality:	Groomed and tracked for classic and skating techniques.
Food and facilities:	The warming room and snack bar at the rustic Pineridge Lodge offers light fare and includes a woodstove, picnic tables, and rest rooms. Ski and snowshoe rentals, accessories, and instructions are available. Fast-food venues, grocery stores, restaurants, and lodging may be found in the nearby villages of Berlin and East Greenbush and in the cities of Troy and Albany. Bentley's General Store and Diner is within a mile of the Nordic center (518–283–6490).
Phone numbers:	Pineridge Nordic Center, (518) 283–3652
Fees:	There is a fee for use of the trails.

Pineridge Cross-Country Ski Area is located in the foothills of the Taconic and Berkshire Mountains between the Massachusetts border and the capital city of Albany. Pineridge is surrounded by thousands of acres of forest land with ski trails winding through groves of hardwoods and evergreen trees. The property is inhabited by abundant wildlife, including deer, fox, turkey, beaver, and otter. The wilderness-like trails offer a wide variety of skiing and snowshoeing for beginners as well as trails that can test even the experts. The trails travel along the picturesque Poestenkill Creek and climb to an elevation of 1,746 feet, offering views of the Taconic Mountain Range in New York and Mt. Greylock in Massachusetts. Snowshoeing is permitted on all trails except two (Round Top and Snow Slide), and there are miles of trails designated for snowshoes only.

The Nordic center is located along a kill (Dutch for "stream"). The steep slopes of the Poestenkill, with its series of waterfalls, jagged rock formations, and depth, create a scene of dramatic visual impact. The Troy/Poestenkill area is rich in history and natural beauty. In the early eighteenth century, the Poestenkill became a man-made canal, its flow directed into the Hudson River. As it entered the city of Troy, the powerful stream formed a deep gorge and created a unique natural environment for wildlife and lush vegetation.

Gravel
Pit

N

420

ROAD

KILL

START/
FINISH

Pineridge
Ski Lodge

Plank Road

450

× 527

View

462

510

480

Round Top Trail
Scale: 1:12,048 or 5.3" = 1 mile
Elevations are in meters.

The Poestenkill powered a variety of mills for more than 300 years, supplying the cities of Troy and Albany with cotton, lumber, flour, paper, plaster of Paris, and tanned goods. Factories were built next to each other along the Poestenkill, contributing to America's industrial age. The Troy Poestenkill Gorge has been appropriately acknowledged by its listing on the National Register of Historic Places.

To access the Round Top Trail, cross the road at the Nordic Center and Lodge, where a sign will direct you to the entrance for the trail. You'll begin a steady climb for about 0.6 mile to an elevation of 150 feet, after which there is a nice downhill slope that crosses a small stream before beginning the final ascent to the base of the Round Top hill. This trail begins in a white birch stand with a short, steep climb to the summit of the mountain. As the trail levels you may take a 0.1-mile side trip on the Pineridge Trail to a steep cliff (about a 200-foot drop-off), where you'll catch a view of the city of Albany in the distance.

Return to Round Top Trail and turn right, continuing on a gradual incline. Summit Trail branches to the left and loops around the summit. Round Top Trail continues downhill for another hundred yards before it intersects with the Taconic Trail, a black diamond route with great views of the Taconic Mountain Range and Maucumber Mountain, the highest peak in Rensselaer County. Round Top Trail continues heading downhill gradually for another 300 yards as you pass the junctions for Stonewall and Telemark Trails. (For a longer trip, you can turn right onto Stonewall and follow it for almost a mile as it circles around the back of the mountain on the former Troy-to-Hoosic Road, reconnecting with Round Top Trail.)

Round Top Trail passes through a dense pine stand and finally begins down a gentle slope as it turns and glides by a natural spring at the edge

Directions at a glance

0.0   Enter trail at roadside.

0.6   Trailhead to Round Top Trail.

0.7   Pineridge Trail (optional side trip).

0.8   Continue straight as Summit Trail to the mountain peak goes left.

1.0   Stonewall Trail option goes right.

1.4   Pass natural spring.

1.5   Steep downhill leads to a plank bridge.

1.7   Turn left on Stagecoach Road Trail.

2.4   Finish at the lodge.

of the trail. From here it is a non-stop downhill ride, steep and fast and separated into two sections. The top section is narrow, with several sharp turns around some large beech trees. The second slope, wider and more open, continues over a plank bridge, leveling off for the final hundred yards and winding through some small pines and hardwood trees. Round Top Trail then joins Stagecoach Road Trail for a downhill trek of about 0..7 mile, returning you to the lodge.

Pineridge provides a designated 1-mile loop for those who wish to ski or snowshoe with their dogs. They are asked to clean up after their pets. Pineridge also offers night skiing and has designated a 6-mile trail for snowshoeing and backcountry skiing.

How to get there

From the west, take I–90 east to exit 8. Take Route 43 east to West Sand Lake. Turn left on Route 351 to Poestenkill. Turn right onto Plank Road. Continue 6 miles to the ski area parking lot.

From the east, take exit B3 of I–90 to Route 22 north to Berlin. Turn left onto Plank Road and drive for 6 miles to the ski area parking lot.

Gideon Putnam Trail

Saratoga Spa State Park, Saratoga Springs, New York

Type of trail:	▬▬ ⬭
Also used by:	Hikers, walkers
Distance:	4.5 miles
Terrain:	Mostly flat
Trail difficulty:	Easiest
Surface quality:	Machine packed and groomed, skier tracked.
Food and facilities:	There is a rustic warming hut on the edge of the trails with heated rest rooms, an open-pit fireplace, and picnic tables for snacks and bag lunches. The building is open to the public and maintained by park staff throughout the winter. Trail maps and brochures may be obtained at the warming hut and the Park Office. Additional rest rooms are located in the Administration Building and the Victoria Pool Building. The Gideon Putnam Hotel, located just off the trail, is open to the public for breakfast, lunch, and dinner as well as lodging (518–584–3000). Fast-food vendors, grocery stores, restaurants, and lodging may be found in downtown Saratoga Springs. For groceries try Price Chopper (518–580–9172), Stewart's Shop (518–584–9525), or XtraMart (518–584–5363). For lodging, Grand Union Motel (518–584–9000) and Springs Motel (518–584–6336) are just outside the park. For light fare try the Spa City Diner (518–584–9833).
Phone numbers:	Saratoga Spa State Park, (518) 584–2535. Park Police, (518) 584–2004. For emergencies call 911.
Fees:	There are no fees to use the trails. The park is a carry-in, carry-out facility.

The mineral waters of Saratoga Springs have long been renowned for their healing powers. The naturally carbonated waters have drawn visitors for hundreds of years. Originating in a layer of limestone 100 to 1,000 feet below you, these waters rise to the surface through the Saratoga Fault. As early as the fourteenth century, Native Americans (Iroquois) frequented the High Rock Spring in "Saratogha," leading the way for those who later came to Saratoga Springs to "take the waters." By the mid-nineteenth century, the village of Saratoga Springs and its waters were drawing wealthy and famous visitors who sought the recuperative benefits.

The unique waters also attracted businessmen. In 1803 Gideon Putnam came to build the first hotel and to lay out streets for a village to

accommodate the increasing number of visitors. By 1880 a process was developed to extract the carbon dioxide gas for the new and rapidly growing carbonated beverage industry. Over-pumping of the precious mineral waters became a major concern, threatening the supply of both the gas and the invaluable waters. To preserve this unique natural resource, the state leg-

Skiers enjoy the spacious grounds of the historic Gideon Putnam Hotel, located at the famous Saratoga Spa State Park.

islature formed the State Reservation Commission (1909) whose purpose was "to acquire and protect the springs and surrounding lands." Noted hydrotherapist Simon Baruch encouraged the Commission to develop a treatment center modeled after many of the European spas. By 1920 the state had acquired thousands of acres of land just south of the city of Saratoga Springs. In 1927 Governor Franklin Roosevelt appointed a state commission to develop a health treatment center at the Spa, adding extensively to the Washington and Lincoln bathhouses. No expense was spared in creating the magnificent new "Saratoga Spa." The elaborate buildings were completed in 1935 with federal funds, becoming the first major project completed under President Roosevelt's New Deal.

In 1962 the world-famous Saratoga Spa became a state park with the addition of the Peerless Pool Complex, picnic area, and a championship golf course. With more than 2,000 acres of land and 1.5 million visitors annually, the Saratoga Spa State Park is noted for its unique waters, diverse culture, and recreational resources. The classical architecture of the Spa has earned it a coveted listing as a National Historic Landmark.

With health and recreation as its major thrust, Saratoga Spa State Park offers miles of multiuse trails over a wide variety of terrain throughout the park. There are more than 12 miles of trails suitable for cross-country skiing and snowshoeing. Although snowshoeing is permitted in the park, participants must make every effort to stay off the tracks made by skiers. Many of the Spa's winter trails are on the golf course; others traverse the park through the picnic areas, passing the famous geyserlike "spouter," several mineral springs, the Performing Arts Center, the world-famous Gideon Putnam Hotel, and the European-style bathhouses. The park is truly a wonderland in winter, with its outdoor ice-skating rink, hockey rink, and miles of picturesque roadways and trails around the mineral springs, streams, and woodlands. Many of the winter trails follow the nature trails used extensively in other seasons for guided and self-guided tours. The park is the home of the only mounted police unit in the state park system. Its officers and horses are often called upon for official state activities. Brochures with a map of the winter trails are available at the Administration Building.

The Gideon Putnam Trail begins at the Warming Hut near the South Broadway Entrance to the park. Turn at the first left off the Avenue of the Pines for the winter parking area, outdoor hockey rink, and Warming Hut. Here winter trail users will find warm rest rooms, picnic tables, and a nice log fire. The building is open during daylight hours and for late-night skiers, snowshoers, and hockey players.

Although it is a two-way trail, it is best to begin the Gideon Putnam Ski Trail at the left of the Warming Hut. Cross the driveway, enter the trail and travel past a small hill, actually a putting green on the thirteenth fairway. You'll be heading toward the Avenue of the Pines, a very picturesque roadway into the famous park. The trail will take you along the edge of an open fairway as it passes a small pump house nestled in the trees. It then bears left and follows the tall white pine trees, traveling along the edge of the next fairway and the Avenue of the Pines. The trail turns sharply left as the roadway turns, leading you to the magnificent Gideon Putnam Hotel. You will certainly be tempted to slow your pace here or stop to enjoy the splendid view of this grand old hotel. You will need to remove your skis to cross the roadway at this point. You may decide to drop in at the hotel for a hot beverage or just to see the charming mansion and conference center while warming up before continuing your tour.

The Gideon Putnam Trail continues on the opposite side of the roadway as it proceeds on another fairway and through a hedgerow of pine trees to the front of the Victoria Pool Complex, the Golf Complex, and the ice-skating rink. To the right is a trail that takes skiers past the rink to the reflecting pool and the Mall Trail. The driveway to the golf buildings is plowed in winter; you may need to remove your skis to cross it.

After crossing the driveway, ski past a small hill (a putting green under the snow), across an open meadow (fairway), and between the rows of trees where the trail switches back to the right, and enters the next open field. At the end of this section there is another switchback, taking you across the open meadow to the edge of the park's North-South Road. Many local skiers join the Gideon Putnam Trail at the trail junction from the parking area near the ice-skating rink. A little further is the junction for the Ferndell Spring Trail, which leads to the more difficult trails in the area of the mineral springs and the geyserlike spouter.

The trail continues to the end of the fairway, then turns left and snakes its way along East-West Road. You'll cross a small bridge and

Directions at a glance

0.0   Begin at winter parking area.

0.2   Pass the pump house near the Avenue of the Pines.

1.2   Cross the roadway beside the Gideon Putnam Hotel.

1.5   Cross driveway beside the Golf Complex.

2.0   Pass junction for Ferndell Trail.

2.5   Cross bridge.

2.8   Turn left at state highway.

3.5   Pass Latour House at tree nursery.

4.0   Cross Marrin Avenue.

4.3   Pass speed-skating rink.

4.5   Finish at Warming Hut and parking lot.

begin a gradual climb to a pond. There is a junction here for a shortcut trail that rejoins the main trail a quarter of a mile later. The Gideon Putnam Trail continues straight ahead for about 50 yards, then turns sharply left and follows a state highway for another 50 yards before turning left again. The trail goes through a narrow grove of trees and along the boundary of the Saratoga Tree Nursery, passing the old Latour House, formerly the home of the superintendent of the tree nursery.

Now paralleling one of the nursery roads, the trail turns right through a couple of open fairways and passes the starter shack as it continues along the hedgerow separating the golf course from the tree nursery. You will cross a pretty snow-covered roadway, used for horse-drawn sleigh rides during the annual Saratoga Spa Winter Fest. After crossing the tree-lined roadway (Marrin Avenue), turn right and follow the open trail to the outdoor speed-skating rink, formerly the Eastern States Championship Rink. Circle left and follow the edge of the rink for about 200 yards before returning to the Warming Hut and parking lot.

How to get there

From the south take the Adirondack Northway (I–87) to Exit 13N. Travel 3 miles north on Route 9 to the Avenue of Pines entrance.

From the north take the Northway (I-87) to Exit 15S. Take Route 50 to Route 9 and travel south through Saratoga Springs 5 miles to the Avenue of the Pines entrance.

From the east or west take Route 29 to Route 9. Take Route 9 south 1.5 miles to the Avenue of the Pines entrance.

Cliff Trail Loop

John Boyd Thacher State Park, Voorheesville, New York

Type of trail:	▬▬▬ ⬭
Also used by:	Walkers, hikers
Distance:	4.8 miles
Terrain:	Mostly flat with some hills
Trail difficulty:	Easiest, except for the start area
Surface quality:	Ungroomed, user tracked
Food and facilites:	The park office is open year-round during regular working hours; winter trail maps and other information are available. A warming room with rest rooms is provided. No food is available at the park. Fast-food vendors, grocery stores, and restaurants may be found in nearby Berne, Voorheesville, and Altamont. For groceries: Settler's General Store & Deli in Berne (518–872–2472) or D.J. Markquette & Pizza in Altamont (518–861–5353). Lodging may be found in and around Albany (16 miles).
Phone numbers:	Park Office, (518) 872–1237. For emergencies call 911.
Fees:	There are no fees to use the winter trails.
Caution:	Thacher Park has dangerous cliffs. Do not venture beyond the fences. Winter trail users are asked not to walk dogs on ski/snowshoe trails.

John Boyd Thacher Park, located 16 miles west of Albany, is situated along the Helderberg Escarpment acknowledged by geologists as one of the richest fossil-bearing formations in the world. Today the park comprises 2,300 acres, including the original 350 acres donated by Emma Treadwell Thacher in 1914 in memory of her husband. John Boyd Thacher was born in Ballston Spa, New York, in 1847. He was mayor of Albany from 1886 to 1887 and again from 1896 to 1897. He was also a New York State senator and historian.

Panoramic views of the Hudson-Mohawk Valley can be seen along the park's escarpment as well as the foothills of the Adirondacks, the Green Mountains of Vermont, and the Taconic Mountains in Massachusetts. On a clear day, the Empire State Plaza, the SUNY campus, and the state office buildings can be viewed from the Overlook parking area.

The names of the various sections of the park commemorate area history. Hop Field and Pear Orchard are named for the crops the settlers grew in the poor, rocky soil. Knowles Flats, La Grange Bush, and Hailes Cave were named for previous owners and explorers.

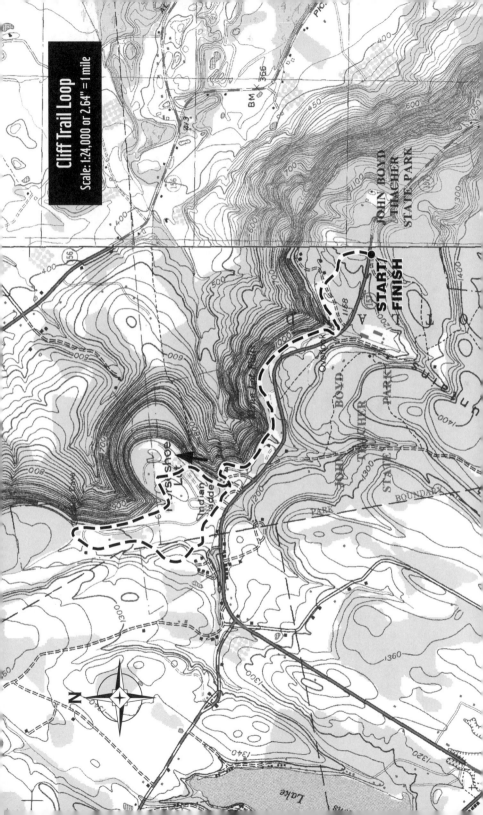

Cliff Trail Loop
Scale: 1:24,000 or 2.64" = 1 mile

JOHN BOYD
THACHER STATE PARK

START/
FINISH

JOHN BOYD THACHER STATE PARK BOUNDARY

N

Lake

Members of the Bill Koch Youth Ski League pose with their coach before a training session on the ski trails.

In colonial times a pass over the Helderbergs was used by the Mohawk Indians to get their furs to Albany from the Schoharie Valley. The Indian Ladder Trail gets its name from the strong notched tree trunks the Indians laid up against the cliff to get up and down the escarpment.

To access the winter trails at John Boyd Thacher Park, skiers and snowshoers are invited to park at Hop Field, where they will find a cozy warming room and heated toilets. The trail begins just across the park's main road from Hop Field, although you may access the Cliff Trail from several points along the highly scenic route. The Cliff Trail includes a sec-

Directions at a glance

0.0 Begin at Hop Field parking lot.

0.1 Ski past Yellow Rocks area.

0.5 Pass Glen Doone pavilion.

0.8 Turn sharply right, cross bridge to Overlook.

1.5 Pass Indian Ladder Trail to parking area, then turn right.

2.0 Ski through Horseshoe area and behind swimming pool.

2.5 Cross maintenance road. Ski between stone pillars.

3.0 Leave wooded trail (Long Path) behind park office.

3.3 Rejoin Cliff Trail at Indian Ladder parking lot.

4.8 Finish at Hop Field parking lot.

tion of the famed Long Path Trail, a trail constructed and maintained by members of the New Jersey–New York Trail Conference.

A caution is in order regarding this loop because the start of the winter trail is rated "not for beginners." There is a fairly steep pitch and twisting path shortly after crossing the road at Hop Field. Snowshoers will be fine on this section but novice and beginning skiers should start at another location. We suggest that inexperienced skiers begin at the Overlook parking area. Snowshoers and advanced skiers should begin at the Hop Field parking area to enjoy and appreciate the full length (4.8 miles) of this unique winter trail.

After crossing the park road you will traverse a flat section through the Yellow Rocks picnic area to a fairly steep downhill run leading to the Glen Doone picnic area. This is a well-marked trail identified with 4-foot plastic posts bearing colorful symbols that indicate direction and appropriate uses. As the trail flattens you pass between two fieldstone pillars and turn sharply right to face a large, round building (kiosk). Here you will get your first look over the cliff at the sheer walls of the Helderberg Escarpment and the valley far below.

After your eyes feast on this fascinating geologic marvel, turn left and continue through the Glen Doone picnic area, perhaps stopping for a rest at the beautiful stone-pillared pavilion with massive beams that support the snow-laden roof. Continuing to the edge of the park road, you will cross a long wooden bridge and turn sharply right to the southern end of the parking area for the Cliff Edge Overlook. Here you'll find several coin-operated binoculars pointed out over the valley toward the capital city of Albany. On a clear day you will see the towers of the State University and the great structures of the massive Empire State Plaza, built during the Rockefeller Administration. You are sure to linger here at least for a bit before continuing your tour. At the north entrance to the Overlook parking lot is a trail marker indicating your direction of travel along the trail. The cliff edge is well fenced with many signs warning park patrons not to venture beyond the fence.

Following the directional arrows, you will soon pass one entrance to the Indian Ladder Trail (closed in winter) and continue along the cliff through the Horseshoe picnic area to the end of the Cliff Trail. Here you'll turn left to cross the maintenance road that leads to the park's treatment plant. Pass through another set of fieldstone pillars and enter a pine grove, following the Haile's Cave Loop around the parking lot. Follow the markers across the baseball field, through the woods and behind the park office.

After crossing the entrance road near the ticket booth, continue past the Indian Ladder picnic area and rejoin the main Cliff Trail. From here you'll retrace your route back to the warming room and parking lot at Hop Field. Remember that the trail from the round kiosk at the Glen Doone picnic area to the Yellow Rock area will be a difficult climb for beginning skiers. They are advised to finish at the Cliff Edge parking area and walk or drive back to the warming room.

How to get there

From Albany take I–90 to exit 4 at New Scotland Road (Route 85). Take route west to Thacher Park Road (Route 157) and follow it to Hop Field parking lot.

From Schenectady take Route 146 to Altamont, then Route 156 to Thacher Park Road (Route 157). Follow Thacher Park Road to Hop Field parking lot.

Wilkinson Trail

Saratoga National Historical Park, Stillwater, New York

Type of trail:	━━ 🔘
Also used by:	Walkers, hikers
Distance:	4.2 miles
Terrain:	Flat
Trail difficulty:	Easiest to more difficult
Surface quality:	Ungroomed, skier tracked
Food and facilities:	The Visitor Center is open to the public daily, providing warm rest rooms, historic exhibits, and a film presentation. Picnic tables are available outdoors under a covered patio with a lovely view of a section of the historic battlefield. Fast-food vendors, restaurants, grocery stores, and lodging may be found in nearby Mechanicville, Saratoga Springs, Schuylerville, and Stillwater. Try Burgoyne Motor Inn and Coffee Shop (518–695–3282), The Marshall House (518–695–3765) for lodging. Pick up groceries at Price Chopper (518–664–1112) and Stewart's Shop (518–695–9226).
Phone numbers:	Visitor Center, (518) 664–9821. For emergencies dial 911.
Fees:	There are no fees for use of the trails.
Caution:	Trail hazards include steep grades, some rough terrain, and slippery slopes.

The Saratoga National Historical Park, site of the turning point of the American Revolution, is located in the hills above the Hudson River between the towns of Schuylerville and Stillwater about 30 miles north of Albany. The park and visitor center are open every day except major holidays. In 1987 the Wilkinson Trail opened as part of the country's National Trail System, giving park visitors the rare opportunity to follow in the footsteps of the British soldiers who used much of the same road system during the decisive battles of 1777. Skiing or snowshoeing on the Wilkinson Trail can be your journey into eighteenth-century America and the events surrounding the battles of Saratoga. We recommend that you stop at the visitor center to pick up a trail map and brochure for information about the historic events identified at more than a dozen stations along the Wilkinson Trail. History buffs may wish to see the twenty-minute documentary film in the auditorium before venturing out on the grounds and Wilkinson Trail.

Access to the winter trails is gained from the patio at the rear of the visitor center. The trail is very well marked with posts of recycled plas-

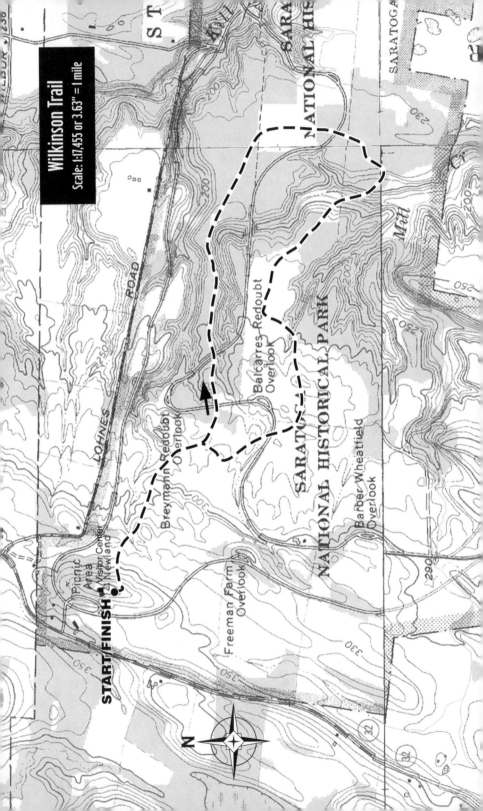

tic, and is designed to be followed in alphabetic order. The letter W is engraved in the posts to signify the Wilkinson Trail, named in honor of Lieutenant John Wilkinson, who drew maps of the battle areas in 1770. The Wilkinson maps made it possible for later historians to locate much of the Revolutionary War road system that the trail attempts to follow.

The trail begins at the far edge of the lawn at a trailhead kiosk marked with the national park's symbol and an emblem of the Boy Scouts of America. A large colored map of the Wilkinson Trail is posted here. Several cannons are positioned on the lawn overlooking the battlefield, the Hudson River Valley, and the mountains of Vermont. From the first gray marker post at the trailhead (Station A), follow the trail to the left.

The Wilkinson Trail descends from the trailhead for about 50 yards before turning sharply left and descending rapidly through a long stretch of pines and mixed hardwood trees. Winter trail users will notice additional gray marker posts along the way to help them stay on the trail. Upon climbing to the top of a knoll, you will have a panoramic view of the battlefields, the Wilkinson Trail before you, and the visitor center behind you. Descending a fairly steep hill, you'll cross a wooden bridge and reach station B and the intersection for a horse trail. This was the site of the McBride Farm during the 1770s. Proceed straight ahead, climbing another knoll and arriving at a trail junction (left) for the site of the Breymann Redoubt (Station C). The redoubt, named for Lieutenant Colonel Breymann, was a temporary fortification built by the Crown forces. On October 7, 1777, it was held by 200 German troops fighting for the British.

As you travel through an open field you will notice some ancient pine trees that may have stood here during the historic battles of the Revolutionary War. Soon you will arrive at a Y in the trail and a directional arrow indicating that trail users are to stay to the left. You'll leave the open field and enter a wooded area, arriving shortly at a service road. The trail crosses the road and heads directly back into the woods. It undulates nicely as it travels through a pine grove. You may observe deer here; they like to use the pine needles for bedding. Traveling through this pine forest, the trail flattens out and travels along the top of a ridge. At station D there is a junction for the Liaison Trail. Trail users may turn right for a shortcut back to the visitor center, shortening the tour by 2 miles.

About 100 yards past this junction you will need to cross the service road again. Both sides of the roadway are quite steep, requiring skiers to snowplow down on one side and use the herringbone or sidestepping ski techniques on the other side. You'll enter a dense forest where the trail meanders through tall evergreens, red oaks, maples, and other hardwoods. This relatively flat section follows a ridge with steep slopes on each side, similar to the eskers found in the central regions of New York State. The ridge follows a small stream as the trail snakes its way toward the end of the ridge. The forest is wide open, giving winter trail users a comfortable and safe feeling. This forest is the habitat of numerous animals, including large herds of deer. Near the end of the forest you will enter a large wetland and cross two bridges before reaching station F, where you will intersect again with a horse trail.

As you leave this station you will cross a bridge with handrails and enter a large farm field. This trail across

The Wilkinson Trail passes by silent cannons at the historic Saratoga Battlefield.

the field is said to be the path taken by British soldiers on September 19, 1777. The field (station G) was cultivated in the eighteenth century with rye, wheat, barley, oats, corn, potatoes, Jerusalem artichokes, pumpkins, and squash. In the woods were an abundance of wild raspberries and blueberries. Other fields here may well have been planted with oats, clover, and timothy for livestock.

Leaving the farm fields you will cross the service road again and reenter the woods at station H, which in 1777 was a campground for the troops. At the end of this narrow forest trail there is a caution sign at the top of a fairly long and steep hill. Skiers and snowshoers may have difficulty negotiating this section of the trail. It is wise for the less experienced winter trail users to exercise extreme caution in crossing over the narrow bridge and climbing the steep hill on the other side. Some may find it best to remove their equipment and walk to the base of the hill where a bench is provided. This bench was constructed by the Youth Conservation Corps (YCC), as noted by the symbol etched in the bench seat. The long hill is often referred to as "killer hill," and is the only difficult section on the Wilkinson Trail. It will be necessary for skiers to uti-

lize herringbone, sidestep, and other climbing techniques on this long hill, which is followed by a difficult sloping section through the woods.

As the Wilkinson Trail comes out of the woods it enters a very large field where you will notice some scattered clumps of white birch trees. In winter the chilling winds often whip across these fields. The change in body temperature is often dramatic here, after the exertion of climbing hills that are protected from the wind by trees. There are no trees as you cross through the center of this expansive farm field unprotected from the cold gusts of the winter winds. Winter trail users should dress in layers, adding or removing clothing as needed.

The Wilkinson Trail crosses a path at the site of John Freeman's Farm and the Balcarres Redoubt, where many soldiers died and were buried. "Some were not buried very well," according to historians. You will notice several cannons at Stop 6 along the park's auto route. You will then encounter another downhill section and come to a final service road crossing. The trail continues to be well marked as it snakes its way through the woods and crosses a horse trail intersection. As you climb a small rise (Station N), the visitor center will come into view. There is a sign indicating the path you must take for your return to the Y intersection at station C. Bearing left, retrace your tracks along the Wilkinson Trail and begin a long and gradual uphill climb back to the lawn and patio of the visitor center.

How to get there

From the south take the Adirondack Northway (I–87) to exit 12 and travel north to Route 9P. Turn right and travel around Saratoga Lake to Route 423. Turn right and go about 4 miles to Route 32. Turn left onto Route 32 and continue 2 miles to park entrance.

From the north take the Adirondack Northway (I–87) to exit 14 and

Directions at a glance

0.0   Begin at lawn of visitor center.

0.1   Bear left at kiosk (A).

0.3   Cross bridge and horse trail.

0.6   Bear left at Interpretive Station C.

0.7   Cross park road.

0.8   Cross park road again and enter woods.

1.0   Cross two bridges.

1.2   Pass Interpretive Station F.

1.65 Cross park road.

2.0   Pass Interpretive Station I.

2.1. Cross bridge.

2.8   Pass Interpretive Station L.

3.6   Complete loop at Station C.

4.2   Finish at visitor station.

travel south on 9P around Saratoga Lake to Route 423. Turn left and go about 4 miles to Route 32. Turn left onto Route 32 and continue 2 miles to the park entrance.

Note: There is also an entrance to the Saratoga National Historical Park on Route 4 in Stillwater.

The Langlauf Trail

Clarkson University, Potsdam, New York

Type of trail:	═══ ⬤ ◄
Also used by:	Hikers, bikers, walkers
Distance:	2.0 miles
Trail difficulty:	Easiest
Surface quality:	Machine groomed for skate skiing
Food and facilities:	There are no facilities on the trail, but the Cheel Campus Center, within walking distance of the trail, has lounges, rest rooms, and a cafeteria/restaurant offering a choice of excellent meals and snacks. Fast-food vendors, grocery stores, restaurants, and lodging may be found in downtown Potsdam and surrounding communities. For groceries try P&C (315–265–2165), the Big M (315–265–6282), or Potsdam Food Co-Op (315–265–4630). Restaurants include Tardelli's (315–265–8446) and Maxfields (315–265–3796).
Fees:	There are no fees to use the trails.
Caution:	This is private property shared with the community. It is not patrolled and is a carry-in, carry-out facility.

The Clarkson family, for which Clarkson University was named, and the Town of Potsdam are linked in the long history of upstate New York. In 1802 David M. Clarkson was one of the original purchasers of the town of Potsdam. Mathew Clarkson, his grandson, was a soldier in the American Army who had the distinction and honor of receiving the sword of surrender from General Burgoyne on October 17, 1777, after the Battle of Saratoga. He was later promoted to Major General. Thomas S. Clarkson, a highly successful businessman, suffered an accidental death while trying to save one of his employees at his Potsdam quarry in 1894. A few months later, his family began planning a school as a memorial to him. In 1896 the Clarksons opened the Thomas S. Clarkson Memorial School of Technology. It grew from a small school with a dozen students to a fully certified college, adding not only many grand facilities but graduate programs in engineering, science, and management. Ph.D. programs were added to accommodate the burgeoning student body. The school moved to its current campus on the hill, where its expanded classroom and residential facilities provide educational programs for almost 3,000 students.

Development of the cross-country ski trails at CU's "hill campus" began in 1973, when it became clear to the organizers of an annual ski race, called the Potsdam Langlauf, that use of two adjacent farms in the

short map X

Clarkson College

Tower

START/FINISH

410

410

412

412

450

450

450

450

450

450

BR 462

N

The Langlauf Trail
Scale: 1:12,288 or 5.16" = 1 mile

township could not continue. Volunteers from the community worked together with staff from the university to blaze and clear 7 kilometers of single-track ski trails through the hills and forest behind the school's new campus. The Potsdam Langlauf was held at the university trails for several years, before moving to Clarkson's Seven Springs Ski Center outside of town. Although the Langlauf race was eventually discontinued, the popularity of the campus ski trails has grown among local skiers as well as the students.

The CU trails are located on campus property that blends into the neighboring countryside. They are well maintained year-round by university staff for a variety of uses, including training programs for the Army ROTC. The trails have been covered with a sandy soil and wood chips and were widened considerably to accommodate trail grooming equipment. The local mountain biking community has developed a network of unimproved bike trails that crisscross the ski area. Motorized vehicles are prohibited. Students as well as hikers and walkers from the community enjoy the quiet, wooded area and its varied terrain, trees, marshes, wildflowers, and wildlife.

For the most part the Langlauf Trail is level, curvy, and gently rolling.

Local residents as well as students enjoy the pristine woods surrounding the Clarkson University ski trails.

This trail actually takes the shape of an elongated figure eight (see map) with two rather pronounced loops connected in the middle. Along the route you may notice several smaller trails intersecting the main trail. These are unmarked, narrow mountain bike trails that are very busy in the other seasons, but should be ignored by skiers and snowshoers.

The CU winter trails may be accessed from the parking lot nearest the water tower, behind the Woodstock Village Townhouse residences. The new Outdoor Recreation Center is also at the edge of the trails. You may start your tour of the winter trails by walking or skiing (depending on conditions) along the water tower fence to the gated entrance where the Nordic ski trails actually begin. The Army ROTC has erected a rappelling tower near the entrance. Pass this unique structure and travel to a Y in the trail. Following the trail to the right you can't help becoming aware of the peace and quiet of the woodlands surrounding the university campus.

The trail turns and meanders through a hardwood forest before beginning a gentle downhill slope. It continues to wend its way through the mixed hardwoods, bearing left and rising gradually before leveling off on a plateau. At the end of the plateau the trail descends, passing a large wetland.

As you arrive near the end of the first loop, you may take a shortcut by bearing left and circling back to the beginning of the trail. We recommend that you continue on the trail as it bears right, providing a nice downhill run with a few wide turns before the trail begins to climb again. This relatively easy climb brings you to the highest point on the CU trail system, where there is a small, open meadow. The trail then takes a nice dip before reaching the end of the college property. It turns sharply left and follows a fence line separating it from private property marked by posted signs.

Directions at a glance

0.0   Begin at gated entrance.

0.1   Bear right at Y intersection.

0.5   Bear right at end of first loop.

0.9   University property ends. Turn left.

1.1   Turn left at end of fence.

1.4   Stay right at end of second loop.

1.9   Return to Y intersection.

2.0   Finish at gated entrance.

After a few hundred yards the trail turns left as if completing the top portion of the figure eight. It descends gently and gradually, then heads to the top of a ridge before circling through a hemlock grove. Finally, the trail continues downhill, circling left and snaking its way through the mixed hardwoods until it reaches the end of the lower loop. There's a long uphill prior to retracing your tracks along the flat section and the last portion of the trail. Returning to the start/finish area, you may walk or ski to the parking lot depending on conditions.

How to get there

From the corner of Clarkson Avenue and Route 11 in Potsdam, travel west 0.4 mile on Route 11 and turn left onto the entrance road for Cheel Arena. Travel 0.5 mile (passing the arena) to the parking lot at the water tower. Follow the water tower fence to the gated trail entrance.

Warm Brook Trail Loop

Higley Flow State Park, Colton, New York

Type of trail:	▬▬ 🌐
Also used by:	Hikers, hunters, walkers
Distance:	1.3 miles, 2.0 miles with optional Beaver Pond Loop
Terrain:	Hilly, rolling
Trail difficulty:	Easiest to more difficult
Surface quality:	Groomed and tracked
Food and facilities:	There are no facilities in winter at Higley Flow State Park. Pack a bag lunch and/or snacks. Fast-food vendors, restaurants, and lodging may be found in the nearby village of Potsdam (16 miles). For groceries (2 miles) try Boyce's Store (315–262–2420) or South Woods Grocery & Deli (315–262–2820). For lodging, the Braeside B&B on Cold Brook Drive (315–262–2553) or Catamount Lodge (315–262–2255). Try the nearby Shoreline Restaurant (315–265–7120).
Phone numbers:	Higley Flow State Park, (315) 262–2880. Park Police, (315) 769–0127. Forest Ranger, (315) 891–0235. For emergencies call 911.
Fees:	There are no fees for use of the trails.
Caution:	New York State park rules and regulations require dogs to have appropriate rabies shots and be kept on a 6-foot leash. Dogs are permitted on park roads, but not on the ski and snowshoe trails. This is a carry-in, carry-out facility.

Higley Flow State Park is located on the banks of the Racquette River in the town of Colton in northern New York. The town dates to the Macomb Purchase of 1790 when the state sold almost four million acres of unappropriated wastelands in the north. The sale was divided into great tracts of 30,000 acres each, several of which comprised the town of Matildaville, created in 1843. The town's name was later changed to honor an early settler, businessman, and town official, Jessie Colton Higley.

In the early 1900s the river was harnessed for its power and several dams were constructed in the town. In 1911 a dam and hydroelectric powerhouse went into operation near the village of Colton, creating a 700-acre body of water called a flow. The Higley Flow, a regulating reservoir for other downriver operations, looks like a pond or lake, but has the mighty Racquette River flowing through it. The state park, 1,250 acres of

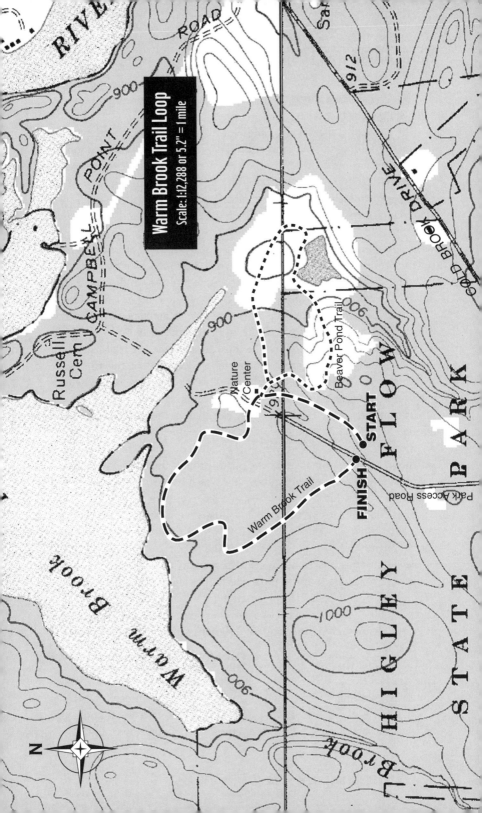

Warm Brook Trail Loop
Scale: 1:12,288 or 5.2" = 1 mile

RIVER

ROAD

900

CAMPBELL POINT

Russell Cem.

900

900

Nature Center

912

Sa

COLD BROOK DRIVE

912

Beaver Pond Trail

900

FLOW

START

PARK

FINISH

Park Access Road

Warm Brook Trail

Brook

Warm

900

1000

900

HIGLEY STATE PARK

Brook

N

former farmland, was created on the edge of the flow. The farmland was purchased in the 1930s by the state and managed as a State Forest Reforestation area. Today it serves as a highly popular campground, beach, and boating area for those who want to enjoy the environment of New York State's north country.

The town of Colton is also noted for its position on the northern edge of the six-million-acre Adirondack Park. A giant rock, which stood for perhaps thousands of years in the center of a path traveled by Native Americans, is now a constant reminder to those passing through of the town's geographic position. Sunday Rock, a 35-ton glacial boulder, is proclaimed to be the dividing line between the everyday world and the great "Southwoods." According to folklore, beyond the rock to the south there were no different days, no formal law, no observance of Sunday—a place where lumbermen toiled seven days a week from sunup until dark. It has twice been moved to accommodate the state highway and now sits in a pleasant rest area alongside the road, awaiting the traveler's attention.

The ski and snowshoe trails at Higley Flow State Park have been cut through old pine and hardwood forests planted in the 1930s by the Civilian Conservation Corps (CCC). The trails are multiple-use trails, shared in winter by hikers, skiers, snowshoers, and snowmobilers, but the snowmobiles do not use the ski/snowshoe trails. Park roads are not plowed in the winter, leaving 4.5 miles of snow-covered roadways through six different campsite loops. Here the public can enjoy a variety of winter recreational activities, including skiing, snowshoeing, and ice fishing. In addition to the unplowed campsite roads, the park has four other ski/snowshoe trails that were developed through the cooperative efforts of the park staff and such volunteer groups as Adirondack Mountain Club, college ski teams, local outing clubs, and town employees.

The Warm Brook Trail Loop is actually a combination of ski and snowshoe trails that can be accessed from the winter parking area. You should begin your tour by signing in at the park register station. A copy of the trail map is posted at the registration kiosk, along with other pertinent information about the trails and their use in winter. To access the Warm Brook Trail Loop from the parking lot, take the Pine Trail, identified with blue trail markers. The Pine Trail begins with a gradual downhill through an old red pine forest and flattens as it reaches the bottom of the first hill.

Continuing through an open meadow, the trail descends again on a long gradual slope, offering some fun downhill skiing. These slopes are quite wide, ending with gradual inclines that allow even beginners to let the skis run without fear of falling. After climbing to a small knoll, you will have another opportunity to enjoy a long, wide downhill run fol-

Skiers enjoy a popular run at Higley Flow State Park.

lowed by a gradual uphill, leading you to a T intersection. Turning left at the intersection, you will reach the park nature center, located in a former farmhouse. A public telephone is located here.

Those who wish to take the mile-long side-trip on the Beaver Pond Trail will turn right here for an enjoyable and challenging experience of snowshoeing or backcountry skiing. Originally laid out in the 1970s as a nature trail, it traverses the wetlands via a long log bridge to a red pine forest. The trail is quite wide with nice climbs, as well as some fun turns and twists through a series of plant and animal habitats. The trail climbs to a large glacial rock then begins a downhill run with a few more wide turns. It enters a dense forest before arriving at a 150-foot boardwalk. The trail begins to climb, then wanders along the edge of the wetlands and a grove of larch trees to a 60-foot-long Adirondack-style bridge over the beaver pond. It continues along the shore of the beaver pond and ascends to traverse a ridge, one of the highest points in the park, before descending to rejoin the Pine Trail.

At the nature center building, cross the unplowed service road and head through a rustic archway to enter the Warm Brook Trail about a half mile from the park office. Follow the old forest road marked with blue trail markers. The trail begins to climb through another old CCC

Directions at a glance

0.0   Sign in at register and begin on the Pine Trail (blue marker).

0.4   Reach junction for Beaver Pond Trail. Turn right to complete optional loop, adding 1 mile to tour.

0.5   Cross road at nature center.

1.1   Reach Higley Flow Overlook on Warm Brook Trail.

1.4   Reach lean-to at the top of the hill.

2.0   Finish at parking lot and register.

hemlock plantation then descends gradually across two small streams (with culverts). As you travel through a hardwood forest, you'll certainly notice hundreds of trees with no tops, a result of the devastating ice storm of 1998. The Warm Brook Trail turns left, taking you through a grove of large black cherry trees. Climbing to the top of the hill, you get a great view of Higley Flow on your right, as well as ahead of you, before the trail makes a sweeping left turn.

As you reach the top of the grade, you will find a rustic log lean-to, a good spot for a rest, lunch break or a look at the splendid view of the valley and the mountains. Soon you will start on another fairly gradual downhill through the hardwoods. You'll arrive at the trail junction for Warm Brook Overlook Trail, where there is a picnic table overlooking the brook. (This trail offers a 1.4-mile side trip and reenters the Warm Brook Trail just after a pine grove.) The terrain here is nicely varied, including some rolling and undulating sections with a bit of turning, twisting, and climbing. You will descend to a mostly flat area before ending at the entrance road and parking lot. Be sure to sign the register before leaving the park.

How to get there

From Potsdam travel south on Route 56 about 14 miles to South Colton. At the park sign turn right on Coldbrook Drive and continue 2.5 miles west to the park entrance.

From Tupper Lake take Route 3 to Route 56. Take Route 56 approximately 19 miles to Coldbrook Drive. Turn left and drive 2.5 miles to the park entrance.

New Trail Loop
Osceola Tug Hill Cross-Country Ski Center, Osceola, New York

Type of trail:	▬▬ ⬭
Also used by:	Hikers, bikers
Distance:	3.1 miles (with options)
Terrain:	Hilly
Trail difficulty:	Easiest to more difficult
Surface quality:	Machine groomed and tracked
Food and facilities:	The lodge features a woodstove and small counter for snacks, soup, and chili. The ski shop offers skis and snowshoes for sale and rent. Ski lessons are available. Fast food, restaurants, groceries, and lodging may be found in nearby Osceola (0.5 mile), Florence (5 miles), and Camden (13 miles). For groceries: General Store (315–245–4791), Osceola Outpost (315–559–4094). Restaurants include Cedar Pines (315–599–7372). For lodging try the Village Inn (315–245–1727).
Phone numbers:	Osceola Tug Hill Ski Center, (315) 599–7377.
Fee:	There is a fee to use the trails.
Caution:	Caution is required for those bushwhacking to the waterfalls.

The Osceola Tug Hill Cross-Country Ski Center is located along New York's Tug Hill region, adjacent to 1,900 acres of state forest land in the town of Osceola, Lewis County. The town was formed in 1844 and named for Chief Osceola, a Seminole war chief from the Florida Everglades. The Tug Hill region encompasses more than 2,000 square miles. Although sometimes referred to as a plateau, the Tug Hill actually rises gradually from an elevation of 250 feet at Lake Ontario to the west to more than 2,000 feet at the eastern escarpment, where it is bordered by the Black River. The area is relatively flat compared to other high elevation areas in New York State, like the Catskills and Adirondack Mountains. The most outstanding characteristic of the Tug Hill region is its undeveloped state. There are several small towns, hamlets, and villages scattered along the outer edges of the region, but the core area is heavily forested and relatively unpopulated. The area is very rural, almost to the point of being remote, with the major land uses being farming and forestry.

Forests in the Tug Hill, most of which are in private ownership, are working forests rather than undisturbed wilderness. These forests are used for logging, hunting, fishing, and other recreational activities such as

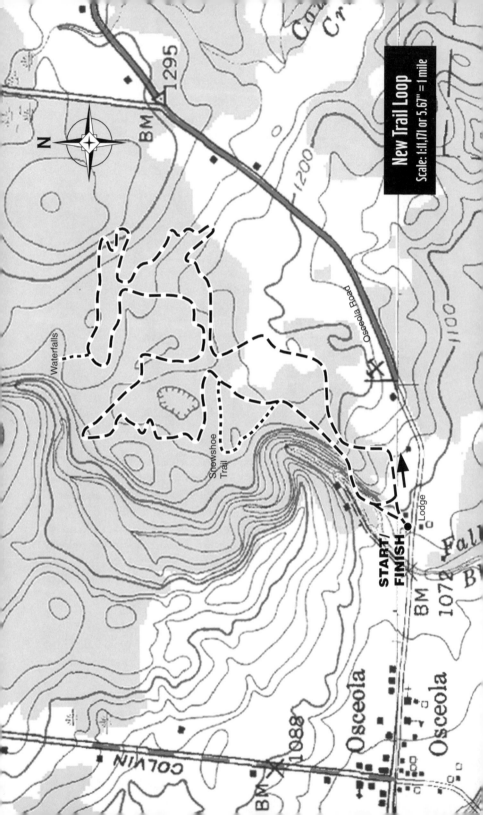

New Trail Loop

Scale: 1:11,171 or 5.67" = 1 mile

N

BM 1295

1200

1100

Osceola Road

Waterfalls

Snowshoe Trail

Lodge

START/ FINISH

BM 1072

Falls Br

BM 1088

Osceola

Osceola

COLVIN

Can Cr

skiing and snowshoeing. Only ten percent of the land on Tug Hill is owned by the state. The Osceola Tug Hill Ski Center grooms and tracks more than 20 miles of trails. The Malloy Trail, a logging trail under the jurisdiction of the Department of Environmental Conservation (DEC), leads to Malloy Brook and miles of state forest trails.

Osceola Tug Hill Ski Center offers cross-country skiing trails for all levels of ability. The ski trails are well maintained throughout the season. They are tracked and groomed daily when conditions permit. Ten miles of separate trails are designated for snowshoeing.

The New Trail Loop is actually a combination of trails. To access the trail from the ski lodge, cross the road and ski around the little red camp to the bottom of the hill. Soon you'll enter a wide trail and travel through a grove of tall pine trees to a junction (left). Continue straight ahead covering some very flat terrain. The trail bears right and climbs gently to a crest where it turns right again, running through a stand of white pines on the right and red pines on the left. As you continue on a gradual uphill, you'll notice a wide, steep hill on your left. You'll enter a woods road with nice undulating terrain that takes you through a hardwood section of mostly maple and cherry trees before reaching an open field. Here is the first of many places on the trail where you may get a glimpse of some of the wild-life (deer, rabbit, grouse) that inhabit the vast Tug Hill Plateau.

Racing on snowshoes is a great fitness activity.

Leaving the open field, you'll enter another reforested section where the trail turns right, followed shortly by a switchback to the left. After bearing to the right again, the trail descends gradually, putting you on the portion of the New Trail Loop known as the Finally Flat Trail. Soon you will see open sky across the pond as the trail cuts sharply left. The trail crosses a culvert and switches back toward the west. The terrain has a rolling feel to it before you come upon the flattest section of this loop.

After this very flat section you'll reach a wide lowland with a meandering stream. Cross the stream, turn right, and follow along its westerly edge. Turn left, and you will begin to hear the crashing sounds of a very powerful waterfall. Soon you reach the spectacular Fall Brook Gorge. The trail continues left and switches back again. However, the adventurous might stop to bushwhack about 200 yards (see map) through the woods to enjoy the boisterous waterfalls and deep gorge. Back on the New Trail Loop, you will continue around a bend as the trail switches back and descends a moderately gradual slope to a trail junction. (You may turn right here to eliminate the Middle of the Road Trail and travel directly to the edge of the Fall Brook Gorge.)

To continue on the New Trail Loop, stay to the left and glide gently down an easy hill on the Middle of the Road Trail until it bottoms out and rises again to the left. Going through a canopy of spruce trees you may get the feeling that you're in a tunnel. After leaving the evergreen grove you'll encounter another downhill followed by a right turn. At the old Four Corners junction the trail turns sharply right. Here you may turn left and retrace your route back to the lodge for a shorter tour (2.5 miles).

The Middle of the Road Trail continues north along an old skid road, skirting a large swamp that's ample for waterfowl to land. Reaching the north end of the swamp, the trail rises and then descends toward the inlet. Here you can experience the fun of slalom skiing around the maple trees. From the inlet the meandering trail rises gradually to the top of the gorge where you'll find the best view at the edge of the magnificent Fall Brook Gorge. This is a great spot to stop and enjoy the peace and beauty of the surroundings, or perhaps to enjoy a snack, hot drink, or picnic lunch. From here you will have a wonderful panoramic view of the brook and the gorge. Here also is the other end of the cutoff trail from the Finally Flat Trail. Novices and beginners may turn right and reconnect with the trail, retracing the route to the lodge. This will lengthen the trip to about 4.5 miles but avoids the more difficult Twist and Shout Trail.

Turning south you'll find yourself at the bottom of the "Shout" portion of the Twist and Shout Trail, facing a 20-foot hill that looks bigger than it really is. There is a gradual dogleg to the left that takes you to the top rim of a small plateau. This is followed by a drop of about 15 feet with a curve to the left. Gliding down a mild slope, you'll cross the outlet from the swamp. The Twist and Shout Trail turns left and runs along the swamp before it reaches the intersection of a snowshoe trail. The

Directions at a glance

0.0 Begin at the red camp across the road from the lodge.

0.33 Pass first junction New Trail Loop.

0.6 Pass old Four Corners junction.

0.8. Cross the stream to reach Finally Flat Trail.

1.4 Reach Bushwhack Trail to the waterfalls.

1.85 Turn right at Four Corners.

2.15 Begin Twist and Shout Trail.

2.55 Snowshoe trail goes right.

2.7 Cutoff goes left, Big Hill Trail goes right.

3.1 Finish at Red Camp.

trail continues gradually downhill with intermittent flat spots, passing the intersection for the lower end of the snowshoe trail. About 50 yards further is a cutoff trail, providing another opportunity for the less able skiers to avoid the steepest sections. The more experienced skiers will bear right, entering the Big Hill section of the trail and continue along the lip of the gorge, ending behind the small red camp across the road from the lodge and parking lot.

How to get there

From the New York State Thruway take exit 34 to Route 13. Travel north Route 13 to Camden. Turn right onto Empey Street at the elementary school. Go two blocks to River Road. Take River Road 6 miles to Florence. Turn left at stop sign and continue 200 yards to Osceola Road. Turn right and travel 6 miles to the village of Osceola. Turn right at the four corners and go 0.5 mile to Osceola Tug Hill Cross-Country Ski Center.

From the north take Route 26 south to West Leyden then west on Osceola Road toward the ski center.

From Rome take Route 69 west to Camden. Turn left onto Route 13 and right onto Empey Street at the elementary school. Go two blocks to River Road. Take River Road 6 miles to Florence. Turn left at stop sign and continue 200 yards to Osceola Road. Turn right and travel 6 miles to the village of Osceola. Turn right at the four corners and go 0.5 mile to Osceola Tug Hill Cross-Country Ski Center.

Lookout Trail Loop

Salmon Hills Cross-Country Ski Resort, Redfield, New York

Type of trail:	▬▬ ◄
Also used by:	Hikers, bikers
Distance:	6 miles (with options)
Terrain:	Hilly
Trail difficulty:	More difficult
Surface quality:	Groomed, double tracked and packed for both classic and skate skiing.
Food and facilities:	The new Log Cabin Lodge houses a restaurant/cafeteria offering quality food (light fare), and a ski shop featuring ski and snowshoe equipment, accessories, sales, and rentals. There are motel rooms and a unique yurt village on the premises. Restaurants, groceries, and lodging may be found in nearby Redfield and Richland. For groceries try Nice & Easy (315–298–3161) or Red & White Market in Richland (315–298–2996). Nearby Century House offers casual dining with a varied menu "from peanut butter to frog legs" (315–298–7714).
Phone numbers:	Salmon Hills, (315) 599–4003. Snow conditions, (888) 976–SNOW.
Fees:	There is a fee to use the trails.
Caution:	Skiing and snowshoeing on the reservoir and creek are prohibited.

One of the finest commercial cross-country ski centers in New York State is also its newest. Established in 1998, the Salmon Hills Cross-Country Ski Resort is located in the state's great Salmon Wilderness, within the snow belt on the Tug Hill Plateau. It's not unusual for Salmon Hills to get 6 or more feet of lake-effect snow in a twenty-four-hour period. While the Syracuse region averages about 150 inches of snow annually, Salmon Hills can get twice or three times as much. Located on 600 acres of forested land adjacent to the 8-mile Salmon River Reservoir, the resort is ideally suited for skiers and snowshoers. Some trails are lighted for night skiing and a few have been designated for snowshoeing. A tubing hill with a lift also adds to the winter fun at this forest resort nestled in the backcountry of Oswego County.

Salmon Hills Resort offers many modern "creature comforts" expected by today's sophisticated winter vacationers, including a modern log cabin ski lodge with a cafeteria, dining area, and full-service ski

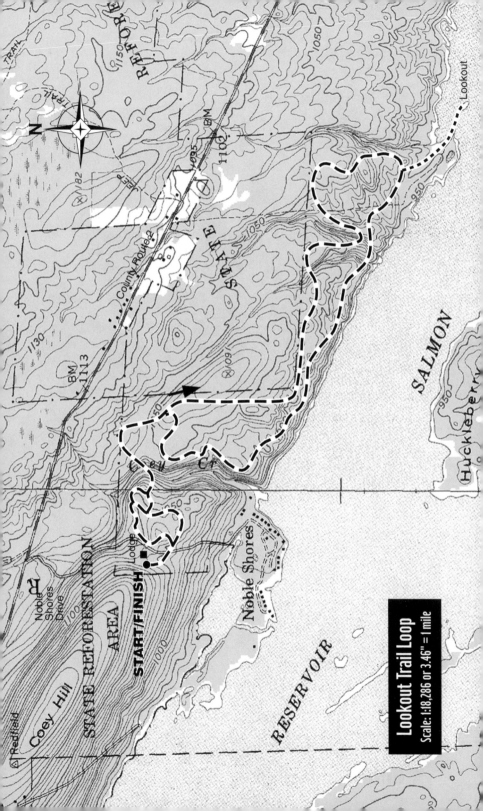

Lookout Trail Loop
Scale: 1:18,286 or 3.46" = 1 mile

The yurt village at Salmon Hills Resort provides a unique experience for skiers and snowshoers.

shop. But the real hallmark of Salmon Hills Resort is its yurt village, the only one of its kind in the nation. Lodging is provided in unique dwellings called yurts. Suitable for individuals, couples, large groups, or families, a yurt is a simple round tent with wood latticed walls covered by canvas or vinyl. Each yurt has a skylight and heat; some have indoor plumbing. Fashioned after the temporary shelters of Mongolian nomads, American yurts have become a popular alternative to tenting. Suitable for up to fifteen people, the rooms at Salmon Hills Yurt Village are fashioned in a pleasant village setting with a hot tub/sauna/shower facility, and are serviced by a large heating system. There are several smaller yurts on the edge of the ski trails, as well as eight full-service rooms in the Log Cabin Lodge.

All ski trails at Salmon Hills begin at the parking lot and Log Cabin Lodge. The trails are mostly wooded, taking skiers and snowshoers through mixed hardwood and evergreen groves. More than 23 miles of trails are cut through the great wilderness, winding throughout several hills nestled against the Salmon River Reservoir. They are expertly designed and personally groomed for skiing by the owners. Several banked turns built into the trails are examples of the innovations at the modern ski center. There are many trails for beginners to experts on a wide variety of terrain. Ski racers love Salmon Hills expert trails. Salmon Hills also has 5 miles of separate snowshoe trails. Pets are not allowed on the trails but owners may walk them on Noble Shores Road.

We have described the Lookout Trail Loop to give skiers a long enjoyable tour with spectacular views of Coey Creek and the Salmon River Reservoir. The Lookout Trail Loop is a combination of trails that leads to a point of land with a secluded and beautiful overview of the Salmon River Reservoir. Although some sections on the route to the Lookout are rated "easiest," the 6-mile loop is most appropriate for intermediate and advanced skiers. There are a couple of cutoff trails for those who desire a shorter tour. The Lookout Trail Loop features very wide double-tracked trails for kick-and-glide classical skiing, packed on one side for the newer skating technique. Trails leading to the Lookout cover mostly rolling terrain with magnificent hemlock and tamarack along the forest trails.

Begin the Lookout Trail Loop by crossing Nobel Shores Drive, near the Log Cabin Lodge, and follow the signs for Mellow Yellow Trail. You will soon pass two left junctions and a large red oak tree. Mellow Yellow Trail crosses the Blue Thunder Trail twice. It then makes a sweeping turn to the right before joining Blue Thunder as the trails go over a bridge to the "Outer Trails." The directional signs are quite good. Here the trail is wide and smooth descending gradually to a wooden bridge crossing Coey Creek. The short up-hill climb on the other side of the bridge may be difficult for some skiers. Herringbone and side step techniques will work fine here. The beauty of the forest and the views from the Lookout will make the extra effort well worthwhile.

After climbing this hill you'll find yourself on the two-way Main Street Trail deep in a beautiful hemlock forest. You will pass two junctions for Hemlock Ridge (on your right) and continue past the next junction to a left turn where Main Street Trail ends and Old Bent Tree Trail begins. About a half mile further is a Y junction offering the first cutoff for those wishing to return to the lodge. Taking this shortcut (right) to Sunset Lane and back to the lodge will shorten your ski tour by approximately 2 miles.

Continuing to the left at the Y, you'll enter the Passeo del Venado Trail (Deer Way), winding through the forest about a half mile to another cutoff over to Sunset Lane. Here you could easily cross over to Sunset Lane and return to the lodge and parking lot (about 2.5 miles).

Continuing past this cutoff, the trail goes left, reaching Frankie's Run, a beautiful ski trail with rolling terrain. It continues northeasterly before turning south around a wide turn. You must bear left at the next Y junction and follow signs to the Lookout. There is a sharp left turn about a hundred yards before reaching the Lookout. This is a great spot to stop and enjoy the peace and beauty of the surroundings, or perhaps to enjoy a hot drink, a snack, or picnic lunch. From here you will have a great panoramic view of the south shore of Salmon River Reservoir, Huckleberry Island, Hall Island State Forest, and the bridge leading to the Village of Redfield.

After leaving the Lookout, retrace your route to a T junction and turn left, returning to the western portion of Frankie's Run. Continue to a four-way intersection and turn left onto Sunset Lane. You may be fortunate to view the sun setting over the reservoir in late afternoon and enjoy the outstanding beauty of the ravine over Coey Creek among the hemlocks and conifers. Shortly you'll pass a narrow maintenance trail to the right and continue to the next Y junction where you'll bear left as Sunset Lane bears right and ends at Main Street Trail. The Lookout Trail Loop continues onto the Hemlock Ridge Trail. Just past the intersection is a one-way trail junction from the Hemlock Ridge Loop. Ski past this junction and continue along Coey Creek to Tie Trail junction. Turn sharply left, continuing on Hemlock Ridge Trail through the woods and back to Main Street Trail. On your left is a great view of Coey Creek.

Back at Main Street Trail, turn left and proceed a short distance to the

Directions at a glance

0.0   Begin your tour at Log Cabin Lodge.

0.1   Cross the road to Mellow Yellow Trail.

0.5   Cross Coey Bridge to Main Street Trail.

1.4   Turn left onto Old Bent Tree Trail.

1.8   Stay to left at Y junction, traveling onto Passeo del Venado Trail.

2.2   Reach Frankie's Run.

2.6   Bear left at Y intersection.

2.8   Turn left onto trail to the Lookout.

3.0   Reach the Lookout.

3.3   Turn left at junction for Sunset Lane Trail.

4.1   Enter Hemlock Ridge Trail at Y junction.

4.5   Turn left at Y junction at Tie Trail.

4.8   Turn left onto Main Street Trail.

5.0   Cross Coey Bridge to Mellow Yellow Trail.

6.0   Finish at lodge.

Coey Bridge crossing. The steep downhill run to the bridge and the climb on the other side will require caution. Novices and intermediate skiers might consider removing skis and walking down the side of the trail to the bridge.

At the other side of the bridge you will follow the trail signs for the Mellow Yellow Trail. The trail will lead you along Blue Thunder for a short while, then turn left onto Mellow Yellow. As you follow the signs to the lodge you'll note that this is a different route on the Mellow Yellow Trail than the one taken on the way to the Lookout. After crossing Nobel Shores Drive you will arrive at the lodge and parking lot.

How to get there

From Syracuse take I–81 north to exit 36 at Pulaski. Take a right onto Route 13 then a left about 1 mile east to Route 2A. Turn left to Route 2 and travel 13 miles to Salmon Hills Cross-Country Ski Resort.

From Watertown take I–81 south to exit 36. Take left onto Route 2; then as above.

Bill's Belly Trail Loop

Tug Hill Tourathon Trails, Boylston, New York

Type of trail:	▬▬▬ 〈⬤〉
Also used by:	Hikers, walkers
Distance:	4.2 miles (with options)
Terrain:	Mostly flat, hilly
Trail difficulty:	Easiest
Surface quality:	Groomed and tracked (usually weekly)
Food and facilities:	Portable toilets are found at the parking lots, courtesy of the Tug Hill Ski Club. Winona Lodge (B&B) and Ski Shop, adjacent to the Wart Road parking lot offers equipment, rentals, and lessons. The River Valley Inn in Mannsville (315–465–7888) is open daily for lunch and dinner and for breakfast on the weekends. The Tug Hill Ski Club has an office at the Inn where you can obtain trail maps and other information about the Tourathon Trails. Fast-food vendors, grocery stores, restaurants, and lodging may be found in nearby Sandy Creek and Pulaski. For lodging try the 1880 House (315–298–6088) or the Winona Lodge (315–387–3886).
Phone numbers:	Tug Hill Ski Club, (315) 456–7888. For emergencies dial 911.
Fees:	There are no fees to use the trails.
Caution:	Stay on the trail. It is quite easy to get disoriented in the forest.

The Tug Hill region of New York is located roughly in a triangle formed by the cities of Watertown, Rome, and Syracuse. It encompasses more than 2,000 square miles. The Tug Hill plateau ranges in elevation from 250 feet to more than 2,000 feet and is relatively flat compared to other high elevation areas in New York State. It is heavily forested and quite rural in nature. Most of the forests in Tug Hill are working forests used extensively for logging, hunting, fishing, and other recreational activities. Because of its landform and location east of Lake Ontario, the area has perfect conditions for lake-effect snowstorms.

The heavy snowfall is one of Tug Hill's most unique recreational assets. While the Tug Hill is not a wilderness area in its strict sense, its densely forested terrain can become confusing even to the most seasoned hiker or cross-country skier. The weather in the region is unpredictable, especially in winter. The plateau is known for its abundant snow, spectacular scenery, and great trail systems. The snow—nearly 300 inches

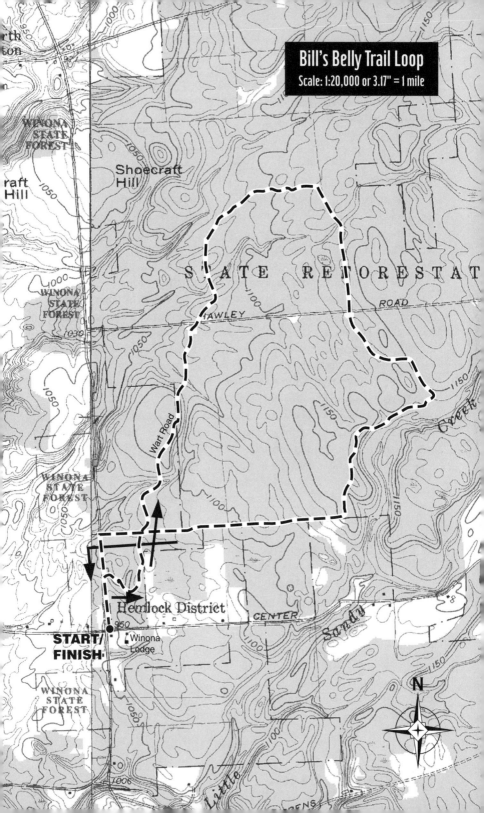

Bill's Belly Trail Loop
Scale: 1:20,000 or 3.17" = 1 mile

Shoecraft Hill

raft Hill

WINONA STATE FOREST

WINONA STATE FOREST

WINONA STATE FOREST

S T A T E   R E F O R E S T A T

ROAD

HAWLEY

Wart Road

Creek

Hemlock District

CENTER

Sandy

START/ FINISH

Winona Lodge

WINONA STATE FOREST

N

annually—comes earlier than in most other areas in New York State and lasts well into April.

For years local cross-country skiers enjoyed their sport on the miles of logging roads, jeep trails, foot paths, abandoned highways, and frozen streambeds that lace the 40,000 acres of state lands, forests, and wildlife areas in the Tug Hill region. Beginning in the early 1980s, Alice Arneson opened a nature center and youth hostel in nearby Boylston. She wanted to do something to utilize the vast state forest lands, at the same time helping tourism in the area during the wintertime. One result was the creation of Tug Hill Tourathon and quality trails to support a 50-kilometer ski race. Little by little, woods trails were designed with the expertise of employees of the state forest, then cut and cleared by volunteers, including Girl Scout and Boy Scout troops, 4-H Clubs, and several winter recreation clubs. Today hundreds of miles of interconnected ski, snowshoe, snowmobile, and dogsled trails crisscross the region.

The Winona State Forest Recreation Area, located in the towns of Lorraine and Boylston, boasts of more than 30 miles of groomed winter trails on unplowed roads and woodland trails through county and state forests. Operations crews at the Department of Environmental Conservation (DEC) maintain the trails with voluntary help from the Tug Hill Ski Club, the Western Edge Recreation Association, and several other community groups. The majority of the trail system is now groomed regularly by members of the ski club. It includes trails for all levels of skiing ability. The ski club uses funds from races and club memberships to help finance season-long trail grooming and track-setting, as well as covering expenses to run major national-level Nordic ski races.

There are three official parking areas designated for skiing and snowshoeing on the Tug Hill Tourathon Trails, although roadside parking is also allowed. Snowshoeing is allowed on all trails, but organizers ask snowshoers to avoid stepping on set ski tracks by walking to the sides of the trails. Other trails are open for snowmobiling and dogsledding. The alternatives for cross-country skiing are numerous and quite varied. We suggest that you stop at the Tug Hill Ski Club office at the River Valley Inn, located on Route 11 in Mannsville, to obtain a Tug Hill Tourathon Trail Map. Orienteering maps prepared for the National Ski Orienteering Championships are also available, giving a higher level of detail to make it easier to stay on the trails. Try to resist the urge to explore. Although the woods here are open, the terrain forgiving, and the snow often firm, it is very easy to get disoriented. On the Tug Hill plateau it is important that you pay particular attention to the weather, even more so than in other areas of the state. Lake-effect snowstorms are intense enough to drench you as surely as if you were in a driving rain. It can snow several

A dad encourages his daughter as she tries the new skate skiing technique.

inches an hour here, obscuring your tracks quickly. At the same time, the snowfall makes for enjoyment and excitement.

Bill's Belly Trail, named as a memorial to Bill Thayer, an honored volunteer, is a very popular ski and snowshoe trail. It is not open to snowmobiles. To access Bill's Belly Trail Loop, start at the trail register just north of the parking lot at the intersection of Wart Road and Center Road in the town of Boylston. After signing the logbook, travel a couple of hundred yards north on the unplowed road to the trailhead. Brown and yellow signs are located at all trailheads. The Tourathon trails are wide and appropriate for two-way skiing. There is no formal ski patrol, but Tug Hill Ski Club members volunteer informally to patrol the trails and check for hazards and maintenance needs.

Entering the woods on the right side of the road, you will follow the round yellow DEC trail markers through a pleasant plantation of mixed hardwoods, including large black cherry trees. Upon reaching the Winona Way Trail intersection, continue through the hardwood grove until you reach Hawley Road at about 0.8 mile. There are two short, steep pitches, both of which are in open forest so you can work around them if you don't want to ski the downhill section.

Hawley Road is also unplowed and can serve as a shortcut (left) for those who wish to return to the register and parking lot via Wart Road. This shorter ski loop, totaling just about 2 miles, has the drawback of following unplowed roads most of the way and sharing the trail with snowmobiles. Another option with fewer roadways is to turn right (east) on

Directions at a glance

0.0 Begin at the trail register and parking lot.

0.06 Cross the creek, turn right onto Bill's Belly Trail.

0.25 Descend small hill heading north.

0.4 Continue straight at intersection with Winona Way Trail.

1.2 Jog right on Hawley Road for 50 feet; continue on Bill's Belly Trail.

1.6 Turn right at Hiscock Trail.

2.0 Turn right at intersection of Hiscock Road and Winona Way.

2.4 Cross Hawley Road to Sally's Ride.

2.8 Reach southern section of Winona Way; turn right.

4.1 Turn left on Wart Road.

4.2 Finish at trail register and parking lot.

Hawley Road from Bill's Belly Trail and then right onto Sally's Ride Trail, shortening this tour by a half mile.

We recommend avoiding all the road travel except a final small stretch on Wart Road by continuing north from Bill's Belly Trail at the Hawley Road intersection. Here you must jog right onto Hawley Road for about 50 feet to find the continuation of the route to Hiscock Trail. Reaching Hiscock Trail, you will turn right and ski east to Winona Way. Turn right again and go south on Winona Way about a half mile to the north end of Sally's Ride at the Hawley Road intersection. Continue south on Sally's Ride to join the southern portion of Winona Way. After turning right, you will continue skiing about a mile before crossing Bill's Belly and arriving at Wart Road. Otter and fisher tracks will often be seen, along with those of deer and porcupine. If you are late leaving the forest you may hear the hoot of a barred owl or even the howl of coyotes.

Upon returning to Wart Road, turn left, ski to the registration kiosk, and sign out before returning to your vehicle. For a winter recreation guide of Winona State Forest, call SnoZone, (800) 847–5263.

How to get there

Take I–81 (north or south) to exit 37 at Sandy Creek/Lacona. Travel east through Lacona to County Route 22 (Orwell Road). Turn left and travel north about .75 mile to Center Road. Turn right and travel about a half mile to the Wart Road parking lot.

Appendix

Other Ski and Snowshoe Trails

New York State holds the record for the greatest number of ski areas in the nation. A 1998 survey by the National Ski Areas Association listed sixty-eight Alpine ski centers in New York followed by Michigan with forty-seven and Wisconsin with thirty-nine. Though no figures were available for Nordic skiing at the time of the publication of this guide-book, we estimate that there are between 400 and 500 cross-country ski/snowshoe trails scattered throughout New York State. For a listing of approximately 200 Nordic ski trails (by region) request a copy of the annual *I Love NY Winter Travel and Ski Guide* from New York State Department of Economic Development, P.O. Box 2603 Albany, NY 12220 (1–800–CALL–NYS) or visit its Web site www.iloveny.state.ny.us.

Winter Trails: New York includes eight commercial cross-country ski and snowshoe centers. For a complete listing of more than two dozen such Nordic centers contact New York State Cross-Country Ski Areas Association, 13 Lake Road, North River, NY 12856; (518) 251–2150. Some commercial Nordic centers are not members of the state associa-tion, but might be located through local chambers of commerce and tourism organizations. For a listing of both commercial and non-com-mercial Nordic ski and snowshoe trails in your county, contact the county department of tourism or department of planning. There are fifty-six county offices in New York State.

New York State is also traversed by a half dozen major national trail systems including the Maine to Georgia Appalachian Trail and the east-west North Country Trail. Other ultra-long trails located within the state include the 500-mile Canalway Trail, the Northville-Placid Trail, the Long Path (see Saratoga/Capital Region), and the Finger Lakes Trail (see Genesse Region). Some sections of these and other long trails are suitable for cross-country skiing/snowshoeing. A color poster "Building Commu-nity Trails Across New York" showing these and several other multi-use trails is available from New York Parks and Recreation Association, 35 Maiden Lane, Albany, NY 12207; (518) 434–1583. For information and maps of these trails, contact the following:

Appalachian Trail
Appalachian Mountain Club
202 East 39th Street
New York City, NY 10016
(212) 986–1430

North Country Trail
RR Box 20B
Forbes Road
Canastoda, NY 13032

Finger Lakes Trail
Finger Lakes Trail Conference
202 Colebourne Road
Rochester, NY 14618
(716) 288–7191

Other Trails Organizations

American Hiking Society (AHS)
P.O. Box 201060
Washington, DC 20041
(800) 972–8608

NYS Trails Council
c/o Parks and Recreation
Agency Bldg 1
Albany, NY 12238
(518) 474–0414

Long Island Trails Conference
23 Deer Path Road
Central Islip, NY 11722
(516) 300–0753

Northville-Placid Trail
Adirondack Mountain Club
Box 3055
Lake George, NY 12845
(518) 668–4447

NYS Canalway Trail
NYS Canal Corporation
P.O. Box 189
Albany, NY 12201
(800) 4CANAL4

Long Path
New York/New Jersey Trail
Conference
P.O. Box 2250
New York, NY 10016

(212) 685–9699
Adirondack Mountain Club (ADK)
Box 3055
Lake George, NY 12845
(518) 668–4447

Appalachian Mountain Club (AMC)
202 East 39th Street
New York City, NY 10016
(212) 986–1430

Rails-To-Trails Conservancy (RTC)
1400 16th Street, Suite 300
Washington, DC 20036
(202) 797–5400

Other Resources

American XC Skiers (AXCS)
P.O. Box 5
Bend OR 97709
(541) 317–0217

U.S. Snowshoe Association
P.O. Box 170 RD
Corinth, NY 12822
(518) 654–7848

Cross-Country Ski Areas
Association (CCSAA)
259 Bolton Road
Winchester, NH 03470
(603) 239–4341
ccsaa@xcski.org

Nordic Ski Patrol
20 Sleepy Hollow Drive
Clifton Park, NY 12065
(518) 371–3762

Olympic Regional Development
Authority (ORDA)
Olympic Center
Lake Placid, NY 12946
(800) 462–6236

Professional Ski Instructors of
America (PSIA)
21A Lincoln Avenue
Albany, NY 12205
(518) 452–6095

U.S. Biathalon Association (USBA)
Camp Johnson
Colchester, VT 05446
(802) 654–0120

Nordic Division NYS Ski Racing
Association
P.O. Box 90
Clifton Park, NY 12065
(518) 383–8565

New York Parks and Recreation
Association
35 Maiden Lane
Albany, NY 12207
(518) 434–1583

NYS Office of Parks and Recreation
Agency Bldg. 1, Empire Plaza
Albany, NY 12238
(518) 474–0456

U.S. Forest Service
P.O. Box 96090
Washington, DC 20090
(202) 205–1426

New England School of Archery
109 School Street
Concord, NH 03301
(603) 224–5768
NESAINC@aol.com

Backcountry Active Vacations
P.O. Box 4029
Bozeman, MT 59772
(800) 575–1540
sroberts@backcountrytours.com

U.S. Olympic Training Center
421 Old Military Road
Lake Placid, NY 12946
(518) 523–2600

U.S. Orienteering Federation
P.O. Box 1444
Forest Park, GA 30051

U.S. Ski & Snowboard
Association (USSA)
P.O. Box 100
Park City, UT 840600
(435) 647–2010

American Volksport
Association (AVA)
1001 Pat Brooker Road
University City, TX 78148
(800) 830–9255

National XC Ski Education
Foundation
1751 Stanford Ave.
St. Paul, MN 55105
(612) 698–1908

All Terrain Dog
P.O. Box 837
Campton, NH 03223
(603) 536–3864/536–7184

Snowsports Industries America (SIA)
8377-B Greensboro Drive
McLean, VA 22102
(703) 506–4212

American Dog Owners Association
1654 Columbia Turnpike
Castleton, NY 12033
(518) 477–8469

Nordic Group International
259 Bolton Road
Winchester, NH
(603) 239–4181/239–6387

New England Sled Dog Club
RR2 Box 262H
Lyme, NH 03768
(603) 353–4601/353–4320

Empire Orienteering Club
Box 51
Clifton Park, NY 12065
(518) 383–8565

Sherpa Snowshoe Company
444 South Pine Street
Burlington, WI 53105
(800) 621–2277

World Masters
P.O. Box 5
Bend, OR 97709

Ski For Light (Blind Skiers)
1455 West Lake Street
Minneapolis, MN 55408
(612) 827–3232
atd@worldpath.net

Tubbs Snowshoes
52 River Road
Stowe, VT 05672
(800) 882–2748

Mutt Mitts
Box 626
Burlington, KY 41005
(800) 697–6084

Nordic Ski Clubs

Bill Koch Youth League
P.O. Box 90
Clifton Park, NY 12065
(518) 383–8565

Adirondack Ski Touring Council
Box 843
Lake Placid, NY 12946
(518) 523–1365

Capital Area Ski Touring Association
(CASTA)
P.O. Box 2012
Albany, NY 12220
(518) 233–0274

Rochester Nordic Ski Club
P.O. Box 22897
Rochester, NY 14692
(716) 473–7888

Cayuga Nordic Club
818 Cayuga Heights Road
Ithaca, NY 14850
(607) 257–7252

Huggers XC Ski Club
P.O. Box 23921
Rochester, NY 14692

Tug Hill Nordic Ski Club
Box 314
Mannsville, NY 13661
(315) 465–7888

Schenectady Winter Sports Club
Box 228
Schenectady, NY 12301
(518) 399–3530

Bibliography

Note: Some of the older titles listed below are now out of print but might still be available at your local library.

Andersen, Steve. *The Orienteering Book.* World Publications, 1977.

Besser, Gretchen R. *The National Ski Patrol.* Backcountry Publications, 1984.

Caldwell, John. *On Competitive Cross-Country Skiing.* Steven Green Press, 1979.

Caldwell, John. *On Cross-Country Sking.* Steven Green Press, 1975.

Conroy, Dennis. *Adirondack Cross-Country Skiing.* Backcountry Publications, 1992.

Corcoran, Malcolm. *Waxing For Cross-Country Skiing.* Intrinsic Publishing, 1988.

Dibelius, Norman. *Winter Sports.* Schenectady Wintersports Club, 1995.

English, Brad. *Total Telemarking.* East River Publishing, 1984.

Fitzgerald, John R. *Cross-Country–Northeast.* Mountain n'Air Books, 1994.

Goodwin, Tony. *Classic Adirondack Ski Tours.* Adirondack Mountain Club, 1994.

Hoffman, Gary. *Happy Trails for You and Your Dog.* ICS Books, 1996.

Kjellstrom, Bjorn. *Be an Expert with Map and Compass.* Simon & Schuster, 1994.

Miner Pelkey, Rosemary. *River, Rails and Ski Trails.* Johnsburg Historical Society, 1994.

Older, Jules. *Cross-Country Skiing for Everyone.* Stackpole Books, 1998.

Petersen, Paul and Richard Lovett. *Essential Cross-Country Skier.* McGraw-Hill, 1999.

Prater, Gene. *Snowshoeing.* Mountaineer Books, 1997.

Quinn, George V. *The Catskills: A Cross-Country Ski Guide.* Purple Mountain Press, 1997.

Rivezzi, Rose and David Trithart. *Kids on the Trail.* Adirondack Mountain Club, 1997.

Wadsworth, Bruce. *Guide to Catskill Trails.* Adirondack Mountain Club, 1994.

Weisel, Jonathan. *Cross-Country Ski Vacations.* John Muir Publications, 1999.

Wilson, Joe Pete. *Complete Cross-Country Skiing and Ski Touring.* Norton & Co., 1983.

Recommended Reading

I Love NY Winter Travel and Ski Guide
New York State Division of Tourism
P.O. Box 2603
Albany, NY 12220
(800) CALL–NYS
This is an excellent guide to ski trails in New York State. It includes names, addresses (postal and electronic), and phone numbers of both Alpine and cross-country ski centers. It also includes names and phone numbers of chambers of commerce, tourism bureaus, and other public information centers throughout the fifty-six counties of the state.

Cross-Country Skier
Box 576
Mt Morris, IL 61054
(800) 827–0607
A great resource for all your needs related to cross-country skiing, including equipment, destinations, and a calendar of events.

Ski Trax
2 Padre Avenue
Toronto, ON M6K 3H5
(416) 530–1350
Produced in Canada, this magazine is filled with important information for Nordic snowsports enthusiasts, including cross-country skiers, ski jumpers, and biathletes.

Orienteering North America
23 Fayette St.
Cambridge MA 02139
(617) 868–7416
A monthly magazine for those involved in the sports of orienteering and ski orienteering.

Adirondack
814 Goggins Rd.
Lake George, NY 12845
(518) 668–4447
A subscription magazine for members of the Adirondack Mountain Club featuring a wide variety of environmental issues, trail related topics, and a calendar listing of trail activities.

The Snowshoer
RCM Enterprises Inc.
P.O. Box 21654
St. Paul MN 55114
(651) 593–0666
This monthly magazine covers a wide variety of topics about snowshoeing and snowshoe activities nationwide. It is a great resource for snowshoers featuring information on equipment, clothing, destinations, and a full calendar of events.

About the Authors

Johanna and Ron Farra have been skiing together since they met at State University Teachers College in the "North Country." They fell in love with skiing and with each other and served as volunteers on the National Ski Patrol and as professional ski instructors at a local Alpine ski center. While their five children were learning to ski, Johanna and Ron coached young racers in the New York State Ski Racing Association (NYSSRA) Alpine Program. In the early 1980s they opened a Nordic ski center and created a cross-country ski racing program for youth in the Saratoga/Capital Region. The couple's children competed on state Alpine racing teams; the youngest competed in Nordic ski racing. Their eldest son became state champion in biathlon and was appointed to the U.S. Biathlon Ski Team, while their youngest son became a national champion in cross-country skiing and competed on the U.S. Olympic Team in 1992.

Ron Farra is a member of the New York State Trails Council, a governor's advisory group. Ron travels extensively and writes "On the Trails," a column appearing in several local, state, and national publications. The column focuses on the "silent sports," including hiking, biking, kayaking, snowshoeing, and skiing. His writings have appeared in official publications of NYSSRA, the Empire State Games, and Ski Areas of New York (SANY). Other publication credits include *Empire Sports Magazine, Warren Miller Magazine, Adirondack Guide, Saratoga Journal*, and several newspapers, including the *Post Star* and the *Lake Placid News*. Ron is co-chairman of the Nordic committees for the Eastern Ski Writers Association and the North American Snowsports Journalist Association, and is the founder of the Nordic division of the New York State Ski Racing Association. He is also the author of *Jockeying for Change*, a biography about jockey/trainer Tommy Luther.

Johanna (Jo) Farra has been a journalist for many years. Her works have appeared in such publications as *Saratoga County Living* magazine, *Saratoga Journal, NYSSRA Nordic Newsletter*, and several newspapers, including the *New England Ski Journal, On The Trail News*, the *Saratogian* and the *Lake Placid News*. With her husband she has co-chaired the Nordic Committee of the Eastern Ski Writers Association and the North American Snowsports Journalist Association. Her column, "Travelog," features travel destinations, family vacations, Olympic profiles, and women in sports.